Marxist Introductions

General Editors
Raymond Williams
Steven Lukes

Marxism and Politics

RALPH MILIBAND

Oxford University Press

Oxford University Press, Walton Street, Oxford OX2 6DP

OXFORD LONDON GLASGOW NEW YORK
TORONTO MELBOURNE WELLINGTON CAPE TOWN
IBADAN NAIROBI DAR ES SALAAM KUALA LUMPUR
SINGAPORE JAKARTA HONG KONG TOKYO DELHI
BOMBAY CALCUTTA MADRAS KARACHI

First published 1977
Reprinted 1978

British Library Cataloguing in Publication Data
Miliband, Ralph
    Marxism and politics.–(Marxist introductions)
    1. Socialism
    I. Title   II. Series
    320.5'315   HX56

ISBN 0–19–876059–0
ISBN 0–19–876062–0 Pbk.

PHOTOTYPESET BY WESTERN PRINTING SERVICES LTD, BRISTOL
PRINTED IN GREAT BRITAIN BY THE PITMAN PRESS, BATH

Preface

I seek to present here what I take to be the main themes and problems of the politics of Marxism, which might also be called the Marxist approach to politics, or Marxist politics. I have attempted to do this by way of a 'theorization' of material drawn mainly from the writings of Marx, Engels, and Lenin, with occasional references to other major figures of Marxism; and I have also drawn on the actual experience of the politics of Marxism—or of what has been claimed to be such—in this century.

I am very conscious that I have not dealt with many things which would have to be included in a book that made any claim to being a comprehensive work on Marxism and politics. I make no such claim and did not set out to write such a book. But I think that the book which I have written may help the interested reader to see more clearly what are the distinctive features of Marxist politics, and what are its problems.

Whatever view may be taken of my text and its arguments, there cannot at least be much doubt that the questions discussed here have been absolutely central to the politics of the twentieth century, and that they are likely to dominate what remains of it.

April 1976   R.M.

For David and Edward

Contents

Abbreviations

EW   K. Marx, *Early Writings*, Pelican Ed., London, 1975.

FI   K. Marx, *The First International and After* in *Political Writings*, vol. 3, Pelican Ed., London, 1974.

Revs.   K. Marx, *The Revolutions of 1848* in *Political Writings*, vol. 1, Pelican Ed., London, 1973.

SE   K. Marx, *Surveys From Exile* in *Political Writings*, vol. 2, Pelican Ed., London, 1973.

SC   K. Marx and F. Engels, *Selected Correspondence*, Moscow, n.d.

SW 1968   K. Marx and F. Engels, *Selected Works*, London, 1968.

SW 1950   K. Marx and F. Engels, *Selected Works*, Moscow, 1950.

CWL   V. I. Lenin, *Collected Works*, Moscow, 1960–70.

SWL   V. I. Lenin, *Selected Works*, London, 1969.

Note: Unless otherwise stated, all italics in the texts quoted in this book are in the original.

I. Introduction

The basic question with which this book is concerned is: 'What are the politics of Marxism?' It is not a simple question, and a preliminary discussion of the reasons why it is not simple may be the best way to begin answering it.

The first difficulty lies in the term 'Marxism' itself. Marx died in 1883 and his own 'Marxism' (a term, incidentally, which he never used) was subsequently greatly enlarged, first of all by Engels in the twelve very active and prolific years by which he survived Marx; and then by a number of other major and not so major figures in the following years up to the present. The most prominent of these figures by far was Lenin, whose own successors invented the term 'Marxism-Leninism', not only to denote Lenin's contribution to the enlargement of Marxism, but also to proclaim as settled what was in fact a highly contentious question, namely how firm was the link between the Marxism of Marx on the one hand and that of Lenin on the other. The question is particularly contentious, as it happens, in regard to some central aspects of the politics of Marxism, for instance the role assigned to the party.

In one way or another, the same problem arises in relation to all the major figures who, by word or deed, have left their stamp on Marxism after Marx. The issue is by no means 'academic'. Given the political importance of Marxism in the twentieth century and its use as a political weapon, it is on the contrary a question which has itself strong and even explosive political implications and consequences.

A second difficulty in the discussion of Marxism and politics has to do with the character of the writings on politics of all the major figures of Marxism, beginning with Marx himself. These writings are for the most part the product of particular historical episodes and specific circumstances; and what there is of theoretical exploration of politics in what may be called classical Marxism (by which I mainly mean the writings of Marx, Engels, and Lenin, and, at a different level, those of some other figures such as Rosa Luxemburg, Gramsci, and Trotsky) is mostly unsystematic and fragmentary, and often part of other work. Some of the most basic texts of the politics of Marxism answer to this description, for instance Marx's *Eighteenth Brumaire of Louis Bonaparte* and *The Civil War in France*, or Lenin's *What is to be Done?* and *The State and Revolution*. In fact, there are very few classical Marxist political texts which do not answer to this description.*

This is not meant to devalue the significance and interest of these works but only to note that none of the greatest figures of classical Marxism, with the partial exception of Gramsci, ever attempted or for that matter felt the need to attempt the writing of a 'political treatise'. Given their total engagement in political struggles, and the vital importance they all attached to theory, this is very remarkable and cannot be taken as accidental. It has in fact to do with the meaning and status of 'politics' in Marxism and requires separate discussion later in this chapter. For the moment, it may be noted that this absence of systematic political theorization on the part of Marx, Engels, and their most prominent successors means in effect that a Marxist politics has to be constructed or reconstructed from the mass of variegated and fragmented material which forms the corpus of Marxism. The danger which this presents of arbitrary selection and emphasis is obvious, and is further enhanced by a strong tendency to extremely one-sided interpretations which Marxism engenders, not least among Marxists. This danger is more easily acknowledged than avoided; but one must do the best one can.

At the same time—and this is another difficulty to bear in mind—it is as well to recognize that what I have just called the 'corpus of Marxism' has very definite limitations in terms of the construction or reconstruction of a Marxist politics. One of these limitations is that the available classical writings are simply silent or extremely perfunctory over major issues of politics and political theory: there is a limit to what can properly be squeezed out of a paragraph, a phrase, an allusion or a metaphor. The point is particularly obvious in regard to a whole range of political experience in the last fifty years or so, which is of crucial importance in any attempt at theorizing the politics of Marxism, but about which classical Marxism is, in any direct way, naturally silent. After all, Marx did die in 1883 and Engels in 1895,

---

* In the short Preface which he wrote in 1869 for the second edition of *The Eighteenth Brumaire*, Marx noted that the work had been written in the form of weekly articles and 'under the immediate pressure of events' (SE, p. 142). This could be said of most of the relevant political texts of classical Marxism.

Rosa Luxemburg in 1919, and Lenin in 1924. Gramsci was in gaol from 1926 until shortly before his death in 1937, and wonderfully suggestive though his *Prison Notebooks* are, it has to be recognized that they are no more than fragments and notes, written under dismal conditions and in the grip of disease. Only Trotsky, until his assassination in 1940, provides a sustained commentary, out of classical Marxism, on a world that encompassed Stalinism and Fascism and much else as well; and this too was written under exceptional pressure and in very special circumstances.

It might well be asked why more by way of a Marxist political theorization of some of the most important experiences of our times, and of a Marxist political theory in general, should not have been constructed in, say, the last fifty years, on the foundations provided by classical Marxism.

At least a part of the answer must be sought in the experience of Stalinism and of Stalinism's domination of Marxism over a period of some thirty years and more from the late twenties onwards. The point is not so much that the Stalinist version of Marxism was a dreadfully impoverished affair, though it was certainly that; but that its version of Marxism, and style of approach to it, were accepted, largely because of extraneous political reasons, by the vast majority of people who then called themselves Marxists, not only in Russia but everywhere else as well.

A particular quality of Stalinism, in this realm as in all others, was its imperative and binding definition of 'the line' to be followed. This served to decide, in catechismal form, what were the 'fundamentals' of Marxism, or rather of 'Marxism-Leninism'; and it also served to specify who was and—even more important—who was not to be regarded as having made a contribution to Marxist thought. Those who were not so regarded constituted a great host—in fact most of the people who have in this century made a serious contribution to the development of Marxism. So they were banned in the Soviet Union and greatly neglected or altogether ignored by most Marxists outside.

Marx and Engels were not banned. But they were read very selectively; and probably less than their accredited interpreters, Lenin and Stalin. The accent was on authoritative interpretations and non-arguable propositions; and on the capacity of 'Marxism-Leninism' and dialectical materialism (another term which Marx never used or even knew) to resolve all theoretical problems, or at the very least to provide a sure guide to their solution. These were not perspectives in which Marxist thought could be expected to flourish, least of all in the highly sensitive area of political theory and political analysis; and it did not.

Things have changed in the last twenty-odd years, at least in those countries where Marxism is not the official ideology, and even up to a point in those where it is. The spell was at long last broken in the fifties; and these two decades have been a period of intense probing and questioning in Marxist thought which is without parallel in its history. But there is a vast amount of ground to make up, most of all perhaps in the area of Marxist politics.

The probing and questioning which have occurred have been fed from many sources. The first of them is the very fact that Stalin's regime came under attack in the Soviet Union itself: however superficial and inadequate that attack was and has remained since the XXth Party Congress of 1956, it did release a vast array of key questions which can never again be ignored or suppressed. There has also been the experience of China and the many challenges which it has posed to the Russian and East European 'models' of socialism. These challenges remain even if one rejects the attempts which have been made to create a Chinese shrine at which to worship in place of the discredited Russian one.

There have also been the liberation struggles all over the 'Third World', and their reverberations in the countries of advanced capitalism. In these countries, class struggles which had in the post-war years been declared to belong to the past have brought back on the agenda the largest questions concerning reform and revolution; and these struggles have been given an added dimension by women's movements, ethnic and student movements, and new forms of expression and action. The inchoate and many-sided 'cultural revolution' which has gripped advanced capitalist countries in these two decades, has also and naturally affected Marxism and forced many reassessments upon it.

Of course, these stirrings within Marxism have their own limitations, particularly in the countries where it is the official ideology. It is in this latter respect a grim and sobering thought that in the infinite number of words produced in Communist countries in the last two decades, not one article could safely appear which, for instance, resolutely attacked Lenin on any issue of importance. As for capitalist countries, the recovery of Marxism has involved the proliferation of coteries and fashionable trends, with different sects and schools proclaiming their own version of Marxism as the only authentic one, or as the only one appropriate to the times we live in, or whatever. But this is the inevitable price which a live and vigorous movement pays for its liveliness and vigour. However it may be in China, Chairman Mao's old injunction to let a hundred flowers bloom has been taken at face value in capitalist countries; and it is of no great account that a fair number of weeds should in the process have grown as well.

The important change, in this realm, is that there is now no 'recognized' Marxist orthodoxy to which general obedience is paid, except where such obedience is capable of being imposed; and this is very different from what happened in the past, when such an orthodoxy was internationally accepted, and not even perceived as an orthodoxy. The change is a great gain. It was after all Marx who once said that his favourite motto was 'Doubt all things'; and it is all to the good that there should be less and less people in favour of amending this to read: 'Doubt all things except what Comrade X, Chairman Y, or President Z pronounces upon.' There are many worse slogans than 'Everyone his own Marx'. For in the end, there is no 'authoritative' interpretation—only personal judgement and evaluation.

In relation to the politics of Marxism, this requires that the first textual priority and attention should be given to Marx himself, and to Engels. This is the essential starting-point, and the only possible 'foundation' of Marxism-as-politics. It is only after this has been done that one can usefully take up Lenin, Luxemburg, Gramsci, and others to try and construct a Marxist politics.

It is worth saying at the outset, however, that the most careful textual scrutiny will not yield a smooth, harmonious, consistent, and unproblematic Marxist political theory. On the contrary, it is only by a very superficial reading, or by fiat, that such a Marxist political theory, of a distorted kind, can be obtained. Not only are the texts susceptible to different and contradictory interpretations: they also do actually incorporate tensions, contradictions, and unresolved problems which form an intrinsic part of Marxist political thought. To ignore or to try and obscure this does not simply distort the real nature of that thought but deprives it of much of its interest.

I noted earlier how remarkable it was that no major Marxist figure had tried to set out systematically the substance and specificity of Marxist political theory. The people concerned were after all among the most gifted and penetrating minds of the last hundred years, men and women utterly immersed in political life, struggle, and ideas; and the same people have always attached the highest importance to theory as an indispensable part of class struggle and working-class politics. 'Without theory, no revolutionary movement' is one of the precepts of Lenin which Marxists have most readily accepted; and they have understood it to mean that without a clear articulation of its theoretical premises and projections, a working-class movement advances blindly. This makes the absence in classical Marxism of a systematic theorization of Marxist politics all the more remarkable. As I have already suggested, the reasons for this must be sought in the concept of politics which informs Marxism, and they are in fact deeply embedded in the structure of Marxist thought concerning social life and the place of politics in it.

On the most general plane, Marxism begins with an insistence that the separation between the political, economic, social, and cultural parts of the social whole is artificial and arbitrary, so that, for instance, the notion of 'economics' as free from 'politics' is an ideological abstraction and distortion. There is no such thing as 'economics'—only 'political economy', in which the 'political' element is an ever-present component.

On this view, politics is the pervasive and ubiquitous articulation of social conflict and particularly of class conflict, and enters into all social relations, however these may be designated. But this very pervasiveness of politics appears to rob it of its specific character and seems to make it less susceptible to particular treatment, save in the purely formal description of processes and institutions which Marxists have precisely wanted to avoid. In reality, it is perfectly possible to treat politics as a specific phenomenon, namely as the ways and means whereby social conflict and notably class conflict is manifested. At one end, this may mean accommodation and agreement between social groups which are not greatly divided (or for that matter which are); at the other end, it may mean civil war which, to adapt Clausewitz, is politics carried out by other means.

There is, however, a more particular and direct reason for the Marxist neglect of political theory, which has to do with the concept of 'base' and 'superstructure', or rather with the implications which have tended to be drawn from it.

One of the most influential formulations in the whole body of Marxist thought occurs in a famous passage of the 'Preface' to *A Contribution to the Critique of Political Economy* of 1859 and goes as follows:

In the social production of their life, men enter into definite relations that are indispensable and independent of their will, relations of production which correspond to a definite stage of development of their material productive forces. The sum total of these relations of production constitutes the economic structure of society, the real foundation on which rises a legal and political superstructure and to which correspond definite forms of social consciousness. The mode of production of material life conditions the social, political and intellectual life process in general. It is not the consciousness of men that determines their being, but, on the contrary, their social being that determines their consciousness.[1]

Another text of Marx, which makes the same point in a somewhat different form, is also worth quoting, given the importance of this whole conceptualization for the status of the political element in Marxism. In the third volume of *Capital*, Marx writes

the specific economic form, in which unpaid surplus-labour is pumped out of direct producers, determines the relationship of rulers and ruled, as it grows directly out of production itself and, in turn, reacts upon it as a determining element . . . it is always the direct relationship of the owners of the conditions of production to the direct producers—a relation always naturally corresponding to a definite stage in the development of the methods of labour and thereby its social productivity—which reveals the innermost secret, the hidden basis of the entire social structure, and with it the political form of the relation of sovereignty and dependence, in short, the corresponding specific form of the state.[2]

Clearly, these texts can easily be interpreted as turning politics into a very 'determined' and 'conditioned' activity indeed—so 'determined' and 'conditioned', in fact, as to give politics a mostly derivative, subsidiary, and 'epiphenomenal' character. At its extreme, this turns Marxism into an 'economic determinism' which deprives politics of any substantial degree of autonomy.

For their part, Marx and Engels explicitly rejected any rigid and mechanistic notion of 'determination'; and Engels specifically repudiated the idea that Marx and he had ever intended to suggest that 'the economic element is the *only* determining one', which he described as a 'meaningless, abstract, senseless phrase'.[3] As for Marx, the passage from *Capital* just quoted goes on to say that 'the same economic basis', because of 'innumerable different empirical circumstances, natural environment, racial relations, external historical influences, etc.', will show 'infinite variations and gradations in appearance, which can be ascertained only by analysis of the empirically given circumstances';[4] and these 'variations' must obviously include the political part of the 'superstructure'.

'Base' and 'superstructure' must be taken, in Gramsci's phrase, as the elements of an 'historical bloc'; and the different elements which make up that 'bloc' will vary in their relative weight and importance according to time, place, circumstance, and human intervention.

But one must not protest too much. There remains in Marxism an insistence on the 'primacy' of the 'economic base' which must not be understated. This 'primacy' is usually taken by Marxists, following Engels,[5] as meaning that the 'economic base' is decisive, or determining, 'in the last instance'. But it is much more apposite and meaningful to treat the 'economic base' as a *starting-point*, as a matter of the *first instance*. In a different but relevant context, Marx noted that

in all forms of society there is one specific kind of production which predominates over the rest, whose relations thus assign rank and influence to the others. It is a general illumination which bathes all the other colours and modifies their particularity. It is a particular ether which determines the specific gravity of every being which has materialized within it.[6]

This formulation may well be applied to the relation which politics, in the Marxist scheme, has to the 'economic base'; and it is then possible to proceed from there, and to attribute to political forms and forces whatever degree of autonomy is judged in any particular case to be appropriate. In this usage, the notion of 'primacy' constitutes an important and illuminating guideline, not an analytical straitjacket. The ways in which that 'primacy' determines and conditions political and other forms remain to be discovered, and must be treated in each case as specific, circumstantial, and contingent; and this also leaves open for assessment the ways in which political forms and processes in turn affect, determine, condition, and shape the economic realm, as of course they do and as they are acknowledged to do by Marxists, beginning with Marx.

Marx's own cast of mind was strongly anti-determinist, and led him to reject all trans-historical and absolute determinations, beginning with the Hegelian 'determination' of the historical process, and including the rejection of any attempt, as he wrote with heavy sarcasm in 1877, to use 'as one's master key a general historico-philosophical theory, the supreme virtue of which consists in being super-historical'.[7] Marx did believe that certain things must come to pass, notably the supersession of capitalism: but a belief in the inevitability of certain events is not the same as a belief in their particular 'determination'.

The question then is not whether Marxism is an 'economic determinism'. I take it that it is not. The point is rather that the entirely legitimate emphasis which Marxists have placed on the importance of the economic 'infra-structure' and the mode of production has resulted, in relation to social analysis and notwithstanding ritual denegations concerning 'economic determinism', in a marked 'economism' in Marxist thought.

The term 'economism' has now come to be used in very loose ways and has been made to cover a multitude of sins, real or imaginary.* But in the present context, it means both the attribution of an exaggerated—almost an exclusive—importance to the economic sphere in the shaping of social and political relations, leading precisely to 'economic determinism'; and it also involves a related underestimation of the importance of the 'superstructural' sphere. In the letter of Engels to Bloch quoted earlier, he also wrote that 'Marx and I are ourselves partly to blame for the fact that the younger people sometimes lay more stress on the economic side than is due to it. We had to

---

*In recent usage, it has meant (a) the belief that the public ownership of the means of production can be equated with, or is at least bound to be followed by, the socialist transformation of the 'relations of production'; (b) the belief that a massive development of the productive forces is an essential precondition for the achievement of socialist 'relations of production'; and (c) that with the abolition of capitalist owners, the state altogether changes its character and comes to reflect or incarnate the 'dictatorship of the proletariat'. How far (or whether) these propositions constitute deformations of Marxism is a matter for discussion.

emphasise the main principle, vis-à-vis our adversaries, who denied it, and we had not always the time, the place or the opportunity to allow the other elements involved in the inter-action to come into their rights.'[8] It may be noted that Engels did not here renounce the 'main principle'; he only regretted the fact that it had sometimes been allowed to obscure or crowd out the 'other elements'.

However, not all the elements of the 'superstructure' suffered equal neglect by Marxists. In intellectual matters, classical Marxism was deeply concerned with economic analysis—but also with history and philosophy, and other areas of thought as well, for instance science. It was political theory which, com-paratively speaking, suffered the greatest neglect; and this has remained so, even in the more recent decades of Marxist intel-lectual growth.

The reason for this may be traced back to a fundamental distinction which Marx drew at the very beginning of his politi-cal life between 'political emancipation' and 'human emancipa-tion'. Political emancipation, by which he meant the achieve-ment of civic rights, the extension of the suffrage, representative institutions, the curbing of monarchical rule, and the curtail-ment of arbitrary state power in general, was by no means to be scorned. On the contrary, it should be welcomed, Marx wrote in his essay On the Jewish Question of 1843, as 'certainly a big step forward' and as 'the last form of human emancipation within the prevailing scheme of things'.[9] The stress is Marx's own and is significant: it points to a major Marxist theme, namely that human emancipation can never be achieved in the political realm alone but requires the revolutionary transforma-tion of the economic and social order. 'Property, etc., in short the whole content of law and the state', Marx also wrote in his Critique of Hegel's 'Philosophy of Right' in the same year, 'is broadly the same in North America as in Prussia. Hence the republic in America is just as much a mere form of the state as the monarchy here. The content of the state lies beyond these con-stitutions.'[10]

There was great strength in the Marxist insistence that sense could not be made out of political reality without probing beneath political institutions and forms; and that insistence was and remains the basis of Marxist political analysis and of Marx-ist political sociology.

But while this in no way *requires* the conclusion that political forms 'within the prevailing scheme of things', are of no great consequence, it produces a *tendency* to draw just such a conclusion; and the tendency *has* been very strong within Marxism to devalue or ignore the importance of 'mere' political forms and to make very little of the problems associated with them.

This tendency was further reinforced by an extraordinarily complacent view of the ease with which political problems (other than mastering bourgeois resistance) would be resolved in post-revolutionary societies. Politics was taken to be an expression of man's alienation. 'Human emancipation' meant, among other things, the *end* of politics. As István Mészáros has summarized it, 'politics must be conceived as an activity whose ultimate end is *its own annulment* by means of fulfilling its determinate function as a necessary stage in the complex process of positive transcendence.'[11]

In *The Poverty of Philosophy* (1846), Marx wrote that 'the working class, in the course of its development, will substitute for the old civil society* an association which will exclude classes and their antagonism, and there will be no more political power properly so-called, since political power is precisely the expression of antagonism in civil society.'[12] Lucio Colletti has rightly noted[13] that this was one of the most consistent themes of Marx throughout his life, from the *Critique of Hegel's 'Philosophy of Right'* to *The Civil War in France* of 1871 and the *Critique of the Gotha Programme* of 1875. It is instructive in this connection to see how contemptuously (and inadequately) Marx answered the very pertinent questions which Bakunin, in his *Statism and Anarchism* of 1874, had raised about some of the problems which he thought must arise in the attempt to bring about the rule of the proletariat, in the literal sense in which Marx meant it.[14] But it was Engels who gave to the notion of the end of politics its most popular Marxist expression in his *Anti-Dühring* of 1878, the relevant part of which was reproduced in *Socialism: Utopian and Scientific*, published in 1892 and probably, after the *Communist Manifesto*, the most widely-read of the works of Marx and Engels. Writing about the state, Engels said that

---

* 'Civil society' here stands for bourgeois society. See K. Marx and F. Engels, *The German Ideology* (London, 1965), p. 48.

when at last it becomes the real representative of the whole of society, it renders itself unnecessary. As soon as there is no longer any social class to be held in subjection; as soon as class rule, and the individual struggle for existence based upon our present anarchy of production, with the collisions and excesses arising from these, are removed, nothing more remains to be repressed, and a special repressive force, a state, is no longer necessary . . . State interference in social relations becomes, in one domain after another, superfluous, and then withers away of itself; the government of persons is replaced by the administration of things, and by the conduct of processes of production. The state is not 'abolished'. *It withers away.*[15]

This optimistic view was reaffirmed in the most extreme form in Lenin's *The State and Revolution*, which was written on the eve of the October Revolution of 1917, and where all the problems of the exercise of socialist power—for instance the danger of the bureaucratization of the revolution and the reproduction of a strongly hierarchical order, not to mention the question of civic freedoms—were either swept aside or simply ignored. This complacency was replaced almost as soon as the Bolsheviks had seized power by a sombre awareness on the part of Lenin and some of the other Bolshevik leaders of how genuine and difficult these problems were, and how real was the threat that they posed to the new Soviet order. But it is significant that neither Lenin nor those around him should have thought it necessary at least to consider these problems seriously in the years preceding the revolution. They did take up many theoretical and organizational problems in the years before 1917, from economic analysis and philosophy to the organization of the party. But save for the debate among Marxists around the issue of the relation of the party to the working class and the danger of 'substitutism', which followed the publication of Lenin's *What is to Be Done?* in 1902, there was comparatively little attention devoted to the theoretical and practical problems posed by the concept of socialist democracy and the 'dictatorship of the proletariat'. It is symptomatic that it was only *after* 1917 that one of the most alert minds among the Bolsheviks, Bukharin, should have become aware of the import of the challenge posed by theories of élite and of bureaucratization which had been posed to Marxists—and left unanswered for a good many years past.[16] Much of the reason for this must be sought in the absence in Marxism of a serious tradition of political inquiry; and in the assumption commonly made by Marxists before 1917 that the socialist revolution would itself—given the kind of overwhelming popular movement it would be—resolve the main political problems presented to it. *The State and Revolution* was the ultimate expression of that belief.

There did occur very extensive and passionate discussion of all such problems after the Russian Revolution, in Russia and in the socialist movements of many other countries; and this would undoubtedly have produced in time a strong Marxist tradition of political thought. But the debates were overtaken by Stalinist 'triumphalism' from the mid-twenties onwards; and this required agreement that the main *political* problems of socialist power had been solved in the Soviet Union, except for the problem presented by the enemies of socialism. To suggest otherwise was to cast doubt on the socialist and proletarian character of Soviet rule, and thus to turn automatically into one of the very enemies of the Soviet Union and socialism. The impact of such modes of thought on the history of Marxism in subsequent years cannot be overestimated.

There is one altogether different explanation for the relative poverty of Marxist political theory which has been advanced over the years, namely and very simply that, whatever the contribution of Marxism may be in other areas of thought, it has little to contribute in this one. This is what anti-Marxist political theorists and others have commonly held to be the case: Marxist politics and political pronouncements might be an object of study, but not much more.

Perhaps more remarkably, a fairly negative verdict on Marxist political theory has also been returned in recent years by Lucio Colletti, who is one of the most interesting modern Marxist writers. In his Introduction to Marx's *Early Writings* which I have already mentioned, Colletti states that Marx, in his *Critique of Hegel's 'Philosophy of Right'*, 'already possesses a very mature theory of politics and the state'. 'The *Critique*, after all', he goes on, 'contains a clear statement of the dependence of the state upon society, a critical analysis of parliamentarism accompanied by a counter-theory of popular delegation, and a perspective showing the need for the ultimate suppression of the state itself.' He then concludes that 'politically speaking, mature Marxism would have relatively little to add to this.'[17]

Colletti also says of Lenin's *The State and Revolution* that it 'advances little beyond the ideas set out in the *Critique*'; and even though he refers to Marx's 'profundity' in connection with the *Critique*; and to the 'marvellous continuation' in *On the Jewish Question* of the theory of the state elaborated in the *Critique*, he takes the view that 'Marxism's most specific terrain of development was the socio-economic one.'[18] For Colletti, the most important progenitor of Marx's political theory was Rousseau; and 'so far as "political" theory in the strict sense is concerned, Marx and Lenin have added nothing to Rousseau, except for the analysis (which is of course rather important) of the "economic bases" for the withering away of the state'.[19]

Claims such as these are too broad and qualified to offer a firm basis of argument, and there does not seem much point in entering into abstract disputation as to whether the originality of Marxism lies in one realm rather than in another. The same applies to the judgements of anti-Marxist writers on the worth of Marxist political theory. The best way to test all such propositions is to show what a Marxist political theory specifically involves; and to indicate how far it may serve to illuminate any particular aspect of historical or contemporary reality.

For this purpose, the developments in Marxist political thinking in recent years have obviously been of great value, not least because the constricting 'triumphalism' of an earlier period has been strongly challenged; and the challenge has produced a much greater awareness among Marxists that Marxism, in this as much as in other realms, is full of questions to be asked and—no less important—of answers to be questioned. Many hitherto neglected or underestimated problems have attracted greater attention; and many old problems have been perceived in a better light. As a result, the beginnings have been made of a political theorization in the Marxist mode.

But these are only beginnings, and in some areas barely even that. One such area is that covered by Communist experience since 1917 and the nature and workings of Communist states and political systems. There has not really been very much, beyond Trotsky's *The Revolution Betrayed* of forty years ago, by way of Marxist attempts to theorize the experience of Stalinism; and the Marxist debate on the nature of the Soviet state (and of other Communist regimes) has long been paralysed by the invocation of formulas and slogans—'degenerate workers' state' versus 'state capitalism' and so forth. The whole area has largely been left for anti-Marxists to explore; and the subject badly requires serious and sustained Marxist political analysis and reinterpretation. This has now begun but needs to be pushed much further.

The position is in many ways rather better in regard to the politics of the many different countries which are arbitrarily subsumed under the label 'Third World'. But here too, it would appear to the non-specialist that, as far as political analysis is concerned, no more than some paths have been cleared, and that the main work of theorizing the known practice remains to be undertaken; and it is only in the undertaking of it that it will be possible to discover which theoretical categories of Marxism are relevant to the experience in question, which need to be modified, and which should be discarded.

Perhaps not surprisingly, it is the countries of advanced capitalism which have received most attention from Marxists in the last two decades, in the area of politics as well as in other areas of inquiry. Even so, it is not the wealth of Marxist political theory and analysis in relation to these societies which is striking, but the fact that it has not proceeded much further. Nothing like enough serious work has yet been done which could be said to constitute a Marxist tradition of political studies.

The present work attempts to make a contribution to the development of such a tradition. It suggests some of the main questions which must be considered and probed in the construction of a Marxist political analysis; and it does so on the basis of a reading of primary Marxist texts, first and foremost on the basis of a reading of Marx himself. Whether the reading is accurate or not must be left for others to judge. So too must the question of the validity of the political argument which, in this reconstruction of Marxist politics, I am inevitably led to put forward and which indeed I want to put forward.

NOTES

1 K. Marx, 'Preface' to *A Contribution to the Critique of Political Economy*, in SW 1968, p. 182.
2 K. Marx, *Capital* (Moscow, 1962), III, p. 772.
3 F. Engels to J. Bloch, 21–2 September 1890, in SW 1968, p. 692.
4 K. Marx, *Capital*, III, p. 772.
5 See e.g. his letter to C. Schmidt, 27 October 1890, in SW 1968, pp. 694–9.
6 K. Marx, *Grundrisse* (London, 1973), pp. 106–7.
7 SC. p. 379. The letter was to the Editorial Board of the journal *Otechestvenniye Zapiski* and is dated November 1877.
8 SW 1968, p. 692.

9 *On the Jewish Question*, in EW, p. 221.
10 K. Marx, *Critique of Hegel's Doctrine of the State*, ibid., p. 89. The usual title of the work is that given in the text above.
11 I. Mészáros, *Marx's Theory of Alienation* (London, 1970), p. 160.
12 K. Marx, *The Poverty of Philosophy* (London, 1946), p.147.
13 See L. Colletti's Introduction to EW.
14 For an extract from Marx's comments on the book, see *FI* (London, 1974). For the full text, see Marx-Engels, *Werke* (Berlin, 1964), XVIII.
15 F. Engels, *Anti-Dühring* (Moscow, 1962), p. 385.
16 See S. F. Cohen, *Bukharin and the Bolshevik Revolution* (London, 1974), p. 21.
17 EW, p. 45.
18 Ibid., p. 46.
19 L. Colletti, 'Rousseau as Critic of "Civil Society"', in *From Rousseau to Lenin* (London, 1972), p. 185.

II. Class and Class Conflict

At the core of Marxist politics, there is the notion of conflict. But this is not what makes it specific and distinct: all concepts of politics, of whatever kind, are about conflict—how to contain it, or abolish it. What is specific about Marxist politics is what it declares the nature of the conflict to be; and what it proclaims to be its necessary outcome.

In the liberal view of politics, conflict exists in terms of 'problems' which need to be 'solved'. The hidden assumption is that conflict does not, or need not, run very deep; that it can be 'managed' by the exercise of reason and good will, and a readiness to compromise and agree. On this view, politics is not civil war conducted by other means but a constant process of bargaining and accommodation, on the basis of accepted procedures, and between parties who have decided as a preliminary that they could and wanted to live together more or less harmoniously. Not only is this sort of conflict not injurious to society: it has positive advantages. It is not only civilized, but also civilizing. It is not only a means of resolving problems in a peaceful way, but also of producing new ideas, ensuring progress, achieving ever-greater harmony, and so on. Conflict is 'functional', a stabilizing rather than a disruptive force.

The Marxist approach to conflict is very different. It is not a matter of 'problems' to be 'solved' but of a state of domination and subjection to be ended by a total transformation of the conditions which give rise to it. No doubt conflict may be attenuated, but only because the ruling class is able by one means or another—coercion, concessions, or persuasion—to prevent the subordinate classes from seeking emancipation. Ultimately, stability is not a matter of reason but of force. The antagonists are irreconcilable, and the notion of genuine harmony is a deception or a delusion, at least in relation to class societies.

For the protagonists are not individuals as such, but individuals as members of social aggregates—classes. In the *Grundrisse*, Marx writes that 'society does not consist of individuals, but expresses the sum of interrelations, the relations within which these individuals stand. As if someone were to say: Seen from the perspective of society, there are no slaves and no citizens: both are human beings. Rather they are that outside society. To be a slave, to be a citizen, are social characteristics, relations between human beings A and B. Human being A, as such, is not a slave. He is a slave in and through society.'[1] A member of one class may well feel no antagonism towards members of other classes; and there may be mobility between classes. But classes nevertheless remain irreconcilably divided, whether conflict occurs or not, and independently of the forms it may or may not assume. It is important not to attribute to the notion of conflict the meaning of 'eruption', or of an interruption of an otherwise smooth, harmonious process. This is often the meaning implicit in the liberal usage of 'conflict'—the expression of a 'problem' or 'problems' that need to be 'solved'. In a Marxist perspective, this is a mystification: conflict is inherent in the class system, incapable of solution within that system. Eruptions, outbursts, revolts, revolutions, are only the most visible manifestations of a permanent alienation and conflict, signs that the contradictions in the social system are growing and that the struggle between contending classes is assuming sharper or irrepressible forms. These contending classes are locked in a situation of domination and subjection from which there is no escape except through the total transformation of the mode of production.

Domination is a central concept in Marxist sociology and politics. But domination, in Marxist thought, is not an inherent part of 'the human condition', just as conflict is not an inherent feature of 'human nature'. Domination and conflict are inherent in class societies, and are based on specific, concrete features of their mode of production. They are rooted in the process of extraction and appropriation of what is produced by human labour. Class domination is not simply a 'fact': it is a process, a continuing endeavour on the part of the dominant class or classes to maintain, strengthen and extend, or defend, their domination.

The focus, always, is on *class* antagonism and *class* conflict. This does not mean that Marxism does not recognize the existence of other kinds of conflict within societies and between them—ethnic, religious, national, etc. But it does consider these rivalries, conflicts and wars as directly or indirectly derived from, or related to, class conflicts; whether it is right to do so is not here the point. The fact is that in Marxism this is the essential, primary focus.

Marx himself greatly underestimated and misleadingly belittled his own contribution and that of Engels to this focusing on class antagonism. In a famous letter to his friend, Weydemeyer, dated 5 March, 1852, he wrote that 'no credit is due to me for discovering the existence of classes in modern society, nor yet the struggle between them. Long before me bourgeois historians had described the historical development of this struggle of the classes and bourgeois economists the economic anatomy of the classes.'[2] True though this may be (and there is something but no more than something in it), it was nevertheless Marx and Engels who so to speak gave to classes their letters of credit as the *dramatis personae* of history and to class struggle as its motor; and it is certainly they who, more than anyone else before them, represented politics as the specific articulation of class struggles.

The protagonists of class struggles have naturally varied, through the ages, from 'freeman and slave, patrician and plebeian, lord and serf, guild-master and journeyman', to bourgeoisie and proletariat in the epoch of capitalism. But throughout, 'oppressor and oppressed' have 'stood in constant opposition to one another, carried on an uninterrupted, now hidden, now open fight, a fight that each time ended, either in a revolutionary reconstitution of society at large, or in the common ruin of the contending classes'.*

The basis of this conflict is somewhat simpler than the endlessly varied forms it assumes in different realms. As already noted, the conflict essentially stems from the determination of the dominant classes to extract as much work as possible from the subject classes; and, conversely, from the attempts of these classes to change the terms and conditions of their subjection, or to end it altogether. In relation to capitalism, the matter is expressed by Marx in terms of the imperative necessity for the owners and controllers of capital to extract the largest possible amount of surplus value from the labour force; and in terms of

* K. Marx and F. Engels, *Manifesto of the Communist Party*, in *Revs.*, p. 68. This early allowance by Marx and Engels that one stage of history, rather than inexorably leading to another, may lead to the 'common ruin of all classes', is worth noting.

the latter's attempts either to reduce that amount, or to bring the system to an end. The first alternative involves the attempt to introduce reforms in the operation of capitalism; the second obviously involves its transcendence.

Class domination is economic, political, and cultural—in other words, it has many different and related facets; and the struggle against it is similarly varied and complex. Politics may be the specific expression of that struggle, but, as I noted in the previous chapter, is in fact involved in all its manifestations. Class domination can never be purely 'economic', or purely 'cultural': it must always have a strong and pervasive 'political' content, not least because the law is the crystallized form which politics assumes in providing the necessary sanction and legitimation of all forms of domination. In this sense, 'politics' sanctions what is 'permitted', and therefore 'permits' the relations between members of different and conflicting classes, inside and outside their 'relations of production'.

In the *Communist Manifesto*, Marx and Engels said that 'the epoch of the bourgeoisie' had 'simplified class antagonisms': 'Society as a whole is more and more splitting up into two great hostile camps, into two great classes directly facing each other: bourgeoisie and proletariat.'[3] Though the formulation is ambiguous and possibly misleading, it ought not to be taken to mean that capitalist society, which is the 'society' that Marx and Engels are talking about, has been or is being reduced to two classes. It is clear from all of their work that they were perfectly well aware of the continued existence of other classes than the bourgeoisie and the proletariat, and that they did not expect these classes simply to vanish. Nor is the formulation to be taken to mean that the *only* antagonism in class society is that between these two classes. They did recognize the existence of other forms of class conflict, and I have already noted that they also recognized the existence of conflicts other than class conflict. The really important point is the insistence by Marx and Engels that the *primary* conflict in capitalist society is that between capitalists and wage-earners, what Marx, in the formulation which I quoted in the first chapter, called 'the direct relationship of the owners of the conditions of production to the direct producers'.[4] It is *this* relationship, Marx claimed, which revealed 'the innermost secret, the hidden basis of the entire social structure';[5] and which also produced by far the most important element of conflict in capitalist society. Whether this is always the case or not is open to inquiry, and it is probably true that too strict an interpretation of the notion of the primacy of the conflict between capitalists and wage-earners has led to the underestimation by Marxists of the importance which other classes and their conflicts have had and still have in capitalist societies, and to an underestimation also of their role in general —notably that of 'intermediate classes', of which more later.

In political terms, however, the more important question is how far Marx was right in speaking of society as 'splitting up into two great *hostile* camps'; indeed, whether he was right about this at all. For it would be possible to think of capitalist society 'simplifying' class arrangements without necessarily turning the different classes into mutually hostile ones; or it would at least be possible to think of this hostility, the 'class antagonism' of which Marx speaks *without* giving it the sharp, warring connotation which he and Engels clearly do give to it—in other words to accept that antagonisms will occur between classes and social aggregates of different kinds without producing 'hostile camps', an imagery that significantly conjures up an actual or incipient state of war. This of course raises the whole question of the validity or otherwise of Marx's and Engels's belief in the inevitability of revolution, in other words of a decisive settlement of accounts between bourgeoisie and proletariat, out of which a new social order and mode of production, namely socialism, would emerge.*

As a preliminary but essential part of the consideration of the many issues which this raises, there is a question which needs to be asked: what is the *meaning* which is to be attached to the names given to the main or subsidiary antagonists in the struggle, whatever its nature? What, above all, do Marx and Engels, and subsequent Marxist writers, *mean* when they speak of 'the working class'? The question is obviously crucial. But despite the constant use of the terms in question, or perhaps because of it, their actual meaning is by no means as clear as

---

* In a letter to the Communist Correspondence Committee in Brussels, written from Paris and dated 23 October 1846, Engels reported that, in argument with upholders of other tendencies, he 'defined the objects of the Communists in this way: (1) to achieve the interests of the proletariat in opposition to those of the bourgeoisie; (2) to do this through the abolition of private property and its replacement by community of goods; (3) to recognize no means of carrying out these objects other than a democratic revolution by force' (SC, p. 37).

their use would suggest or than is assumed. Nor indeed is it at all easy to find a ready and obvious answer to the question in the classic writings. In fact, it is quite *difficult* to find out precisely what Marx meant by the terms 'working class' or 'proletariat'; and later work has not advanced matters very far. The first thing is therefore to try and clarify this and also to identify more closely the other antagonists in the class conflict: this is the basis on which a Marxist politics obviously has to build.

2

How genuine and basic the problem is of identifying the exact meaning which is to be attached to the Marxist concept of working class may first of all be gauged from the fact that, for Marx, the very notion of it as a class is in some degree contingent: it is only by fulfilling certain conditions that the working class may properly be said to have become a class. In *The Poverty of Philosophy*, a passage which refers to the early development of English industrial capitalism makes the point as follows:

Economic conditions had first transformed the mass of the people of the country into workers. The domination of capital has created for this mass a common situation, common interests. This mass is thus already a class as against capital, but not yet for itself. In the struggle . . . this mass becomes united, and constitutes itself as a class for itself. The interests it defends become class interests.[6]

It is thus in a united struggle, which presupposes a consciousness of its interests, that the proletariat becomes a 'class for itself', as distinct from a mere 'mass' in a common situation and with common interests. In the *Communist Manifesto*, Marx and Engels went further and spoke of the 'organisation of the proletarians into a class, and consequently into a political party';[7] and the *Manifesto* also insists that 'the proletariat during its contest with the bourgeoisie is compelled, by the force of circumstances, to organize itself as a class.'[8] Rightly or wrongly, a political criterion is thus assigned to the notion of class, and this remained a fundamental theme in Marx's thought. In 1871, the Resolution of the First International on Political Action of the Working Class, drafted by Marx and Engels, still insists that against the 'collective power of the propertied classes the working class cannot act, as a class, except by constituting itself into a political party'.[9] The ambiguity presented by the formulation whereby the working class constitutes *itself* as a party will be discussed in Chapter V. But it is worth emphasizing that, for Marx, the working class is not truly a class unless it acquires the capacity to organize itself politically. In so far as this involves will and consciousness, as it obviously does, it can be said that there is in Marx a 'subjective' dimension to the notion of the working class as a class, as well as an 'objective' determination of it. The point might be summarized by saying that, without consciousness, the working class is a mere mass: it becomes a class when it acquires consciousness. What 'consciousness' entails will be discussed presently.

To turn first to this 'objective' determination of the working class: the crucial notion for Marx is that of 'productive worker', which is given its most extensive treatment in *Capital* and *Theories of Surplus Value*. The 'productive worker' is he who produces surplus value: 'that labourer alone is productive, who produces surplus-value for the capitalist, and thus works for the self-expansion of capital.'[10] Similarly, 'only that wage-labour is productive which produces capital';[11] and 'only the wage-labour which creates more value than it costs is productive.'[12]

It will immediately be seen that this extends the notion of 'worker' far beyond that of the industrial and factory wage-earner. It does so in two ways. Firstly, it covers a large number of people who are not engaged in the industrial process at all, for instance writers, or at least some writers, since, as Marx put it, 'a writer is a productive labourer not in so far as he produces ideas, but in so far as he enriches the publisher who publishes his works, or if he is a wage-labourer for a capitalist.'[13] In other words, the definition of what constitutes a productive worker has in this conception nothing to do with what he produces: what matters is whether the worker produces surplus value.[14]

The second extension of the notion of 'productive worker' concerns the actual process of production. Marx writes that

the characteristic feature of the capitalist mode of production . . . separates the various kinds of labour from each other, therefore also mental and manual labour—or kinds of labour in which one or the other predominates—and distributes them among different people. This however does not prevent the material product from being the *common product* of these persons, or their common product embodied in material wealth; any more than on the other hand it prevents or in any way alters the relation of each one of these persons to capital being that of wage-labourer and in this pre-eminent sense being that of a *productive labourer*.[15]

In *Capital*, Marx also succinctly notes that 'in order to labour productively, it is no longer necessary for you to do manual work yourself; enough if you are an organ of the collective labourer, and perform one of its *subordinate* functions.'[16]

On this view, it is clear that the 'working class' extends far beyond industrial and manual workers. But this extension also creates certain major difficulties for Marxist sociology and politics. For not only does the designation now cover white-collar workers and 'service' workers of every sort, which is not a major difficulty: it also encompasses many other people as well, for instance managerial staff, executive personnel of high rank and even the topmost layers of capitalist production. 'We are all working class now' may be useful conservative propaganda —but it would be odd to have it legitimated by Marxist concepts; and, more serious, the notion of 'working class' would cease, on this basis, to make possible the differentiations which the class structure of capitalist societies obviously requires.

What is needed here is a set of criteria which do make possible these differentiations—in this instance between the various aggregates of people who constitute different elements of the 'collective labourer', and which allow the necessary distinction to be made between the 'working class' elements of the 'collective labourer' and the rest: between, say, the corporation executive and the factory worker. The criteria in question are partly —but hardly exhaustively—provided by Marx himself when he refers in the above quotation from *Capital* to those people who perform the 'subordinate functions' of the 'collective labourer'. The notion of subordination is here crucial, though other criteria of differentiation may be linked to it, for instance income and status, and are usually related to it.

The 'working class' is therefore that part of the 'collective labourer' which produces surplus value, from a position of subordination, at the lower ends of the income scale, and also at the lower ends of what might be called the 'scale of regard'.

This designation does not by any means solve all problems. But neither does any other. One such problem, which is embedded in the notion of class itself, is that of heterogeneity. Like all other classes, the 'working class' is divided into many different strata and by a whole set of differences, which vary according to time and place, but some of which at least are always present. In the present designation, the main difference would be between industrial wage-earners on the one hand (themselves greatly differentiated) and 'white collar' and 'service' workers on the other—and the latter terms obviously cover a wide variation of occupations and grades.

Another such problem, which is a constantly recurring one in the discussion of class, is where to 'cut off'—in this instance to decide at what point (if any) it is appropriate or necessary to draw the line between the 'workers' just mentioned and the large and growing number of 'workers' who perform a variety of technical, intellectual, supervisory, and managerial tasks. As already noted, these people are indeed part of the 'collective labourer': but whether they are part of the 'working class' is an open question. The point is far from a mere matter of pedantic denomination. On the contrary, it has important political implications, in terms of political strategy and alliances.

As far as classical Marxism is concerned, the 'working class' is basically constituted by industrial wage-earners, factory workers, the 'modern proletariat'. For Marx, Engels, Lenin, and their followers, here is the 'working class', or at least its 'core'. For the purpose of discussing Marxist politics, this will do well enough, provided full account is taken of the many problems which the term presents, precisely in the discussion of politics and such questions as the relation of the working class to its political agencies.

The middle strata of the 'collective labourer' must be distinguished from the so-called 'intermediate' strata of capitalist society of which Marx occasionally spoke* and which comprise a wide range of people often also described in Marxist usage as the *petty bourgeoisie* of capitalist society—medium and small businessmen, shopkeepers, self-employed craftsmen and artisans, small and medium farmers; in other words, that vast and diverse array of people who have not been 'proletarianized', in the sense that they have not become wage and salary earners, and are not therefore part of the 'collective labourer', even though they do of course fulfil definite economic tasks.

In its turn, this petty bourgeoisie must be distinguished from

---

* In *Capital*, for instance, Marx notes the existence in England of 'middle and intermediate strata' which 'obliterate lines of demarcation everywhere' (op. cit. III, p. 862).

the large and growing army of state employees, engaged in administration and in police and military functions.* On the criteria of classification referred to earlier, these state employees are neither part of the working class nor of the petty bourgeoisie: they are, so to speak, a class apart, whose separateness from other classes is bridged by the factor of *ideology*, which will be considered presently.

To complete this brief enumeration of the main protagonists of class struggle in capitalist society, there remains the capitalist class. This is the class which, for Marx, was so designated by virtue of the fact that it owned and controlled the means of production and of economic activity in general—the great manufacturing, financial and commercial 'interests' of capitalist enterprise. The 'capitalist class', however, extends well beyond these 'interests' and includes many people who fulfil specific professional and other functions on behalf of these 'interests', and who are in various ways—by virtue of income, status, occupation, kinship, etc.—associated with them. It is this variegated totality which is also called the 'ruling class' in Marxist parlance, a concept which needs further discussion.

The point has already been made, but needs to be stressed, that the capitalist class or bourgeoisie (the two terms are used here interchangeably, unless the text requires specific use) is in functional, sociological and in most other terms an heterogeneous class, with many different elements or 'fractions'; and while the development of capitalism has fostered an ever-greater interrelationship between different forms of capital, it has by no means obliterated their differences. There are many issues over which the capitalist class as a whole is more or less united, and this unity may assume a more or less solid political expression, and does assume such expression in times of acute class conflict, 'when the chips are down'. But the economic divisions of the class endure, and so do other divisions of various kinds, according to the particular country in question. The importance of these divisions, from a political point of view, is considerable.

A second question, which has already been encountered in relation to the working class, arises here too, namely the 'cut off' point at which the capitalist class ends and the petty bourgeoisie

---

* This is not the case for state employees who are engaged in the economic activities covered by the 'public sector', nationalized industries, public services etc., and who obviously *are* part of the working class.

begins. Marx noted that 'the stratification of classes does not appear in its pure form'[17] and this is certainly true here. Clearly a concept of the 'capitalist class' which covers a small entrepreneur, employing half a dozen workmen and the owner of a corporation employing thousands leaves something to be desired. There is no conclusive answer to the problem and some degree of arbitrariness in deciding who, in this context, belongs to the capitalist class is inevitable.

Much more important is the by now well-worn question of ownership and control, or ownership versus control, and the degree to which capitalism and the notion of a capitalist class have been affected by the coming into being of an ever-growing stratum of managers, controlling the most important units of business life, yet doing so without owning more than a minute fraction of the assets they control, and sometimes not even that.

There is no point in rehearsing here the arguments which have been advanced on both sides of the question.* My own view of the matter is that managerialism, which had already been noted in its early manifestations by Marx,† is indeed a major and growing feature of advanced capitalism; and that the separation of ownership and control which it betokens—when it does betoken it—does not affect in any substantial way the rationale and dynamic of capitalist enterprise. Those who manage it are primarily concerned, whatever they may or may not own, with the maximization of long-term profit and the accumulation of capital for their particular enterprise: ownerless managers are from this point of view practically indistinguishable from owning ones. What matters in both cases are the constraints imposed upon those involved by the imperative and objectively determined requirements of capitalist activity. This being the case, it is perfectly legitimate to speak of a 'capitalist class', occupying the upper rungs of the economic ladder, whatever its members may own, and controlling the operations of capitalist enterprise. It is the more legitimate to do so in that the ideological and political differences between non-owning

---

* For a useful recent survey of the argument, see M. Zeitlin, 'Corporate Ownership and Control: The Large Corporation and the Capitalist Class' in *American Journal of Sociology*, 1974, vol. 79, no. 5.

† On the basis of the formation of joint stock companies, Marx speaks in *Capital* of the 'transformation of the actually functioning capitalist into a mere manager, administrator of other people's capital' and of 'private production without the control of private property' (op. cit. III, 427, 429).

controllers and the rest have never been more than negligible, if that.

The class struggles in which these classes are engaged occur within the territorial boundaries of the nation-state, and the role of the state in class struggle is of course one of the main objects of attention of Marxist politics. On the other hand, it is as well to stress at the outset that these struggles are deeply and often decisively influenced by external forces. This has been the case throughout the history of capitalism but the point is rendered ever more important by the ever-greater inter-relatedness of capitalism, in a process of 'internationalization' which makes national boundaries an economic anachronism of a constantly more pronounced kind. But the nation state endures, and it is within its boundaries that the encounter occurs.

One or two further preliminary points arise. What encounter? To speak of class conflict is to speak of a central reality by way of metaphor. For classes, as entities, do not enter into conflict—only elements of it do, though it is the case that very large parts of contending classes are on rare occasions directly drawn into battle. For the most part, however, the conflict is fought out between groups of people who are part of a given class, and possibly, though not certainly, representative of it.

Another important question is: What kind of class conflict? For the antagonism between classes does assume many different forms of expression, and many different levels of intensity and scope. It often is strictly localized and focused on immediate, specific and 'economic' demands, and forms part of the 'normal' pattern of relations between employer and wage-earners—with strike action as a familiar part of that pattern. Or it may be fought at the 'cultural' level, and indeed is permanently fought at that level, in so far as there occurs a permanent struggle for the communication of alternative and contradictory ideas, values and perspectives. Or it may be fought at the 'political' level, and bring into question existing political arrangements, large or small. And it may of course assume peaceful or violent forms, and move from one form or level to another.

The distinction between various forms and levels of class conflict is certainly not artificial. But it is nevertheless a misconception to ascribe such labels as 'economic' or 'ideological' to this or that form of conflict. For any event in class conflict, large or small, includes and expresses all manifestations of social life, and is in this sense an economic, cultural/ideological, social, and political phenomenon. And it is even more important to stress the concomitant proposition, which is a basic part of Marxist perspectives, namely that *all* manifestations of social life are permanently present in the permanent class conflict of capitalist society.

The class profile which has been outlined here refers to advanced capitalist countries. The very large question which arises is how far that profile and the propositions which relate to it have application to other types of society—the countries of the 'Third World' (using that term with the reservations mentioned earlier) and, even more problematically, the countries of the Communist world. As was noted in Chapter I, the gaps and shortcomings which affect the Marxist theorization of capitalist countries are greatly multiplied in relation to these other forms of society; and I can in any case do no more here than make some cursory remarks about the comparisons and contrasts that may be drawn, in the present context, between these societies and advanced capitalist ones.

In regard to 'Third World' countries, it is clear that class relations are for most of them too the central determinant of their mode of being. But it is equally clear that the classes involved in these relations are in some major ways different or of different importance from those in advanced capitalist societies; and also that, in part because of this and in part for different reasons, the class conflicts engendered by their class relations assume other forms than those encountered in capitalist societies.

The development of these countries has been exceedingly distorted by colonialism and external capitalist domination, direct and indirect; and this has been naturally reflected in their economic, social and political structures. But this also means that Marxism, primarily fashioned in and for a bourgeois/ capitalist context has, to say the least, to be adapted to the very different circumstances subsumed under the notion of 'under-development'.

One of these different circumstances is that in a large number of these countries, there has existed no strong indigenous class of large-scale capitalists, since the major industrial, extractive, financial, and commercial enterprises are likely to be mainly owned and controlled by foreign interests. The indigenous capitalist class has often tended to be economically rooted in medium- and small-scale enterprise, and partially dependent upon the foreign interests implanted in the country. Correspondingly, the working class is relatively small, compared with the population of the countryside, and concentrated on the one hand in a number of large enterprises and dispersed on the other in a multitude of small ones.

In effect, the mass of the working population is of peasant character, and the main 'relations of production' in these countries tend to be between landlord and peasant, in a multitude of different patterns and connections. But this also means that class conflicts in these economies occur on a very different basis and assume a very different form from those encountered in advanced capitalist countries. This does not mean that Marxist 'guidelines' are inoperative in the analysis of these conflicts. But it does very strongly emphasize the danger of a simple transposition of the Marxist mode of analysis of advanced capitalist societies to countries whose capitalism is of a very different nature.

The same point applies to Communist countries; and it may have to be made with even greater force since there has been a fashion in recent years, strongly encouraged by the Chinese Communists, to claim that the categories of analysis used for capitalist countries would do quite well for the Soviet Union and East European regimes. These, the claim goes, are 'essentially' capitalist countries, and the differences between them and other capitalist countries are sufficiently indicated by affixing to them the label 'state capitalist'. Their social structure is one where a 'state bourgeoisie', similar if not identical to the bourgeoisie of Western capitalist countries, exploits and oppresses the working class in the same way as it is oppressed and exploited in classical capitalist countries, and indeed more so. This being so, these regimes are equally susceptible to class conflict, and are only able to contain it by ruthless repression.*

That there is conflict and repression in these societies is not in question. Nor is the fact of marked disparities of resources,

---

* One of the most explicit recent examples of this kind of categorization is C. Bettelheim, *Les Luttes de classes en URSS* (Paris, 1974). For a critical review, see R. Miliband, 'Bettelheim and Soviet Experience', in *New Left Review*, no. 91, May–June 1975.

status and power. What is however very questionable indeed is the notion that it is possible to equate these societies with capitalist ones. These are collectivist societies in which the absence of a class which actually owns the means of economic activity, and in which the question of control of these means poses considerable problems, is sufficient to suggest that any such equation is arbitrary and misleading, an exercise in propaganda rather than analysis. Whether the people in these regimes who are at the top of the pyramid are called a class, an élite, a bureaucracy or whatever, it cannot be analysed in the terms which are used to analyse the 'ruling class' of either advanced capitalist societies or of under-developed ones. Nor can the political systems of these collectivist societies. I propose to take up the subject later, and only wish to note here the existence of the problem which it poses for Marxism, and to reiterate the point that it has so far been very inadequately discussed within the Marxist 'problematic'. For the present, the question to which I want to proceed is that of 'class-consciousness' in that 'problematic'.

3

Whether or not a class may only be said 'properly' to exist if it has a certain kind of consciousness, it is clear that the element of consciousness is of crucial importance in political terms; and 'class-consciousness' is certainly such an element in Marxist politics. Yet the point has to be made once again that here too there are many more unresolved difficulties than ready usage would suggest.

In Marxist language, class-consciousness may be taken to mean the consciousness which the members of a class have of its 'true' interests—the notion of 'true' interests being one which itself requires elucidation.

The matter is in a sense least complicated in relation to the capitalist class and the bourgeoisie in general. Its true interests presumably consist in the maintenance and defence of capitalism; and its class-consciousness is on this score very easy to achieve. As a matter of historical fact, privileged classes have always been perfectly class-conscious, at least in this sense. On the other hand, the clear perception of the interests of a class in no way betokens a clear perception of the ways in which these interests may best be defended. Also, as a matter of historical fact, privileged classes have very often been short-sighted in this respect, and have needed the skills and adroitness of agents acting on their behalf but with a sufficient degree of independence to mitigate if not to overcome the short-sightedness of their masters.[18]

Also, there is in Marxist terms a sense in which the bourgeoisie is falsely conscious, not because it is unable to perceive its true interests, but because it proclaims and believes that these partial and class interests have a universal and classless character. In The German Ideology (1846), Marx and Engels wrote that 'each new class which puts itself in the place of one ruling before it, is compelled, merely in order to carry through its aim, to represent its interest as the common interest of all the members of society, that is, expressed in ideal form: it has to give its ideas the form of universality, and represent them as the only rational, universally valid ones'.[19] In writing thus, Marx and Engels were thinking primarily of the bourgeoisie's struggles against feudal rule, and particularly of the French bourgeoisie's protracted struggles for intellectual as well as economic and political ascendancy under the ancien régime. 'Ideology', for Marx and Engels, is precisely the attempt to 'universalize' and give 'ideal' form to what are no more than limited, class-bound ideas and interests: it is in this sense that they use the word 'ideology' pejoratively, as meaning a false representation of reality. At the same time, they did not hold to the vulgar view that this false representation was necessarily deliberate. Deliberate deception does indeed occur, whereby the spokesmen of a dominant class act as the 'ideologues' of that class, and try to persuade the subordinate classes of the universal validity of ideas and principles which these spokesmen know to be partial and class-bound but useful in the maintenance of the given social order. But alongside deliberate deception, there is also much, and perhaps more, of self-deception, in so far as the spokesmen of a dominant class, and those for whom they speak, do deeply believe in the universal truth of the ideas and ideals which they uphold, and will therefore fight for them all the more vigorously and, if need be, ferociously.

The obvious question which arises here is why the point should not also apply to the working class—in other words why should the working class be thought of and claim to be a 'universal' class, whose interests are indistinguishable from those of society at large, which Marx and Engels did claim to be the case, and which has remained a central Marxist claim ever since.

The answer which they gave to that question has many facets and ramifications which need to be examined and followed through, but the basis of it is that the working class is not only the vast majority of the population but that it is also the only class in history whose interests and well-being do not depend on the oppression and exploitation of other classes. 'All previous historical movements', they said in the *Communist Manifesto*, 'were movements of minorities, or in the interest of minorities. The proletarian movement is the self-conscious, independent movement of the immense majority, in the interest of the immense majority'.[20] Indeed, the proletariat, having swept away the old conditions of production, 'will, along with these conditions, have swept away the conditions for the existence of class antagonisms and of classes generally, and will thereby have abolished its own supremacy as a class'.[21] All previous revolutions had by necessity been limited in scope, because of the narrow class interests of those who had made them. By contrast, 'the communist revolution is the most radical rupture with traditional property relations'; and, Marx adds, 'no wonder that its development involves the most radical rupture with traditional ideas'.[22] Related to this, and reinforcing the notion of the working class as a 'universal' class, there is the Marxist view that the working class alone is capable of acting on behalf of the whole of society and remove from it the greatest and weightiest of all impediments to its boundless development, namely the capitalist mode of production. How far some of these claims are themselves tainted with 'ideology' is an interesting and important question.

What then *is* class-consciousness in reference to the working class—the class with which Marxists in this context have been mainly concerned? A great deal, in terms of Marxist politics, hinges on the answer to this.

In the Marxist perspective, proletarian class-consciousness may be taken to mean the achievement of an understanding that the emancipation of the proletariat and the liberation of society require the overthrow of capitalism; and this understanding may also be taken to entail the will to overthrow it. It is in this sense that proletarian class-consciousness is also revolutionary consciousness.

It is of course possible to invest the notion of revolutionary consciousness with any meaning one chooses; and to argue that no one can be said to be 'truly' or 'really' class-conscious who does not subscribe to this or that idea, precept, strategy, party, and whatever else. But it is essential to realize that Marx himself did not define it with any such specificity, and that it did remain for him, as for Engels, a general concept, without any more precise meaning than that suggested above. In fact, it is very striking that Marx and Engels consistently and vigorously dismissed the notion that there was a set of ideas which specifically defined revolutionary consciousness. In the *Communist Manifesto*, they said that the Communists 'do not set up any sectarian principles of their own, by which to shape and mould the proletarian movement';[23] and they also insisted that 'the theoretical conclusions of the Communists are in no way based on ideas or principles that have been invented, or discovered, by this or that would-be reformer'.* Many years later, Marx wrote in *The Civil War in France* that the working class 'have no ready-made utopias to introduce *par décret du peuple*' and even that 'they have no ideals to realize, but to set free the elements of the new society with which old collapsing bourgeois society itself is pregnant'.[24] Soon after, Marx and Engels, in a Circular concerning 'The Alleged Splits in the International' (1872), noted that, while the rules of the International gave to its constituent societies a common object and programme, that programme was 'limited to outlining the major features of the proletarian movement, and leaving the details of theory to be worked out as inspired by the demands of the practical struggle, and as growing out of the exchange of ideas among the sections, with an equal hearing given to all socialist views in their journals and congresses'.†

---

* Ibid., p. 80. In his *Class Struggles in France* (1850), Marx contemptuously referred to 'petty-bourgeois socialists' for whom 'the coming historical process' appeared 'as an *application* of systems, which the thinkers of society, either in company with others, or as single inventors, devise or have devised. In this way they become the eclectics or adepts of existing socialist *systems*, of *doctrinaire socialism*, which was the theoretical expression of the proletariat only as long as it had not yet developed further and become a free, autonomous, historical movement' (SE, p.122). The italics, it will be recalled, are in the text.

† Ibid., p. 299. Note also Marx's warning in a private letter to his daughter and son-in-law in 1870: 'Sectarian "etiquettes" must be avoided in the International. The general aims and tendencies of the working class arise from the general conditions in which it finds itself. Therefore, these aims and tendencies are

The general point is one of extreme importance. In relation to revolutionary consciousness, it means that, for Marx and Engels at least, the concept did not entail the kind of devout and categorical adherence to given formulas which became the hallmark of later Marxism. Indeed, they never even claimed that the achievement of class-consciousness required adherence to something specifically called Marxism—Marx's cast of mind suggests that he would have found the idea rather laughable.*

Unfortunately, later developments turned the issue into anything but a laughing matter. For the attempt *was* made from many quarters, and has not ceased to be made, to stipulate exactly what revolutionary consciousness means in terms of convictions on a vast range of questions; and also what convictions on an equally vast range of questions such revolutionary consciousness must exclude. One consequence of this is to turn class-consciousness into a catechismal orthodoxy, departure and dissent from which become grave—and punishable—offences. Another consequence is to enhance tremendously the role of the keepers of the orthodoxy, namely the party leaders and their appointees: if revolutionary consciousness *can* be so precisely defined, there must be an authority to define it, and to decide when and in what ways it must be modified.

Even the notion of class-consciousness as something to be 'achieved' is not free from question-begging connotations. For it suggests a *state* to be reached, a *thing* to be appropriated; or at least this is what it may well imply. But in this meaning, it robs the concept of its dynamic nature, deprives it of its character as a process, which is constantly changing, and which is susceptible not only to advance but to regress, and certainly in no way unilinear. In other words, revolutionary consciousness is not some kind of Marxist state of grace which, once achieved, is total and irreversible. It is a certain understanding of the nature of the

---

found in the whole class, although the movement is reflected in their heads in the most varied forms, more or less imaginary, more or less related to the conditions. Those who best understand the hidden meaning of the class struggle which is unfolding before our eyes—the Communists—are the last to commit the error of approving or furthering Sectarianism' (K. Marx to Paul and Laura Lafargue, in K. Marx and F. Engels, *Werke* (Berlin, 1965), vol. XXXII, p. 671).

* The case has occasionally been made that it was Engels who, after Marx's death, first 'invented' Marxism as a political creed and as *the* political doctrine of the working-class movement. For an extreme but scholarly statement of this thesis, see M. Rubel, *Marx critique du marxisme* (Paris, 1974), particularly Ch. I.

social order and of what needs to be done about it. As such, it comprises many uncertainties, tensions, contradictions, open questions, and possibilities of error and regression. This at least is how it has always been in reality.

These qualifications do not, however, deprive the notion of class-consciousness, in its Marxist sense, of considerable and distinctive meaning. For it does after all denote a commitment to the revolutionary transformation of society, an 'interiorization' of the need to achieve that 'most radical rupture' with traditional property relations and traditional ideas of which Marx and Engels spoke in the *Communist Manifesto* and to which they held throughout. This meaning of class-consciousness does not carry in its train specific answers to many questions of great importance to the working-class movement. But it does carry certain definite perspectives and establishes certain firm delimitations. No more—but no less either.

The class with whose class-consciousness Marxists, beginning with Marx and Engels, have always been preoccupied is of course the working class; and the latter's relation, so to speak, to class-consciousness needs to be considered. But before doing so, it is worth noting that it is not only the proletariat which, in Marxist terms, can achieve class-consciousness. Again in the *Communist Manifesto*, Marx and Engels said that

in times when the class struggle nears the decisive hour, the process of dissolution going on within the ruling class, in fact within the whole range of old society, assumes such a violent, glaring character, that a small section of the ruling class cuts itself adrift, and joins the revolutionary class, the class that holds the future in its hands . . . a portion of the bourgeoisie goes over to the proletariat, and in particular, a portion of the bourgeois ideologists, who have raised themselves to the level of comprehending theoretically the historical movement as a whole.[25]

Half a century later, Lenin echoed this in relation to 'educated representatives of the propertied classes, the intellectuals', and noted that 'the founders of modern scientific socialism, Marx and Engels, themselves belonged to the bourgeois intelligentsia.'[26]

Such instances of 'class betrayal' on the part of members of the bourgeoisie, whether intellectuals or not, have been quite common in the history of the working-class movements; and many of the leaders of these movements have been of bourgeois origin. But for the present discussion, the more important question is that posed by the class orientations of other classes, notably the middle strata of the 'collective labourer' referred to earlier; and of the petty bourgeoisie.

About the latter, Marx and Engels were generally scathing, and their view of the petty bourgeoisie has been endorsed by later Marxists—and for that matter confirmed by historical developments. 'The lower middle class, the small manufacturer, the shopkeeper, the artisan, the peasant, all these fight against the bourgeoisie', said Marx and Engels, but only 'to save from extinction their existence as fractions of the middle class'; and this meant that 'they are therefore not revolutionary, but conservative. Nay more, they are reactionary for they try to roll back the wheel of history.*

Summary though the characterization may be, it does quite accurately pinpoint the general position adopted by members of the petty bourgeoisies of advanced capitalism—certainly most of them have been fierce opponents of organized labour, and unwilling allies, but allies none the less, of the large-scale capitalist interests which threaten their economic existence. This 'intermediate' class may be wooed and even pacified by a workers' movement, but its members can hardly be expected fundamentally to change a class-consciousness which is deeply rooted in their economic and social circumstances, and which sets them at odds with proletarian class-consciousness.

The issue presents itself very differently in regard to the vast and ever growing number of people who man the technical, scientific, supervisory, and cultural posts of advanced capitalist societies. This 'new working class', as it has been called, is sharply pulled in contrary directions. On a variety of economic, social, and cultural criteria, it is markedly differentiated from the 'traditional' working class; and some of its members may have plausible hopes of access to the upper layers of the social pyramid. On the other hand, it has undergone a steady process of 'proletarianization', in so far as it is a salaried and subordinate part of the 'collective worker': and it has in recent decades learnt the virtues of collective organization and collective action in

---

* *Revs.*, p. 77. Marx and Engels were equally or even more scathing about the 'lumpenproletariat', the 'social scum, that passively rotting mass thrown off by the lowest layers of society', most of whom could be expected to become 'the bribed tool of reactionary intrigue' (ibid., p. 77).

defence of its sectional interests. Such barriers as do exist to its development of 'class-consciousness' are not insuperable, or for that matter particularly high; and this may have very large repercussions indeed on the political plane, since an organic linkage between this part of the 'collective worker' and the rest of the working class is bound to make a considerable difference to the nature and impact of the political organizations of the working class. This is one of the most important open areas of the political sociology of Marxism, and of its politics.

But the really big question still remains: why should the working class have or acquire revolutionary class-consciousness —the understanding that it must do away with capitalism to emancipate itself and society? Why should it not *reject* the call to revolution, and seek reform of various kinds within the loose confines of capitalism, in accordance with what Lenin and others after him described as mere 'trade union consciousness'? These questions are the more relevant since the working class has, or so it is claimed, generally chosen this second path and resolutely refused to act out the revolutionary role assigned to it by Marxism.

An early answer to this kind of question was given by Marx in his introduction to the *Critique of Hegel's 'Philosophy of Right'*. Discussing the inability of the German bourgeoisie to make a thoroughgoing revolution, Marx asked: 'Where is the *positive* possibility of German emancipation?'; and he goes on to say that the answer lies 'in the formation of a class with *radical chains*, a class of civil society which is not a class of civil society, a class which is the dissolution of all classes, a sphere which has a universal character because of its universal suffering and which lays claim to no *particular right* because the wrong it suffers is not a *particular wrong* but *wrong in general* . . .'[27]

That class, he said, was the proletariat. As if to anticipate later developments and objections, Marx and Engels also wrote in *The Holy Family* (1844) that 'the question is not what this or that proletarian, or even the whole of the proletariat at the moment *considers* as its aim. The question is *what the proletariat is*, and what, consequent on that *being*, it will be compelled to do. Its aim and historical action is irrevocable and obviously demonstrated in its own life situation as well as in the whole organisation of bourgeois society today.'[28]

Marx's early formulations of the 'role' and the 'mission' of the proletariat as an agent of emancipation do undoubtedly have a fairly heavy Hegelian imprint, with the proletariat almost occupying in the unfolding of history the role which Hegel assigned to the Idea. But even in these early formulations, there is in Marx and Engels a concept of the proletariat as destined to become a revolutionary class because revolution is its only means of deliverance from the oppression, exploitation and alienation which existing society imposes upon it. These features of existing society are inherent to it, an intrinsic part of *this* social order, and can therefore only be got rid of by the disappearance of the social order itself. From this point of view, the proletariat's role is not determined by any extra-historical agency: it is determined by the nature of capitalism and by the concrete conditions which it imposes upon the working class and upon society at large.

Against this, it has often been argued that conditions have greatly changed over time, and that Marxists, beginning with Marx, have always had too strong a tendency to under-estimate the capacity of capitalism to assimilate far-reaching reforms in every area of life.

However true this may be, it misses the real argument, which is that capitalism, however many and varied the reforms it can assimilate, is unable to do without exploitation, oppression, and dehumanization; and that it cannot create the truly human environment for which it has itself produced the material conditions.

This, on the other hand, leaves unanswered the objection that the working class has not, over a period of a hundred years and more, developed the class-consciousness which Marxists have expected of it and turned itself into a revolutionary class. This needs to be looked at more closely, since it relates to the meaning of class-consciousness as it concerns the working class.

One fairly common element of confusion in this discussion is the equation of revolutionary consciousness with the will to insurrection—the absence of such a will in the working class being automatically deemed to demonstrate a lack of class-consciousness. But this is precisely the kind of arbitrary designation of what does not *specifically* constitute such consciousness, which Marx never sought to lay down. It may well be that class-consciousness and revolutionary consciousness must eventually come to encompass a will to insurrection; and Marx himself, without being dogmatic about it, and while allowing for some possible exceptions, did believe that the abolition of capitalism would require its violent overthrow. But the will to insurrection which this would entail must be seen as the ultimate extension of revolutionary consciousness, as its final strategic manifestation, produced by specific and for the most part unforeseeable circumstances. That the working class has only seldom, and in some countries never, manifested much of a will to insurrection is not in Marxist terms a decisive demonstration of a lack of class-consciousness.

Nor for that matter is the pursuit of specific and partial reforms within the ambit of capitalism and through the constitutional and political mechanisms of bourgeois regimes. Marx himself vigorously supported the pursuit of such reforms and it may be recalled that, in the Inaugural Address of the First International, which he wrote in 1864, he hailed one such reform, the Ten Hours Bill, as 'not only a great practical success' but as 'the victory of a principle; it was the first time that in broad daylight the political economy of the middle class succumbed to the political economy of the working class'.[29] Nor did Engels have the slightest difficulty in giving his support to the parliamentary, electoral, and quite 'reformist' endeavours of the German Social Democratic Party, notwithstanding certain reservations—and even these should not be exaggerated.[30] As for Lenin, his whole work is permeated by firm approval for the struggle for partial reforms of every sort, including the most modest 'economic' reforms; and so is his work peppered with contemptuous denunciations of the all-or-nothing approach to the revolutionary struggle, culminating in *'Left-Wing' Communism—An Infantile Disorder* of 1920.

The question is not one of support for reforms: to designate such support as an example of 'false consciousness' is as arbitrary as the equation of 'false consciousness' with the absence of a will to insurrection. The real issue is the perspective from which reforms are viewed, what they are expected to achieve, and what else than reforms is being pursued. What Lenin called 'trade union consciousness', and which he counterposed to revolutionary consciousness was a perspective which did not go beyond the achievement of partial reforms and was content to seek the amelioration and not the abolition of capitalism.

Marxists have always believed that the working class *would* eventually want to go beyond partial reforms inside the system—that it would, in other words, come to acquire the 'class-consciousness' needed to want a thoroughgoing, revolutionary transformation of capitalist society into an entirely differently based and differently motivated system.

In some meanings of 'class-consciousness' and of 'revolutionary consciousness', this hope might well amount to what C. Wright Mills scathingly called a 'labour metaphysic', grounded in nothing more than faith. But in the meaning which it had for Marx and Engels, this is not what it amounts to. It simply derives from the conviction that the working class, confronted with the shortcomings, depredations, and contradictions of capitalism, would want to get rid of it, in favour of a system which, as Marx put it, transformed 'the means of production, land and capital, now chiefly the means of enslaving and exploiting labour, into mere instruments of free and associated labour'.[31]

These propositions leave open many questions, but there is no 'labour metaphysic' about it; so little, indeed, in the case of Lenin, that he bluntly said in 1902 that 'the working class, exclusively by its own effort, is able to develop only trade-union consciousness'.[32] This too has very large implications for Marxist politics. But it may be said at this stage that a strict reading of the record, both of capitalism and of the working class, suggests that the expectation of a growing development in the working class (and in other large segments of the 'collective labourer') of a will for radical change is not in the least unreasonable or 'metaphysical'.

Neither Marx nor any of the classical Marxist writers had any illusion about the massive obstacles which the working class would have to overcome on the way to acquiring this class-consciousness, and about the difficulties that there would be in breaking through the fog of what Gramsci called the 'common-sense' of the epoch. They knew well, as Marx put it in *The Eighteenth Brumaire of Louis Bonaparte* of 1852 that 'the tradition of the dead generations weighs like a nightmare on the minds of the living';[33] and that enormous efforts would be undertaken by those in whose interest it was to do so to make the weight heavier still. I now propose to discuss the nature of the obstacles which obstruct and retard the acquisition of class-consciousness by the working class.

NOTES

1 K. Marx, *Grundrisse*, p. 265.
2 SW 1968, p. 679.
3 *Revs.*, p. 68.
4 K. Marx, *Capital*, III, p. 772.
5 Ibid., p. 772.
6 K. Marx, *The Poverty of Philosophy*, p. 145.
7 *Revs.*, p. 76. My italics.
8 Ibid., p. 87.
9 *FI*, p. 270.
10 K. Marx, *Capital* (Moscow, 1959), I, p. 509.
11 K. Marx, *Theories of Surplus Value* (Moscow, 1969), Part I, p. 152.
12 Ibid., p. 154.
13 Ibid., p. 158.
14 Ibid., p. 157.
15 Ibid., p. 411.
16 K. Marx, *Capital*, I, p. 508. My italics.
17 K. Marx, *Capital*, III, p. 862.
18 See below, Ch. IV.
19 K. Marx and F.Engels, *The German Ideology*, p. 63.
20 *Revs.*, p. 78.
21 Ibid., p. 87.
22 Ibid., p. 86.
23 Ibid., p. 79.
24 *FI*, p. 213.
25 *Revs.*, p. 77.
26 *What is to be Done?* in CWL, vol. 5 (1961), p. 375.
27 EW, p. 256.
28 K. Marx and F. Engels, *The Holy Family* (Moscow, 1956), p. 53.
29 *FI*, p. 79.
30 See below, pp. 79–80.
31 K. Marx, *The Civil War in France*, in *FI*, p. 213.
32 V. I. Lenin, *What is to be Done?*, op. cit., p. 375.
33 *SE*, p. 146.

III. The Defence of the Old Order: I

1

In the last chapter, I noted that the classical Marxist writers had been well aware of the importance of tradition in shaping the consciousness of the working class—in shaping it, of course, in ways which made much more difficult a 'radical rupture' with the established order. But it is also necessary to note that classical Marxism did not really make very much of this phenomenon and that, with the signal exception of Gramsci, it did not seriously try to theorize, or even to identify, the many different ways in which the shaping of consciousness contributed to the stabilization and legitimation of capitalism.

This neglect may be related to that of political theory, which was discussed in the Introduction; and as in the case of political theory, the neglect was further accentuated in subsequent years by the kind of Marxism which Stalinism produced and was able to impose. This Marxism had a very pronounced tendency to provide whatever answer to any given question was most convenient to the people in power, which did not encourage the serious probing of difficult and often uncomfortable questions.

As a result, Marxism as a theory of domination remained poorly worked out. It was presented with the very large question of why capitalism was able to maintain itself, despite the crises and contradictions by which it was beset; and it tended to return a series of answers which were manifestly inadequate. In particular, it relied on an explanation based upon the Marxist view of the state as an instrument of capitalist coercion and repression. But coercion and repression could not possibly, in the case of many if not most of these regimes, explain why they endured. Nor did a second main line of explanation serve the purpose, namely betrayal by 'reformist' labour leaders, since this left whole the question why the working class allowed itself so regularly and so blatantly to be betrayed.

The notions of state coercion and repression, and of betrayal, are not wrong; but they need to be integrated into a wider theory of domination, comprising both 'infra-structural' and 'super-structural' elements. These elements can mostly be found in various parts of the corpus of Marxist writing, but have never been properly integrated. Until they are, a Marxist theory of politics will remain seriously deficient. The present chapter does not of course purport to fill the gap, but only to indicate some of the major ways in which the established order achieves legitimation.*

Tradition is not a monolith. On the contrary, it always consists of a large and diverse accumulation of customary ways of thought and action. In other words, there is not in any society one tradition but many: some of them are more congruent with others, some less. Thus, to take an instance which has direct relevance in the present context, there is in most societies a tradition of dissent as well as a tradition of conformity; or several of each. Traditional ways are never uniformly conservative.

But from a Marxist point of view, this 'polymorphous' nature of tradition is not particularly helpful. For however many forms it may assume, none of them is likely to afford a very helpful path to Marxist thought and to the revolutionary project which it proclaims: the Marxist notion of a 'most radical rupture' with traditional ideas, however attenuated it may be, signifies a break with all forms of tradition, and must expect to encounter the latter not as friend but as foe.

In this respect, the perpetuation of capitalism for well over a century after Marx and Engels began to write about it has produced an ironical twist in the story. One of the most important features of capitalism on which they fastened was precisely the universal uprooting of all aspects of life for which it was responsible. It is with something approaching exultation that they wrote in the *Communist Manifesto* that

constant revolutionizing of production, uninterrupted disturbance of all social conditions, everlasting uncertainty and agitation distinguish the bourgeois epoch from all earlier ones. All fixed, fast-frozen relations, with their train of ancient and venerable prejudices and opinions, are swept away, all new-formed ones become antiquated before they can ossify. All that is solid melts into air, all that is holy is profaned, and

---

* This discussion is based on and continues the analysis which is to be found in *The State in Capitalist Society* (London, 1969).

man is at last compelled to face with sober senses, his real conditions of life, and his relations with his kind.*

The clear message is of an irresistible movement, sweeping everything before it, including before long the forces which had set it going. In actual fact, the uprooting of tradition was not quite as thorough as Marx and Engels had claimed it to be; nor in any case were its consequences nearly as dramatic as they suggested. Furthermore, capitalism soon came to create, and has not ceased to reinforce, its own traditions, which were fused with or superimposed upon what remained of the older ones—and a lot did.

It was only a few years after the *Manifesto* that Marx, in the aftermath of the defeats of 1848, wrote of tradition weighing like a mountain upon the minds of the living, and of men making their own history not as they choose but 'under the given and inherited circumstances with which they are directly confronted';[1] and this was to be a recurrent theme with him. Indeed, we find in *Capital* two very different views of the impact of capitalist production itself upon the working class.

In the first of these, 'capitalist production develops a working class, which, by education, tradition, habit, looks upon the conditions of that mode of production as self-evident laws of Nature ... the dull compulsion of economic relations complete the subjection of the labourer to the capitalist';[2] and this process is much enhanced by the very nature of the capitalist mode of production which, much more than its predecessors, veils and mystifies the exploitative nature of its 'relations of production' by making them appear as a matter of free, unfettered, and equal exchange. The point is crucially important in the Marxist view of capitalist society and of its politics, and must be taken a little further.

There is an extremely strong sense in Marx of the *falsity of perception* which is woven into the tissue of capitalist society, the disjunction between appearance and reality, form and substance. In *Capital*, Marx writes as follows:

* *Revs.*, p. 70. Note also, in the same vein, Marx's famous description of England's impact upon India, which 'separates Hindustan, ruled by Britain, from all its ancient traditions, and from the whole of its past history', and which 'produced the greatest, and, to speak the truth, the only *social* revolution ever heard of in Asia' ('The British Rule of India' in K. Marx and F. Engels, *The First Indian War of Independence* (Moscow, 1959), pp. 16, 19).

If, as the reader will have realized to his great dismay, the analysis of the actual intrinsic relations of the capitalist process of production is a very complicated matter and very extensive; *if it is a work of science to resolve the merely external movement into the true intrinsic movement*, it is self-evident that conceptions which arise about the laws of production in the minds of agents of capitalist production and circulation will diverge drastically from these real laws and will merely be the conscious expression of the visible movements.[3]

Marx then goes on to say that 'the conceptions of the merchant, stockbroker, and banker, are necessarily quite distorted'. As for manufacturers, 'competition likewise assumes a completely distorted role in their minds'.[4] But this distortion also occurs in a generalized form in the production of commodities, and engenders what Marx, in a famous section of *Capital*, called 'the fetishism of commodities'; and this 'fetishism' obviously affects those who produce the commodities, namely the workers. A commodity, Marx said, was 'a mysterious thing',

simply because in it the social character of men's labour appears to them as an objective character stamped upon the product of that labour; because the relation of the producers to the sum total of their own labour is presented to them as a social relation, existing not between themselves, but between the products of their labour . . . it is a definite social relation between men, that assumes, in their eyes, the fantastic form of a relation between things.[5]

In the *Grundrisse*, Marx had made the same point, in a more general form still, with reference to the circulation of commodities produced as exchange values: 'The social relations of individuals to one another as a power over the individuals which has become autonomous, whether conceived as a natural force, as chance or in whatever other form, is a necessary result of the fact that the point of departure is not the free social individual.'[6]

It is thus the capitalist system of production itself which also produces mystification as to the real nature of its 'relations of production'. This mystification is then further enhanced by intellectuals of one sort or another; and this incidentally indicates the role which revolutionary intellectuals should play, namely in helping to demystify capitalist reality.

There is, however, another view of the impact of capitalism in Marx. For he also believed that the working class becomes ever more 'disciplined, united, organized by the very mechanism of the process of capitalist production itself', and that this must ultimately lead to a situation where 'the expropriators are expropriated'.[7]

These statements do not really contradict each other: they simply reflect different and contradictory facets of a complex reality, in which the opposing forces of tradition and actuality on the one hand, and of change on the other, do constant battle for the consciousness of the working class. From that battle, neither of these forces can emerge totally victorious, or totally secure in such victories as they may achieve. Tradition can never be completely paralysing: but neither can it be rapidly overcome. The problem, for victorious revolutions, is to prevent tradition from corroding them and ultimately defeating them from within. To topple a regime is seldom easy and is often very difficult indeed. But it is nevertheless easier to do so and to proclaim a new social order than actually to bring one into being. This is the point at which Lenin and Mao Tse-tung meet—in a common awareness that the revolution each led was under threat from the most deeply ingrained traditions of thought and behaviour. Lenin's last years were overshadowed by that awareness, and illness and death cut short whatever attempt he might have made to do more about it. Mao Tse-tung was more fortunate; but to what extent is far from clear.

At any rate, the enduring and pervasive importance of traditional ways, in a multitude of areas, is not in doubt, even in circumstances of very rapid economic, social, and political change. Some of these ways are so deeply woven into the texture of life that they can survive more or less indefinitely without visible means of support and under conditions of extreme adversity. Two obvious cases in point are persecuted religious creeds and suppressed national sentiments. But for the most part, traditions are sustained and mediated by a network of particular institutions, which are actively involved in the performance of a process of transmission—institutions such as the family, schools, the mass media, and so on. It might be added that no reasonable government would seek to obliterate *all* traditions: the notion is both absurd and abhorrent.

The churches were the first mass media in history and the message they made it their business (in more senses than one) to transmit has generally tended to preach acceptance and obedience rather than questioning and rebellion. This is too summary for what is a complex and tortuous history; but it undoubtedly holds as a generalization. At any rate, Marxism, from the earliest days, has had a consistent record of opposition to religion and the churches, and this has been richly reciprocated by the latter. It was in the 'Introduction' to his *Critique of Hegel's 'Philosophy of Right'* that Marx made the famous statement that religion is 'the opium of the people',[8] a phrase which does not begin to do justice to the many different grounds of Marx's and Engels's opposition to religion and to their understanding of it as an historical fact, but which serves well enough to indicate what is in effect their paramount objection to it, namely that it stands as an obstacle to a proper appreciation by the working class of what is really wrong with the world it inhabits, so that 'the abolition of religion as the illusory happiness of the people is a demand for their true happiness.'[9] 'The critique of religion disillusions man so that he will think, act, and fashion his reality as a man who has lost his illusions and regained his reason, so that he will revolve about himself as his own true sun.'[10] The formulation is very much an 'early Marx' one: but the general sentiment remains at the core of the Marxist view of religion; so essentially does the view expressed in the *Communist Manifesto* that 'the parson has ever gone hand in hand with the landlord.'[11]

Marx and Engels were equally scathing about the early (and for that matter the later) forms of Christian Socialism they encountered. But earnest attempts have been made over the years, and particularly in more recent times to attempt a 'reconciliation' between Christianity and Marxism by way of some kind of syncretic humanism. The results of these endeavours seem to have been philosophically and politically exceedingly thin. The question has of course nothing to do with the attempts of Communist regimes, particularly in Eastern Europe, to bring to an end their *Kulturkampf* with the churches and to find some mode of understanding with them.

A substantial part of Gramsci's concern with popular culture and with the degree to which it was permeated by a conservative 'common sense' had to do with the hold of religion upon the people, and with the need for Marxists to diffuse their own alternative 'common sense' as part of the battle for 'hegemony'. Religion was by no means the only part of the 'superstructure' with which he was concerned; but it was this which, in relation to popular culture, preoccupied him most, which is hardly sur-

prising in the Italian context of the first decades of the twentieth
century.

On the other hand, the notion of religion as the main ideological line of defence—or of attack, which is here the same
thing—of the conservative forces in class society clearly does
not accord with the ever-greater secular nature of this kind of
society. Whether the religious 'opium' was ever as potent as it
was declared to be in the first half of the nineteenth century (and
before) is a question that cannot be answered in general: the
impact of religion was obviously much greater on some parts of
'the people' than on others, depending on many different factors. But in any case, religion in advanced capitalist countries
must now be reckoned, with obvious exceptions, to be one of the
less effective forces which shape working-class consciousness,
and certainly less than a good many others.

It is not my purpose here to discuss these forces in any detail,
but only to indicate how they are, or might be, viewed in a
Marxist perspective. The qualification is required because of the
dearth of sustained Marxist work in analysing and exposing the
meanings and messages purveyed in the cultural output produced for mass consumption in, say, the thirty-odd years since
the end of World War II—not to speak of the virtual absence of
such work in the years preceding it.* Gramsci was exceptional
in his stress on the importance that must be attached to every
artifact of this production, however trivial; and in his insistence
that the struggle for 'hegemony' must be waged at every level,
and include every single level of the 'superstructure'.

The key text on this whole issue was provided by Marx and
Engels in *The German Ideology*, which was written in 1845–6,
but which was only published in 1932 (save for one irrelevant
chapter published earlier). In a Section entitled 'Concerning the
Production of Consciousness', they wrote that

The ideas of the ruling class are in every epoch the ruling ideas: i.e., the
class, which is the ruling *material* force of society, is at the same time its
ruling *intellectual* force. The class which has the means of material
production at its disposal, has control at the same time over the means
of mental production, so that thereby, generally speaking, the ideas of
those who lack the means of mental production are subject to it.[12]

* For a remarkable example of such analysis (by a non-Marxist), see George
  Orwell's essay on the reactionary values of boys' magazines in Britain, 'Boys'
  Weeklies', in G. Orwell, *Collected Essays, Journalism and Letters*, vol. I (Lon-
  don, 1970). The essay was written in 1939.

As will be argued presently, these formulations now need to be amended in certain respects. But there is at least one respect in which the text remains remarkably fresh, and points to one of the dominant features of life in advanced capitalist societies, namely the fact that the largest part of what is produced in the cultural domain in these societies is produced by capitalism; and is also therefore quite naturally intended to help, one way and another, in the defence of capitalism.

The point may be put quite simply: whatever else the immense output of the mass media is intended to achieve, it is *also* intended to help prevent the development of class-consciousness in the working class, and to reduce as much as possible any hankering it might have for a radical alternative to capitalism. The ways in which this is attempted are endlessly different; and the degree of success achieved varies considerably from country to country and from one period to another—there are other influences at work. But the fact remains that 'the class which has the means of material production at its disposal' does have 'control at the same time of the means of mental production'; and that it does seek to use them for the weakening of opposition to the established order. Nor is the point much affected by the fact that the state in almost all capitalist countries 'owns' the radio and television—*its* purpose is identical, namely the weakening of opposition to the established order. There is absolutely nothing remarkable about all this: the only remarkable thing is that the reality of the matter should be so befogged; and that Marxists should not have done more to pierce the fog which surrounds what is after all a vital aspect of the battle in which they are engaged.

Nor is that 'battle for consciousness' only waged in terms of traditions and communications. It has other facets which come under neither of these rubrics. One of the most important of these is the work process itself, to which Marx devoted some of his most searing pages—see for instance his denunciation of a system of division of labour which 'seizes labour-power by its very roots' and 'converts the labourer into a crippled monstrosity, by forcing his detail dexterity at the expense of a world of productive capabilities and instincts'.*

* K. Marx, *Capital*, I, p. 360. Here too, however, there is another side to the story. For 'Modern Industry', Marx also writes, 'compels society, under penalty of death, to replace the detail-worker of today, crippled by life-long repetition of

Division of labour is one major aspect of the work process. Divisions within the working class, related to the division of labour, are another aspect of it. These concern skills, function, pay, conditions, status; and they add further to the erosion of class solidarity. Also, capitalist 'relations of production' are strongly hierarchical, not to say authoritarian (though this is not only true of capitalist ones), and subordination at work forms an important and diffuse—but complex and contradictory—element of working-class culture, going far beyond the work process. Its existence as a daily fact breeds frustrations which seek compensation and release in many different ways, most of them by no means conducive to the development of class-consciousness.

One of these ways is undoubtedly sport, or rather spectator and commercialized sport, some forms of which have assumed a central place in working-class life. For instance, vast numbers of people in the countries of advanced capitalism turn out on Saturdays and Sundays to watch soccer being played. Most of them are members of the working class, and so, in social origin, are the players, trainers, and managers. There is no other form of public activity which is capable of attracting even a fraction of those who attend football matches week in week out. A very large number of the people concerned are deeply involved, intellectually and emotionally, in the game, the players and one or other club; and their involvement, with all that informs and surrounds it, constitutes a *sport culture* which is an important part of the general culture. With this or that variation (e.g. baseball instead of soccer in the United States), this is a major modern phenomenon, which radio and television have greatly helped to foster. The sport culture of capitalist countries, like every other mass activity, is big business for the various industries associated with sport, from sports gear and the pools industry to advertising. This is a very strong reason for the encouragement of its development by business.

But whether by design or not, there is an important amount of what might be described as cultural fall-out from the sports

---

one and the same trivial operation, and thus reduced to the mere fragment of a man, by the fully developed individual, fit for a variety of labours, ready to face any change of production, and to whom the different social functions he performs, are but so many modes of giving free scope to his own natural and acquired powers' (ibid., p. 488).

industry and spectator involvement. The nature of this fall-out is not quite as obviously negative as Marxists are often tempted to assume. The subject lends itself to simplistic and prim-sounding attitudes, which are often over-compensated by hearty demagogic-populist ones. In fact, the sport culture deserves, from the point of view of the making and unmaking of class-consciousness, much more attention than it has received. The elaboration of a Marxist sociology of sport may not be the most urgent of theoretical tasks; but it is not the most negligible of tasks either.*

The easiest assumption to make is that working-class involvement in sport as spectacle in the context of capitalism (the role and organization of sport in Communist countries raise questions of a different order) is most likely further to discourage the development of class-consciousness. But this is a bit too simple. For it rests on the antecedent assumption that a deep interest in the fortunes of, say, Leeds United Football Club is incompatible with militant trade unionism and the pursuit of the class struggle. This does not seem *a priori* reasonable and is belied by much evidence to the contrary; and to murmur 'bread and circuses' is no substitute for serious thinking upon the matter.

What may well be advanced in relation to sport and the sport culture in capitalist countries is that it is very strongly pervaded by commercialism and money values; that this is very generally accepted and unquestioned as a 'natural' part of the life of sport; and that it is also likely to strengthen an acceptance of social life in general as being 'naturally' and inevitably pervaded by commercialism and money values. In this sense, it may well be that the sport culture does help to block off the perception of a mode of social existence which is not thus pervaded. But how important this is in the total production of culture in these societies is a matter for surmise.

The formulations from *The German Ideology* which were quoted earlier have a serious defect in relation to present-day conditions, and indeed to earlier ones as well; and this defect is

---

* This would involve work on the evident 'sexist' bias and influence of most mass spectacle sports, for instance soccer, baseball and rugby, and of their celebration of 'manly' qualities. 'So what?' is a question to which it would be useful to have a detailed answer.

also shared by the Gramscian concept of 'hegemony', or at least by some interpretations of it.

What is involved is an over-statement of the ideological predominance of the 'ruling class', or of the *effectiveness* of that predominance. As I have noted earlier, it is at least as true now as it was when the words were written that 'the class which has the means of material production at its disposal has control at the same time over the means of mental production.' But it is only partially true—and the variations are considerable from country to country—that 'thereby, generally speaking, the ideas of those who lack the means of mental production are subject to it.' The danger of this formulation, as of the notion of 'hegemony', is that it may lead to quite inadequate account being taken of the many-sided and permanent challenge which is directed at the ideological predominance of the 'ruling class', and of the fact that this challenge, notwithstanding all difficulties and disadvantages, produces a steady erosion of that predominance.

A useful historical illustration of this process may be found in the ideological battle conducted in the eighteenth century against the *ancien régime*. The changes which occurred in the ideological climate of the *ancien régime* from year to year were almost imperceptible; but the difference between 1715, the year of the death of Louis XIV, and, say, 1775, is very great indeed. There are many closely related reasons for this: but one of them is the ideological battle that was conducted by a host of individuals, great and small, against the hegemony represented by the *ancien régime*. It is they who form the human link between 'infra-structure' and 'superstructure.'

On an enormously larger canvas, an ideological battle against bourgeois hegemony has been proceeding for 150 years and more; and even if only the relatively short span of the last fifty years is taken into account, it is obvious that, notwithstanding the dreadful battering to which it has been subjected, not least from its own side, what may for brevity's sake be called the socialist idea has vastly grown in strength in this period, immeasurably so in terms of its extension to every part of the globe, and also in the extent and depth of its penetration in the countries of advanced capitalism. However much more slowly and tortuously than he could ever have anticipated, Marx's 'old mole' has continued to burrow—so much so that the real question is progressively coming to be what kind of socialism towards which it is burrowing and, as a related question, how it is to be realized.

At any rate, the discussion of hegemony and class-consciousness more than ever requires the inclusion of the concept of a battle being fought on many different fronts and on the basis of the tensions and contradictions which are present in the actual structures or work and of life in general in capitalism as a social formation. The manifestations of that battle are endlessly diverse;* but the fact is that it does occur. The ideological terrain is by no means wholly occupied by 'the ideas of the ruling class': it is highly contested territory.

In capitalist societies with bourgeois democratic regimes, ideological struggles are mainly waged in and through institutions which are not part of the state system. This point has in recent years been controverted by Louis Althusser and others who have opposed to it Althusser's notion of 'Ideological State Apparatuses' (ISA), according to which a vast number of institutions involved in one way or another in the dissemination of ideology are not only 'ideological apparatuses' but '*state* ideological apparatuses', which must be distinguished from the 'Repressive State Apparatus'. Althusser lists these 'Ideological State Apparatuses' as 'the religious ISA (the system of the different churches), the educational ISA (the system of the different public and private 'Schools'), the family ISA, the legal ISA, the political ISA (the political system, including the different Parties), the trade union ISA, the communications ISA (press, radio, and television, etc.), the cultural ISA (Literature, the Arts, sports, etc.)'.†

Calling all these '*state* ideological apparatuses' is based on or at least produces a confusion between *class power* and *state power*, a distinction which it is important not to blur.

Class power is the general and pervasive power which a

* This diversity lends added significance to Marx's distinction between 'the material transformations of the economic conditions of production' which can be 'determined with the precision of natural science', and 'the legal, political, religious, esthetic or philosophical—in short, ideological forms' in which men become conscious of conflict and fight it out. (K. Marx, *Preface to A Contribution to the Critique of Political Economy*, in SW 1968, p. 183.)

† L. Althusser, 'Ideology and Ideological State Apparatuses (Notes Towards an Investigation)', in *Lenin and Philosophy* (London, 1972) p. 143. The listing seems a little superfluous, since it is difficult to think of anything that has been left out.

dominant class (assuming for the purpose of exposition that there is only one) exercises in order to maintain and defend its predominance in 'civil society'. This class power is exercised through many institutions and agencies. Some of these are primarily designed for the purpose, e.g. political parties of the dominant class, interest and pressure groups, etc. Others may not be specifically designed for the purpose, yet may serve it, e.g. churches, schools, the family. But whether designed for the purpose or not, they are the institutions and agencies through which the dominant class seeks to assure its 'hegemony'. This class power is generally challenged by a counter-power, that of the subordinate classes, often through the same institutions, and also through different ones. Instances of the former case are the family, schools and churches; and of the latter, parties of the working class and trade unions. That some institutions are 'used' by opposite classes simply means that these institutions are not 'monolithic' but that on the contrary they are themselves arenas of class conflict; and some institutions which are designed to further class power may well play another role as well (or even altogether), for instance that of 'routinizing', stabilizing, and limiting class conflict. But this too only shows that institutions may assume different roles than those for which they were brought into being, and may have other effects than those which they were intended to have.

The important point, however, is that the class power of the dominant class is not exercised, in some important respects, by state action but by class action, at least in 'bourgeois democratic' regimes, and in a number of other forms of capitalist regimes as well. Of course, there are other, crucial respects, in which that power *is* exercised through the agency of the state; and the state is in *all* respects the ultimate sanctioning agency of class power. But these are different issues. I am concerned to point here to the fact that the dominant class, under the protection of the state, has vast resources, immeasurably greater than the resources of the subordinate classes, to bring its own weight to bear on 'civil society'. The following quotation from Marx's *Class Struggles in France* provides a good illustration of the meaning of class power. Writing about the election campaign of 'the party of Order' in 1849, Marx notes:

The party of Order had enormous financial resources at its disposal; it had organised branches throughout France; it had all the ideologists of the old society in its pay; it had the influence of the existing government power at its disposal; it possessed an army of unpaid vassals in the mass of the petty bourgeoisie and peasants, who, still separated from the revolutionary movement, found in the high dignitaries of property the natural representatives of their petty property and their petty prejudices. Represented throughout the country by innumerable petty monarchs, the party of Order could punish the rejection of its candidates as insurrection, and could dismiss rebellious workers, recalcitrant farm labourers, servants, clerks, railway officials, registrars and all the functionaries who are its social subordinates.[13]

Clearly, much of this would now have to be amended, extended or qualified, and much that is more 'modern' by way of resources would have to be added: but the basic conception remains valid and important about this kind of capitalist regime, as opposed to other kinds, where class power is mainly or mostly exercised by way of the state. The extreme example of class power in capitalist society being 'taken over' and exercised by the state is Fascism and Nazism, with other forms and degrees of authoritarian rule in between.

In periods of acute social crisis and conflict, class power does tend to be taken over by the state itself, and indeed gladly surrenders to it; and it may well be argued that, even in the 'normal' circumstances of advanced capitalism, the state takes over more and more of the functions hitherto performed by the dominant class, or at least takes a greater share in the performance of these functions than was the case in previous periods. I am not here referring to state intervention in the economy, where this is obviously true,[14] but rather to the shaping of consciousness.

The enormous advances in communication techniques have in any case tempted governments to use these techniques in order to try and influence 'public opinion', and to intervene much more directly in the shaping of consciousness. This is done both positively and negatively. Positively in the sense that there now exists a governmental and state communications industry, which actually disseminates or influences the dissemination of news, views, opinions and perspectives; and negatively in so far as governments try as best they can to prevent the dissemination of news, views etc. which they consider 'unhelpful'. The range of means and techniques for doing this varies from country to country but is everywhere formidable.

This communications industry run by the state does not produce *any* kind of commodity: its range of products, unlike its range of means and techniques, is fairly narrow, in ideological terms, and the products quite naturally bear mostly a conformist and 'helpful' label—helpful, that is, to the maintenance of stability, the discrediting of dangerous thoughts and the defence of things as they are. The state is now in the consciousness industry in a big way, and thus plays its role in a permanent battle of ideas which is a crucial element of class conflict.

Even so, and even if the process of 'statisation' is taken fully into account, as it obviously must be, there is absolutely no warrant for speaking of 'state ideological apparatuses' in regard to institutions which, in bourgeois democratic societies, are not part of the state; and much which is important about the life of these societies is lost in the obliteration of the distinction between ideological apparatuses which are mainly the product of 'civil society' and those which are the product and part of the state apparatus. The point, it may be added, does not only bear on capitalist societies: it has large implications for the way in which ideological apparatuses are viewed in relation to a future socialist society, their connection to and independence from the state, and so on. As Althusser might say, these are not 'innocent' discussions.

2

If it is agreed that a crucially important battle for consciousness is waged, or occurs, day in day out in capitalist societies (and in others as well for that matter), it also follows that a great deal of importance must be attributed to those people who play the main part in articulating and giving expression to the terms of that battle—intellectuals.

'Intellectual' is a notoriously difficult designation. Gramsci noted that all men were in a way 'intellectuals'. 'In any physical work, even the most degraded and mechanical', he wrote, 'there exists a minimum of technical qualification, that is, a minimum of creative intellectual activity';[15] and, rather more positively,

there is no human activity from which every form of intellectual participation can be excluded: *homo faber* cannot be separated from *homo sapiens*. Each man, finally, outside his professional activity, carries on some form of intellectual activity, that is, he is a 'philosopher', an artist, a man of taste, he participates in a particular conception of the world, has a conscious line of moral conduct, and therefore contributes to sustain a conception of the world or to modify it, that is, to bring into being new modes of thought.[16]

This is broadly speaking true and points to the fact that everyone, in his and her daily life and utterances, does mediate social reality for other people and thereby helps, in however so small a way, to shape the character of that reality. But Gramsci also observed that though all men might in some sense be said to be intellectuals, 'not all men have in society the function of intellectuals'.[17]

As for that function, he defined it as being two-fold, 'organisational and connective': 'The intellectuals are the dominant group's "deputies" exercising the subaltern function of social hegemony and political government'; in other words, as involving *two* major superstructural levels, one of these being the organization of 'hegemony' and the second being the organization of political functions.[18]

'This way of posing the problem', Gramsci said, 'has as a result a considerable extension of the concept of intellectual, but it is the only way which enables one to reach a concrete approximation of reality.'[19]

This is not particularly convincing; and it would seem rather less confusing, without any loss, to confine the notion of 'intellectual' to the first of Gramsci's two categories and levels, namely to the cultural-ideological domain.* This is how Marx and Engels saw it, in *The German Ideology*, when they spoke of a 'division of labour' in the ruling class,

so that inside this class one part appears as the thinkers of the class (its active, conceptive ideologists, who make the perfecting of the illusion of the class about itself their chief source of livelihood), while the others' attitude to these ideas and illusions is more passive and receptive, because they are in reality the active members of this class and have less time to make up illusions and ideas about themselves.[20]

---

* There is another important distinction of Gramsci's, that between 'organic' and 'traditional' intellectuals, which does not seem to be very helpful either. Roughly speaking, 'organic' intellectuals are those which a 'new class' needs because they 'give it homogeneity and an awareness of its own function not only in the economic but also in the social and political fields'. 'Traditional' intellectuals are those which are linked to already established classes. (See, ibid., p. 5 ff.) Gramsci had in mind the bourgeoisie and the landed aristocracy respectively, but the terminology and for that matter the conceptualization becomes unhelpful when the bourgeoisie is counterposed to the working class.

The general view expressed here is that intellectuals/
ideologists are mainly (though not exclusively, as will be seen
in a moment) the 'deputies' of the ruling class, in Gramsci's
formula. Marx's own resounding phrase in *Capital* about economists was that the latter had, after the heyday of political
economy, turned themselves into the 'hired prize-fighters' of the
bourgeoisie;[21] and this is obviously capable of application to
intellectuals and ideologists other than economists. Gramsci
also called intellectuals the 'managers of legitimation', which
fixes their role in this perspective with adequate precision; for it
is indeed the management, fostering, and consolidation of the
legitimacy of the existing social order that most intellectuals
have in one way or another been about. The impression has often
been purveyed in this century that intellectuals were for the
most part left-wing dissidents; and the term 'intellectual' was
itself invented in France at the time of the Dreyfus Affair to
designate (pejoratively) those journalists or men of letters who
were 'Dreyfusards' and who subversively attacked sacred
institutions such as the French Army and cast doubt on its
honour.

The Marxist assessment is the more realistic one: the majority
of those who could properly be called intellectuals in bourgeois
society, not to speak of professional people of one sort or
another, lawyers, architects, accountants, doctors, scientists,
etc., *have* been the 'managers of legitimation' of their society.
Nor have they been the less such because they were for the most
part unaware that this *was* the role they were performing. In
other words, they not only propagated but shared to the full in
the illusion of universalism which was described earlier as the
'false consciousness' of the bourgeoisie, or of any class which
cloaks its partial interests, deliberately or not, in the garb of
universal principles, sacred and eternal verities, the national
interest, and so on.

However, the Marxist view of intellectuals is rather more
complex, even ambiguous, than this might suggest. To begin
with, Marx and Engels, it will be recalled, said in the *Communist Manifesto* that, in 'times when the class struggle nears
the decisive hour', 'a portion of the bourgeoisie goes over to
the proletariat, and in particular a portion of the bourgeois
ideologists'.[22] This notion was subsequently widened to include
the possibility that some ideologists would join the socialist

cause even in periods when the class struggle did not near its decisive hour; and this has more recently become a major element of the Marxist perspective in regard to the struggle against capitalism: with the vast increase in the numbers of people who perform 'intellectual' tasks under capitalism, and do so as 'proletarianized' members of the 'collective labourer', the question of their alliance with the working class, and enlistment in its cause, becomes a matter of crucial importance. On the other hand, it is true that we are not here speaking of the 'bourgeois ideologists' that Marx and Engels had in mind, and are moving somewhat closer towards Gramsci's much wider definition.

As far as 'bourgeois ideologists' are concerned, Marx noted, as shown in the last quotation, that many (or some) of them might be particularly prone to 'go over to the proletariat' in times of crisis: they would do so because they had 'raised themselves to the level of comprehending theoretically the historical movement as a whole'.[23] Marx and Engels also noted that these sections of the bourgeoisie that were 'proletarianized' would 'supply the proletariat with fresh elements of enlightenment and progress',[24] and the point would presumably apply with particular force to 'ideologists', but this is no more than a presumption—Marx and Engels attributed no special 'role' to the intellectuals-cum-ideologists who had 'gone over' to the proletariat.

By the end of the nineteenth century, however, there were many such intellectuals occupying positions of influence in mass working-class parties, to the point of forming, so to speak, their own informal 'International' inside the Second International which had been formed in 1889. The question of intellectuals and their relation to the working-class movement had now assumed a much greater importance than it had ever had for Marx; and it was about them that Karl Kautsky wrote at the turn of the century what Lenin described in *What is to be Done?* as 'the following profoundly true and important words':

. . . Socialism and the class struggle arise side by side and not one out of the other; each arises under different conditions. Modern socialist consciousness can arise only on the basis of profound scientific knowledge . . . The vehicle of science is not the proletariat but the *bourgeois intelligentsia* . . . it was in the minds of individual members of this stratum that modern socialism originated, and it was they who communicated it to the more intellectually developed proletarians who, in their turn, introduce it into the proletarian class struggle where conditions allow that to be done. Thus, socialist consciousness is something introduced into the proletarian class struggle from without, and not something that arose within it spontaneously.[25]

There is more than a faint echo of these 'profoundly true and important words' in Lenin's own insistence that 'the theory of Socialism . . . grew out of the philosophic, historical and economic theories elaborated by the educated representatives of the propertied classes, by intellectuals.'*

Even so, the similarities with Kautsky are misleading. For Lenin had a poor view of intellectuals, not excluding Marxist ones. He was perfectly willing to acknowledge the debt which the development of socialist theory owed to bourgeois intellectuals. But he was exceedingly critical of what he saw as the intellectuals' 'flabbiness', individualism, lack of capacity for discipline and organization, tendency to reformism and opportunism, and so forth. He was also given to contrast their uncertain and vacillating commitment to the revolutionary movement with the sturdier and more reliable attitude of revolutionary workers. This is a 'workerist' tendency which has to a greater or lesser degree affected most Marxist writing and thinking. In Lenin's vision of the dictatorship of the proletariat, as expressed for instance in *The State and Revolution* on the eve of the Bolshevik seizure of power, it is the working class which fills the stage, together with peasants and soldiers: 'experts' are expected to serve the revolution under the watchful (and distrustful) eye of the people. Nor was his perspective different after the Bolshevik seizure of power. In so far as intellectuals played a role in the leadership of the revolution, and a large number of them, in the Bolshevik party, did, they did so not as intellectuals but, precisely, as members of the party. Whatever Lenin thought of the merits of bourgeois intellectuals in an earlier epoch of socialist development, it is *as members of the Party* and through its mediation that he saw later generations of intellectuals involved in the service of the workers' cause.

This notion is further extended and articulated by Gramsci, for whom the emergence of a class of intellectuals 'belonging' to

* Ibid., p. 375. Lenin also notes that 'in the very same way, in Russia, the theoretical doctrine of Social-Democracy arose altogether independently of the spontaneous growth of the working-class movement; it arose as a natural and inevitable outcome of the development of thought among the revolutionary socialist intelligentsia' (ibid., p. 375).

the working class was a matter of the first importance: in its bid for hegemony, the working class must produce its own intellectuals, and it is indeed one of the prime tasks of the revolutionary party to form such 'organic' intellectuals of the working class. These intellectuals play a major role in the formulation and the implantation of a new 'common sense'. But they play that role as members of a party which is itself the directing centre of the revolutionary movement, the 'modern prince', who is also the 'collective intellectual' of the working class. Here too it is the revolutionary party which performs the crucial task of bringing together and fusing in a common endeavour the working class and its intellectuals.

These and similar formulations do very little to resolve the real problems involved in the relation of intellectuals to the revolutionary movement, and this relation is in fact a major point of tension in Marxist theory, or at least in Marxist theory after Marx, and it has been a major point of tension, to put it mildly, in Communist practice.

Intellectuals are required to 'serve the people': this has been the injunction of Communist leaders to intellectuals from Lenin to the present day. The injuction may be entirely unobjectionable. The problems begin when the question is asked *how* the objective is to be served—not because the question is necessarily difficult, but because the answer to it is reserved, in the main, to the party leaders. It is they who have, in Communist practice, arrogated to themselves the prerogative of defining what serving the people means, and what it does not mean. This is much less true for Lenin, who tended to be cautious in such matters. But it has formed an intrinsic part of Communist practice ever since Lenin, and is in fact one characteristic feature of Stalinism, and for that matter of Maoism. Thus, one of the most authoritative of Chairman Mao's texts on the subject includes the following passage:

Empty, dry dogmatic formulas do indeed destroy the creative mood; not only that, they first destroy Marxism. Dogmatic 'Marxism' is not Marxism, it is anti-Marxism. Then does not Marxism destroy the creative mood? Yes, it does. It definitely destroys creative moods that are feudal, bourgeois, petty-bourgeois, liberalistic, individualistic, nihilistic, art-for-art's sake, aristocratic, decadent or pessimistic, and every other creative mood that is alien to the masses of the people and to the proletariat. So far as proletarian writers and artists are concerned, should not these kinds of creative moods be destroyed? I think they should; they should be utterly destroyed. And while they are being destroyed, something new can be constructed.*

This text dates from 1942, but there is plenty in Chairman Mao's pronouncements on intellectuals and intellectual and artistic work before and after that date which shows it to be typical of a mode of thought. The point about pronouncements such as these is not whether they are true, or false, or indeed whether they actually *mean* anything: it is rather that there is an external authority which is able to decide what is 'feudal, bourgeois, petty-bourgeois . . .' etc., and to impose its decisions upon intellectuals. The manner of imposition has varied, and assumed different forms in Russia under Stalin from those it has assumed in China, or in Cuba. But the prerogative of party leaders or of their representatives to decide what, in intellectual productions, 'serves the people', and even more so what does not, has not come under serious question in Communist regimes.

For a long time, that prerogative was also asserted, though it could not of course be imposed, by Communist Party leaders outside Communist regimes. The position has in recent years become much more open and fluid, and the notion of freedom of intellectual and artistic endeavour has by now gained a very considerable measure of acceptance and recognition by the leaderships, for instance, of the Italian and French Communist parties. The idea that intellectuals and artists should 'serve the people' has not been abandoned by these leaderships, as indeed why should it be? But the idea that they or some Cultural Commission of the Party should define what this does or does not involve has come to be increasingly discredited, together with the idea that the Party (meaning Party leaders) have any business to pass judgement on what, in artistic matters, is or is not 'acceptable'. This more relaxed approach to artistic and cultural

---

* 'Talks at the Yenan Forum on Literature and Art', in *Selected Works of Mao Tse-tung* (Peking, 1967), III, p. 94. Chairman Mao also noted that 'wrong styles of work still exist to a serious extent in our literary and art circles and that there are still many defects among our comrades, such as idealism, dogmatism, empty illusions, empty talk, contempt for practice and aloofness from the masses, all of which call for an effective and serious campaign of rectification' (ibid., p. 94). Such a comprehensive and vague indictment offers of course a formidable weapon against intellectuals, whose work is bound to be vulnerable to one or other such description.

work which has no direct and obvious political connotations has even come to affect, up to a point, intellectual work which is directly political and politically 'sensitive'. The general tendency is obviously towards a loosening up and the toleration of differences.

On the other hand, intellectuals in Western Communist parties are still expected, like other Party members, to behave in accordance with the principles of 'democratic centralism', at least where directly political utterances are involved. This may not render 'deviation' from party policy altogether unacceptable to party leaders, but it makes serious and sustained debate, and particularly organized debate, with defined platforms, next to impossible. This, which is one feature of the weakness or absence of internal democracy in these parties, affects and is intended to affect all Party members. But it affects Party intellectuals more than others in so far as criticism and probing are intrinsic elements of their being as intellectuals, or at least ought to be. The weight of 'democratic centralism' upon them is not as heavy as it was: but it is still very real; and the pressures and temptations to 'tighten up' which will arise when these parties come to office, and in the extremely difficult circumstances which will follow their accession to office, are bound to be very considerable.

Even so, the point may be worth making that the place and role of intellectuals is not a question determined by the nature of Marxism. It has been determined in Communist regimes—very adversely for the most part, namely at the price of conformity—by the conditions in which regimes which claim to be inspired by Marxism have come to power and developed. Ruthless repression of dissident intellectual work—and of every other kind of dissidence as well—has occurred in the name or 'under the banner' of Marxism. But there is no warrant for the view that such repression is somehow inscribed in the nature of Marxism. Assertions of this sort are merely propaganda.

This propaganda is part of the 'battle for consciousness' to which reference was made earlier, and which is part of the daily life of class societies. But this battle is only one facet of class conflict. There are other battles which proceed alongside this one, and in which the state plays a central role. Nor indeed is it really possible to separate any of these battles from each other; and the state intervenes, at one level or another, in all of them.

Here is the first and the last defender of the old order; and it is therefore to the state that we must now turn.

NOTES

1 *The Eighteenth Brumaire of Louis Bonaparte* in *Surveys from Exile*, op cit., p. 146.
2 K. Marx, *Capital*, I, p. 737.
3 K. Marx, *Capital*, III, p. 307. My italics.
4 Ibid., p. 308.
5 *Capital*, I, p. 72.
6 K. Marx, *Grundrisse*, p. 197.
7 *Capital*, I, p. 763.
8 K. Marx, *Critique of Hegel's 'Philosophy of Right'*, p. 131.
9 Ibid., p. 131.
10 Ibid., p. 132.
11 Revs., p. 89.
12 K. Marx and F. Engels, *The German Ideology* (London, 1965), p. 60.
13 SE, p. 90.
14 See below, pp. 92 ff.
15 A. Gramsci, *Selections from the Prison Notebooks* (London, 1971), p. 8.
16 Ibid., p. 9.
17 Ibid., p. 9.
18 Ibid., p. 12.
19 Ibid., p. 12.
20 K. Marx and F. Engels, *The German Ideology*, p. 61.
21 K. Marx, *Capital*, I, p. 15.
22 Revs., p. 77.
23 Ibid., p. 77.
24 Ibid., p. 77.
25 Lenin, *What is to be Done?*, CWL, vol. 5, p. 383. Italics in Kautsky's original text.

IV. The Defence of the Old Order: II

1

In the politics of Marxism, there is no institution which is nearly as important as the state—so much so that concentration of attention upon it has helped to devalue in Marxist theory other important elements of politics, for instance the cultural elements discussed in the last chapter.

Nevertheless, there is no question that it is right to emphasize the central role of the state in any given social system. Nor of course is the emphasis specific to Marxism: it is also found in other and opposed theories of politics.

Most of these theories, however large their differences from each other may be, have in common a view of the state as charged with the representation of 'society as a whole', as standing above particular and necessarily partial groups, interests, and classes, as having the special function of ensuring both that the competition between these groups, interests, and classes remains orderly and that the 'national interest' should not be impaired in the process. Whether the state discharges these tasks well or not is not here at issue: the point is that most theories of politics do assign the tasks in question to the state, and thereby turn it into the linchpin of the social system.

The starting point of the Marxist theory of politics and the state is its categorical rejection of this view of the state as the trustee, instrument, or agent of 'society as a whole'. This rejection necessarily follows from the Marxist concept of society as class society. In class societies, the concept of 'society as a whole' and of the 'national interest' is clearly a mystification. There may be occasions and matters where the interests of all classes happen to coincide. But for the most part and in essence, these interests are fundamentally and irrevocably at odds, so that the state cannot possibly be their common trustee: the idea that it can is part of the ideological veil which a dominant class draws upon the reality of class rule, so as to legitimate that rule in its own eyes as well as in the eyes of the subordinate classes.

In reality, so the Marxist argument has always been, the state is an essential means of class domination. It is not a neutral referee arbitrating between competing interests: it is inevitably a deeply engaged partisan. It is not 'above' class struggles but right in them. Its intervention in the affairs of society is crucial, constant and pervasive; and that intervention is closely conditioned by the most fundamental of the state's characteristics, namely that it *is* a means of class domination—ultimately the most important by far of any such means.

The most famous formulation of the Marxist view of the state occurs in the *Communist Manifesto*: 'The executive of the modern state is but a committee for managing the common affairs of the whole bourgeoisie.'[1] But this is not nearly so simple and straightforward a formulation as it has commonly been interpreted to be. In fact, it presents, as do all Marxist formulations on the state, many problems which need careful probing. I do not mean by this that the general perspective is false: on the contrary, I think that it is closer to the political reality of class societies than any other perspective. But it is not a magic formula which renders the interpretation of that reality unproblematic. There is no such formula.

One immediate problem concerns the notion of 'ruling class' in its Marxist usage. In that usage, the 'ruling class' is so designated by virtue of the fact that it owns and controls a predominant part of the means of material and 'mental' production; *and* that it thereby controls, runs, dictates to, or is predominant in the state as well. But this *assumes* that class power is automatically translated into state power. In fact, there is no such automatic translation: the question of the relation between class power and state power constitutes a major problem, with many different facets. Even where that relation can be shown to be very close, a number of difficult questions remain to be answered, or at least explored. Not the least of these questions concerns the forms which the state assumes, and why it assumes different forms, and with what consequences.

But the very first thing that is needed is to realize that the relation between the 'ruling class' and the state *is* a problem, which cannot be assumed away. Indeed, the problem is implicit in the formulation from the *Manifesto* which I have quoted earlier. For the reference to 'the common affairs of the whole bourgeoisie' clearly implies that the bourgeoisie is a social totality made up of different and therefore potentially or actually conflicting elements, a point which, as was suggested in Chapter II, must be taken as axiomatic for all classes; while 'common affairs' implies the existence of particular ones as well. On this basis, there is an absolutely essential function of mediation and reconciliation to be performed by the state; or rather, it is the state which plays a major role in the performance of that function, the qualification being required because there are other institutions which help in its performance, for instance the parties of the bourgeoisie.

But if the state is to perform this mediating and reconciling function for what are, in effect, different elements or fractions of the bourgeoisie, which have different and conflicting interests, it clearly must have a certain degree of autonomy in relation to the 'ruling class'. In so far as that class is not monolithic, and it never is, it cannot act as a principal to an agent, and 'it' cannot simply use the state as 'its' instrument. In this context, there is no 'it', capable of issuing coherent instructions, least of all in highly complex, fragmented and 'old' societies, where a long process of historical development has brought to predominance a 'ruling class' which harbours many different interests and fractions. This is not to deny the acceptability, with various qualifications, of the term, but only to suggest that the relation of the 'ruling class' to the state is always and in all circumstances *bound* to be problematic.

The best way to proceed is to ask the simplest possible question, namely why, in Marxist terms, the state should be thought to be the 'instrument' of a 'ruling class'; and an answer to this question should also yield an answer to the question of the validity of the concept of 'ruling class' itself.

Marxists have, in effect, given three distinct answers to the question, none of which have however been adequately theorized.

The first of these has to do with the *personnel* of the state system, that is to say the fact that the people who are located in the commanding heights of the state, in the executive, administrative, judicial, repressive and legislative branches, have tended to belong to the same class or classes which have dominated the other strategic heights of the society, notably the economic and the cultural ones. Thus in contemporary capitalism, members of the bourgeoisie tend to predominate in the three main sectors of social life, the economic, the political and the cultural/ideological—the political being understood here as referring mainly to the state apparatus, though the point would apply more widely. Where the people concerned, it is usually added, are not members of the bourgeoisie by social origin, they are later recruited into it by virtue of their education, connections, and way of life.

The assumption which is at work here is that a common social background and origin, education, connections, kinship, and friendship, a similar way of life, result in a cluster of common ideological and political positions and attitudes, common values and perspectives. There is no necessary unanimity of views among the people in question and there may be fairly deep differences between them on this or that issue. But these differences occur within a specific and fairly narrow conservative spectrum. This being the case, it is to be expected, so the argument goes, that those who run the state apparatus should, at the very least, be favourably disposed towards those who own and control the larger part of the means of economic activity, that they should be much better disposed towards them than towards any other interest or class, and that they should seek to serve the interests and purposes of the economically dominant class, the more so since those who run the state power are most likely to be persuaded that to serve these interests and purposes is also, broadly speaking, to serve the 'national interest' or the interests of 'the nation as a whole'.

This is a strong case, easily verifiable by a wealth of evidence. The bourgeois state *has* tended to be run by people very largely of the same class as the people who commanded the 'private sector' of the economic life of capitalist societies (and for that matter the 'public sector' as well). What I have elsewhere called the state élite *has* tended to share the ideological and political presumptions of the economically dominant class. And the state in capitalist society *has* tended to favour capitalist interests and capitalist enterprise—to put it thus is in fact to understate the bias.

Yet, strong though the case is, it is open to a number of very serious objections. These do not render the consideration of the nature of the state personnel irrelevant. Nor do they in the least affect the notion of the state as a class state. But they do suggest that the correlation which can be established in class terms between the state élite and the economically dominant class is not adequate to settle the issue.

One major objection is that there have been important and frequent exceptions to the general pattern of class correlation. These exceptions have occurred, so to speak, at both the upper and the lower levels of the social scale.

Britain provides the most notable example of the former case. Here, a landowning aristocracy continued for most of the nineteenth century to occupy what may accurately be described as an overwhelmingly preponderant place in the highest reaches of the state apparatus; while Britain was in the same period turning into the 'workshop of the world', the most advanced of all capitalist countries, with a large, solid, and economically powerful capitalist class. The phenomenon was of course familiar to Marx and Engels, who frequently remarked upon it. Thus in an article, 'The British Constitution', written in 1855, Marx observed that 'although the bourgeoisie, itself only the highest social stratum of the middle classes', had 'gained *political* recognition as the *ruling class*', 'this only happened on one condition; namely that the whole business of government in all its details—including even the executive branch of the legislature, that is, the actual making of laws in both Houses of Parliament—remained the guranteed domain of the landed aristocracy';[2] and he went on to add that 'now, subjected to certain principles laid down by the bourgeoisie, the aristocracy (which enjoys exclusive power in the Cabinet, in Parliament, in the Civil Service, in the Army and Navy . . .) is being forced at this very moment to sign its own death warrant and to admit before the whole world that it is no longer destined to govern England'.[3]

Of course, the aristocracy was then neither signing its death warrant nor admitting anything of the kind Marx suggested. But even if we leave this aside, there are here very large theoretical as well as empirical questions which remain unanswered concerning the relations of this new 'ruling class' to a landed aristocracy which, according to Marx, remained in complete charge of state power; and also concerning the ways in which the 'compromise' of which Marx also spoke in this article worked themselves out.

The same phenomenon of an aristocratic class exercising power 'on behalf' of capitalism occurred elsewhere, for instance in Germany, and was discussed by Marx and Engels, though in different terms. But it is obvious that this presents a problem for the thesis that the bias of the state is determined by the social class of its leading personnel.

The problem is at least as great where an important part of the state apparatus is in the hands of members of 'lower' classes. This too has frequently been the case in the history of capitalism. In all capitalist countries, members of the petty bourgeoisie, and increasingly of the working class as well, have made a successful career in the state service, often at the highest levels.* It may well be argued that many if not most of them have been 'absorbed' into the bourgeoisie precisely by virtue of their success; but the categorization is too wide and subjective to be convincing. In any case, there are telling instances where no such 'absorption' occurred: the most dramatic such instances are those of the Fascist dictators who held close to absolute power for substantial periods of time in Italy and Germany. This will need to be discussed later, but it may be noted here that whatever else may be said about them, it cannot be said about Hitler and Mussolini that they were in any meaningful way 'absorbed' into the German and Italian bourgeoisies and capitalist classes.

In other words, the class bias of the state is not determined, or at least not decisively and conclusively determined, by the social origins of its leading personnel. Nor for that matter has it always been the case that truly bourgeois-led states have necessarily pursued policies of which the capitalist class has approved. On the contrary, it has often been found that such states have been quite seriously at odds with their economically dominant classes. The classic example is that of Roosevelt after his election to the Presidency of the United States in 1932. In short, exclusive reliance on the social character of the state personnel is unhelpful—it creates as many problems as it solves.

The second answer which Marxists have tended to give to the question why the state should be thought to be the 'instrument' of a capitalist 'ruling class' has to do with the economic power which that class is able to wield by virtue of its ownership and control of economic and other resources, and of its strength and influence as a pressure group, in a broad meaning of the term.

* In the *Prison Notebooks*, Gramsci asks: 'Does there exist, in a given country, a widespread social stratum in whose economic life and political self-assertion . . . the bureaucratic career, either civil or military, is a very important element?'; and he answered that 'in modern Europe, this stratum can be identified in the medium and small rural bourgeoisie, which is more or less numerous from one country to another', and which he saw as occasionally capable of 'laying down the law' to the ruling class (op. cit., pp. 212, 213).

There is much strength in this argument too, to which is added by virtue of the growth of economic giants as a characteristic feature of advanced capitalism. These powerful conglomerates are obviously bound to constitute a major reference point for governments; and many of them are multi-national, which means that important international considerations enter into the question. And there is in any case a vital international dimension injected into the process of governmental decision-making, and in the power which business is able to exercise in the shaping of that process, because governments have to take very carefully into account the attitudes of other and powerful capitalist governments and of a number of international institutions, agencies and associations, whose primary concern is the defence of the 'free enterprise' system.

Capitalist enterprise is undoubtedly the strongest 'pressure group' in capitalist society; and it is indeed able to command the attention of the state. But this is not the same as saying that the state is the 'instrument' of the capitalist class; and the pressure which business is able to apply upon the state is not in itself sufficient to explain the latter's actions and policies. There are complexities in the decision-making process which the notion of business as pressure group is too rough and unwieldy to explain. There may well be cases where that pressure is decisive. But there are others where it is not. Too great an emphasis upon this aspect of the matter leaves too much out of account.

In particular, it leaves out of account the third answer to the question posed earlier as to the nature of the state, namely a 'structural' dimension, of an objective and impersonal kind. In essence, the argument is simply that the state is the 'instrument' of the 'ruling class' because, *given its insertion in the capitalist mode of production*, it cannot be anything else. The question does not, on this view, depend on the personnel of the state, or on the pressure which the capitalist class is able to bring upon it: the nature of the state is here determined by the nature and requirements of the mode of production. There are 'structural constraints' which no government, whatever its complexion, wishes, and promises, can ignore or evade. A capitalist economy has its own 'rationality' to which any government and state must sooner or later submit, and usually sooner.

There is a great deal of strength in this 'structural' perspective, and it must in fact form an integral part of the Marxist view of the state, even though it too has never been adequately theorized. But it also has certain deficiencies which can easily turn into crippling weaknesses.

The strength of the 'structural' explanation is that it helps to understand why governments do act as they do—for instance why governments pledged to far-reaching reforms before reaching office, and indeed elected because they were so pledged, have more often than not failed to carry out more than at best a very small part of their reforming programme. This has often been attributed—not least by Marxists—to the personal failings of leaders, corruption, betrayal, the machinations of civil servants and bankers, or a combination of all these. Such explanations are not necessarily wrong, but they require backing up by the concept (and the fact) of 'structural constraints' which do beset any government working within the context of a particular mode of production.

The weakness of the case is that it makes it very easy to set up arbitrary limits to the possible. There *are* 'structural constraints'—but how constraining they are is a difficult question; and the temptation is to fall into what I have called a 'hyperstructuralist' trap, which deprives 'agents' of any freedom of choice and manoeuvre and turns them into the 'bearers' of objective forces which they are unable to affect. This perspective is but another form of determinism—which is alien to Marxism and in any case false, which is much more serious.* Governments can and do press against the 'structural constraints' by which they are beset. Yet, to recognize the existence and the importance of these constraints is also to point to the *limits of reform*, of which more later, and to make possible a strategy of change which attacks the mode of production that imposes the constraints.

Taken together, as they need to be, these three modes of explanation of the nature of the state—the character of its leading personnel, the pressures exercised by the economically dominant class, and the structural constraints imposed by the

* See R. Miliband, 'Poulantzas and the Capitalist State' in *New Left Review*, no. 82, Nov.–Dec. 1973, for a critical assessment of what I take to be an example of this type of determinism, namely N. Poulantzas, *Political Power and Social Classes* (London, 1973). For a reply, see N. Poulantzas, 'The Capitalist State: A reply to Miliband and Laclau', in *New Left Review*, no. 95, Jan.–Feb. 1976.

mode of production—constitute the Marxist answer to the question why the state should be considered as the 'instrument' of the 'ruling class'.

Yet, there is a powerful reason for rejecting this particular formulation as misleading. This is that, while the state does act, in Marxist terms, *on behalf* of the 'ruling class', it does not for the most part act *at its behest*. The state is indeed a class state, the state of the 'ruling class'. But it enjoys a high degree of autonomy and independence in the manner of its operation as a class state, and indeed *must* have that high degree of autonomy and independence if it is to act as a class state. The notion of the state as an 'instrument' does not fit this fact, and tends to obscure what has come to be seen as a crucial property of the state, namely its *relative autonomy* from the 'ruling class' and from civil society at large. This notion of the relative autonomy of the state forms an important part of the Marxist theory of the state and was, in one form or another, much discussed by Marx and Engels. The meaning and implication of the concept require further consideration.

2

As a preliminary to the discussion of the relative autonomy of the state in Marxist thought, it should be noted that Marx and Engels duly acknowledged, as they could hardly fail to do, the existence through history and in their own times of different *forms of state*, not only in different modes of production and social formations, but also in the capitalist mode of production itself. In historical terms, they identified forms of state ranging from 'Asiatic' despotism to the Absolutist State, and including the states of Antiquity and of feudalism; and in their own times, they distinguished between such forms of state as the bourgeois republic, the Bonapartist and Bismarckian states, the English and Czarist forms of state, etc.

On the other hand, these distinctions are *never* such, for Marx and Engels and for most of their disciples, as to nullify the one absolutely fundamental feature that these states all have in common, namely that they are all class states. This twin fact about the state, namely that it assumes many different and sharply contrasting forms but also that it remains a class state throughout, has been a source of considerable tension in Marxist political thought and debate, and has also had a considerable influence at one time or another on the strategy of Marxist parties and organizations.

The problem, for revolutionaries, is obvious. The distinctions which clearly must be made between different forms of state—if only because they are too great to be ignored—may lead to a disappearance from view of the central idea of the class nature of *all* forms of state, whether they are dictatorships or bourgeois democratic regimes. But the attempt to avoid this error of appreciation may also lead—and has indeed led—to the assertion that there is *really* no difference between different forms of state, and that, to take a specific example, there is *really* no difference, or at least no really serious difference, between Fascist regimes and bourgeois democratic ones. This is what the Comintern 'line' provided as a perspective during a crucial part of inter-war history, with utterly catastrophic results for working-class movements everywhere, and most notably in Germany. It was only at the Seventh World Congress of the Third International in 1935, long after the Nazis had conquered Germany, that Georgy Dimitrov, speaking on behalf of that disastrous organization, gave the official seal of approval to a drastic change of course, and declared that 'accession to power of fascism is not an *ordinary succession* of one bourgeois government by another, but a *substitution* of one state form of class domination of the bourgeoisie—bourgeois democracy—by another form—open terrorist dictatorship'; and he also proclaimed that 'now the toiling masses of the capitalist countries are faced with the necessity of making a definite choice, and making it today, not between proletarian dictatorship and bourgeois democracy, but between bourgeois democracy and fascism'.[4] In fact, the choice had presented itself years before and had been stated quite clearly inside the ranks of Marxism, most notably by Leon Trotsky.[5]

Since those days, many different varieties of 'ultra-leftism' have included, as part of their creed, the insistence that there was no *real* difference between bourgeois democratic regimes and authoritarian ones. That this *is* an ultra-left deviation seems to me evident. But rather than simply dismiss it as such, one should see it as an expression of the real theoretical and practical problems which the existence of different forms of class state poses to Marxists: not the least of these problems is that, in so far as some of these forms are infinitely preferable to others, choices often have to be made, as Dimitrov said, which involve the defence of bourgeois democratic regimes against their opponents on the right. The terms on which that defence should be conducted has always been a major strategic problem for revolutionary movements, even when they were agreed that the defence itself must be undertaken.

On this latter point, there never was any question for classical Marxism, beginning with Marx and Engels. The latter were not at all taken with bourgeois democracy, and denounced it in utterly uncompromising terms as a form of class domination. Indeed, Marx in The Class Struggles in France wrote of the bourgeois republic of 1848 that it 'could be nothing other than the perfected and most purely developed rule of the whole bourgeois class . . . the synthesis of the Restoration and the July monarchy'.[6] Also, a recurrent theme in Marx's writings on the subject is how repressive and brutal this form of state can turn as soon as its upholders and beneficiaries feel themselves to be threatened by the proletariat. With the June days in Paris, the Republic, Marx wrote in the same text, appeared 'in its pure form, as the state whose avowed purpose it is to perpetuate the rule of capital and the slavery of labour'; and 'bourgeois rule, freed from all fetters, was inevitably transformed, all at once, into bourgeois terrorism'.[7] In the same vein, Marx wrote in The Civil War in France more than two decades later that the treatment meted out to the Communards by the government of Thiers showed what was meant by 'the victory of order, justice and civilization': 'The civilization and justice of bourgeois order comes out in its lurid light whenever the slaves and drudges of that order rise against their masters. Then this civilisation and justice stand forth as undisguised savagery and lawless revenge'.[8]

But when this has been said, it remains true that Marx and Engels saw considerable virtues in bourgeois democratic regimes as compared with other forms of class domination, and notably with Bonapartism, to which Marx in particular devoted much attention. Twenty years of his life, the years of his intellectual maturity, were spent in the shadow, so to speak, of this form of dictatorship; and just as capitalist Britain served as Marx's laboratory for the analysis of the political economy of capitalism, so did France under Louis Bonaparte serve him between 1851 and 1871 as a frame of reference for one kind of capitalist politics.

The Bonapartist state was distinguished by an extreme inflation and concentration of executive power, personified in one
individual, and nullifying the legislative power. This executive
power, Marx wrote in *The Eighteenth Brumaire of Louis
Bonaparte*, possessed 'an immense bureaucratic and military
organisation, an ingenious and broadly based state machinery,
and an army of half a million officials alongside the actual army,
which numbers a further half million'; and he further described
this state machinery as 'this frightful parasitic body, which
surrounds the body of French society like a caul and stops up all
its pores . . '[9]

There is, in Marx's writings on the Bonapartist state, a strong
sense of the life of 'civil society' being stifled and suppressed in
ways which the class state of bourgeois democratic regimes
cannot in 'normal' circumstances adopt—a sense epitomized in
his description of France after the *coup d'état* of December 2: '. . .
all classes fall on their knees, equally mute and equally impo-
tent, before the rifle butt.'[10]

Closely related to this, and crucially important in the
approach of Marx and Engels to the bourgeois republican form
of state, as compared with other forms of bourgeois state power,
was their belief that the former provided the working class with
opportunities and means of struggle which it was precisely the
purpose of the latter to deny them. One of the most specific and
categorical statements connected with this issue occurs in *The
Class Struggles in France*:

The most comprehensive contradiction in the Constitution (of the Second Republic) consists in the fact that it gives political power to the
classes whose social slavery it is intended to perpetuate: proletariat,
peasants and petty bourgeoisie. And it deprives the bourgeoisie, the
class whose old social power it sanctions, of the political guarantees of
this power. It imposes on the political rule of the bourgeoisie democratic conditions which constantly help its enemies towards victory and
endanger the very basis of bourgeois society. It demands from the one
that it should not proceed from political emancipation to social emancipation and from the other that it should not regress from social
restoration to political restoration.[11]

The main feature of the bourgeois democratic regimes on
which Marx and Engels fastened was universal suffrage. Still in
The Class Struggles in France, Marx pointed to the problem
which this presented, or could present, to the bourgeoisie:

But does the Constitution still have any meaning the moment that the content of this suffrage, this sovereign will, is no longer bourgeois rule? Is it not the duty of the bourgeoisie to regulate the franchise so that it demands what is reasonable, *its* rule? By repeatedly terminating the existing state power and by creating it anew from itself does not universal suffrage destroy all stability; does it not perpetually call all existing powers into question; does it not destroy authority; does it not threaten to elevate anarchy itself to the level of authority? [12]

Marx himself answered that the moment must arrive when universal suffrage was no longer compatible with bourgeois rule, and that this moment had indeed arrived in France with the elections of 10 March 1850. The bourgeoisie was now forced to repudiate universal suffrage, he said, and to confess: 'Our dictatorship has existed hitherto by the will of the people; it must now be consolidated against the will of the people'.[13] Nevertheless, he also noted, 'universal suffrage had fulfilled its mission, the only function it can have in a revolutionary period. The majority of the people had passed through the school of development it provided. It had to be abolished—by revolution or by reaction'.[14]

There are many different questions which this conjures up and which will be discussed in Chapter VI. But it may be useful at this point to pursue a little further the issue of universal suffrage and bourgeois democracy as it appeared to Marx and Engels.

Marx himself always held fast to the view that the suffrage, in so far as it helped to sharpen the contradictions of bourgeois society and provided a 'school of development' of the working class, offered definite but limited possibilities to the revolutionary movement.* On the other hand, he also described 'the

---

* In an article on the Chartists published in the *New York Daily Tribune* of 25 August 1852, Marx went as far as the following: '. . . universal suffrage is the equivalent for political power for the working class of England, where the proletariat forms the large majority of the population, where, in a long, though underground, civil war, it has gained a clear consciousness of its position as a class, and where even the rural districts know no longer any peasants, but only landlords, industrial capitalists (farmers) and hired labourers. The carrying of universal suffrage in England would, therefore, be a far more socialistic measure than anything which has been honoured with the name on the Continent' ('The Chartists' in SE, p. 264). Both he and Engels came, particularly after the passage of the Second Reform Act of 1867, to take a rather less sanguine view of the workings of universal suffrage. (See K. Marx and F. Engels, *On Britain* (Moscow, 1953), *passim*.)

general suffrage' in class society as 'abused either for the parliamentary sanction of the Holy State Power, or a play in the
hands of the ruling classes, only employed by the people to
sanction (choose the instruments of) parliamentary class rule
once in many years', instead of being adapted, as he thought it
would have been by the Commune, 'to its real purpose, to choose
by the communes their own functionaries of administration and
initiation'.[15]

The question of the suffrage and its uses is also connected
with that of the 'transition to socialism'; and Marx, as noted
earlier, was willing to allow that there might be some isolated
cases where that transition would be achieved by non-violent
means, and therefore presumably through electoral means made
available by the suffrage. But he was clearly very sceptical about
such a process, and took it for granted that it would not be the
common pattern. 'The workers' he said in a speech after the last
Congress of the First International in 1872, 'will have to seize
political power one day in order to construct the new organisation of labour; they will have to overthrow the old politics which
bolster up the old institutions'. But 'we do not claim', he went on,
'that the road leading to this goal is the same everywhere':

We know that heed must be paid to the institutions, customs and
traditions of the various countries, and we do not deny that there are
countries, such as America and England, and if I was familiar with its
institutions, I might include Holland, where the workers may attain
their goal by peaceful means. That being the case, we must recognize
that in most continental countries the lever of the revolution will have
to be force; a resort to force will be necessary one day in order to set up
the rule of labour.[16]

The weight of the argument is unmistakably on the non-
peaceful side of the line. The case of Engels is a little more
complicated, the complication arising from pronouncements
made in the course of developments, notably the growth of German Social Democracy, which postdate Marx's death. By far
the most important such pronouncement is Engels's famous
Introduction of 1895 to Marx's *Class Struggles in France*. That
Introduction was subjected to some expurgation before it was
published in *Vorwärts*, the main organ of the German Social
Democratic Party; and Engels strongly complained to Kautsky
that the expurgated version made him appear as a 'peaceful
worshipper of legality *quand même*'.[17] But even though Engels

had every right to complain that the editing of his text was misleading, the fact remains that the unexpurgated version unques-
tionably shows a major shift of emphasis from earlier pronouncements of Marx and Engels on the question of the suffrage
and its uses. Engels emphatically denied that he was in any way
suggesting that 'our foreign comrades' should 'in the least renounce their right to revolution'.[18] But he went on to say that
'whatever may happen in other countries, the German Social-
Democracy occupies a special position and therewith, at least in
the immediate future, has a special task'.[19]

This 'special task' was to maintain and preserve the growth of
German Social Democracy and its electoral support:

Its growth proceeds as spontaneously, as steadily, as irresistibly, and at
the same time as tranquilly as a natural process. All government intervention has proved powerless against it. We can count even today on
two and a quarter million voters. If it continues in this fashion, by the
end of the century we shall conquer the greater part of the middle strata
of society, petty bourgeois and small peasants, and grow into the decisive power in the land, before which all other powers will have to bow,
whether they like it or not. To keep this growth going without interruption until it of itself gets beyond the control of the prevailing governmental system, not to fritter away this daily increasing shock force in
vanguard skirmishes, but to keep it intact until the decisive day, that is
our main task.[20]

Engels's reference to 'the decisive day' suggests that he had by
no means given up the notion that a revolutionary break might
yet occur. So does his reference a little later in the text to the
likelihood that the powers-that-be would themselves be forced
to break through the 'fatal legality' under which Social Democracy thrived, and which it therefore was its bounden duty to
maintain. But the shift of emphasis from an earlier perspective is
nevertheless quite clear; and whatever Engels himself may have
thought, his rejection of notions of 'overthrow', even if bound up
with specific conjunctural circumstances, was sufficiently decisive to give considerable encouragement to a much more positive view of what was possible under bourgeois democracy than
had earlier been envisaged by Marx and Engels. Not, it should be
added, that the shift would not have occurred without Engels's
text. The text only gave, or appeared to give, legitimation to a
process that was inscribed in the evolution of the German labour
movement in the conditions of a bourgeois democratic regime
even as incomplete and stunted as the German Imperial one.

In the present context, however, the critical point is that there was no real question for Marxists until the outbreak of the First World War that working-class parties and movements must seize every opportunity of electoral and representative advance offered to them by their respective regimes;[21] and that they must do whatever was in their power to further the 'democratization' of these regimes. In Marxist thought, bourgeois democracy, for all its class limitations, remained a vastly superior form of state to any existing alternative.

Lenin's changing perspectives, in this connection, are particularly interesting, since they considerably affected later debates. At the time of the Russian Revolution of 1905, he pressed hard the case for proletarian support—indeed for the leadership—of the bourgeois revolution in Russia:

In countries like Russia the working class suffers not so much from capitalism as from the insufficient development of capitalism. The working class is, therefore, *most certainly interested* in the broadest, freest, and most rapid development of capitalism ... That is why a *bourgeois revolution is in the highest degree advantageous to the proletariat.* The more complete, determined and consistent the bourgeois revolution, the more assured will the proletariat's struggle be against the bourgeoisie and for socialism.[22]

Moreover, Lenin was then very concerned to stress the differences that were to be found within bourgeois democracy itself:

There are bourgeois-democratic regimes like the one in Germany, and also like the one in England; like the one in Austria and also like those in America and Switzerland. He would be a fine Marxist indeed, who in a period of democratic revolution failed to see this difference between the degrees of democratism and the difference between its forms, and confined himself to 'clever' remarks to the effect that, after all, this is 'a bourgeois revolution', the fruit of 'bourgeois revolution'.[23]

Nor was this in any way a purely tactical or debating standpoint. In 1908 he was referring casually to America and Britain as countries 'where complete political liberty exists';[24] and in 1913, writing in the context of the national question, he suggested that 'advanced countries, Switzerland, Belgium, Norway, and others, provide us with an example of how free nations under a really democratic system live together in peace or separate peacefully from each other'.[25]

These glowing remarks should not be taken too literally: Lenin never ceased to make the sharpest distinction between bourgeois democracy and what he envisaged that the proletarian form of democracy could be. But it was only under the impact of the First World War that he adopted a much more undiscriminating stance towards all forms of bourgeois democracy. Thus in the Preface which he wrote in August 1917 to *The State and Revolution*, he said that

the imperialist war has immensely accelerated and intensified the process of transformation of monopoly capitalism into state-monopoly capitalism. The monstrous oppression of the working people by the state, which is merging more and more with the all-powerful capitalist associations is becoming increasingly monstrous. The advanced countries—we mean their hinterland—are becoming military convict prisons for the workers;[26]

and in the pamphlet itself, he specifically said, in connection with his insistence on the need to 'smash' the bourgeois state, that

both Britain and America, the biggest and the last representatives—in the whole world—of Anglo-Saxon 'liberty', in the sense that they had no militarist cliques and bureaucracy, have completely sunk into the all-European filthy, bloody morass of bureaucratic-military institutions which subordinate everything to themselves, and suppress everything.[27]

Even so, he had also noted, a little earlier in the pamphlet, that 'we are in favour of a democratic republic as the best form of state for the proletariat under capitalism', though with the qualification that 'we have no right to forget that wage slavery is the lot of the people even in the most democratic bourgeois republic'.[28] This was the more or less 'traditional' view. The other, which saw all capitalist countries as 'sunk in the bloody morass of bureaucratic-military institutions' represented a different appreciation, whose 'ultra-leftist' tinges had considerable consequences in terms of policy decisions later. As noted earlier, it was the same trend of thought which led to the adoption, or which at least served as a justification for the adoption, of the 'class against class' Comintern policies of the 'Third Period', in which all bourgeois regimes, of whatever kind, were assimilated for strategic purposes under the same rubric, with results that materially contributed to the Nazi conquest of power in Germany.

There are of course many different reasons why this assimilation was easily accepted by the overwhelming majority of members of Communist parties and organizations. One general reason, as I also already noted earlier, has to do with an attitude of mind to which Marxists have been prone. This is the belief that because A and B are not *totally* different, they are not *really* different at all. This error has not only been made in relation to the state, but in other contexts as well, with damaging effects. More specifically, there is a permanent Marxist temptation to devalue the distinction between bourgeois democratic regimes and authoritarian ones. From the view that the former are class regimes of a more or less repressive kind, which is entirely legitimate, it has always been fairly easy for Marxists to move to the inaccurate and dangerous view that what separates them from truly authoritarian regimes is of no great account, or not 'qualitatively' significant. The temptation to blur the distinction has been further enhanced by the fear that to do otherwise would make more difficult an intransigent critique of the class limitations and inherent shortcomings of bourgeois democracy; and by the fear that it would conceal the fact that bourgeois democracy can be turned with the assent and indeed encouragement of ruling classes into authoritarian or Fascist regimes.

Different forms of state have different degrees of autonomy. But all states enjoy some autonomy or independence (the terms are used interchangeably here) from all classes, including the dominant classes.

The relative autonomy of the state was mainly acknowledged by Marx and Engels in connection with forms of state where the executive power dominated all other elements of the state system—for instance the Absolutist State, or the Bonapartist or Bismarckian one. Where Marx and Engels do acknowledge the relative autonomy of the state, they tend to do so in terms which sometimes exaggerate the extent of that autonomy. Later Marxist political thought, on the contrary, has usually had a strong bias towards the underestimation of the state's relative autonomy.

What this relative autonomy means has already been indicated: it simply consists in the degree of freedom which the state (normally meaning in this context the executive power) has in determining how best to serve what those who hold power conceive to be the 'national interest', and which in fact involves the service of the interests of the ruling class.

Quite clearly, this degree of freedom is in direct relation to the freedom which the executive power and the state in general enjoy *vis-à-vis* institutions (for instance parliamentary assemblies) and pressure groups which represent or speak for either the dominant class or the subordinate ones. In this sense, the relative autonomy of the state is greatest in regimes where the executive power is least constrained, either by other elements within the state system, or by various forces in civil society. Of such regimes, Bonapartist France was the example with which Marx was most familiar. Its extreme version in capitalist society has been Fascism in Italy and Nazism in Germany, with many other less thorough examples in other capitalist societies. But it may be worth stressing again that *all* class states do enjoy *some* degree of autonomy, whatever their form and however 'representative' and 'democratic' they may be. The very notion of the state as an entity separate from civil society implies a certain distance between the two, a *relation* which implies a disjunction. The disjunction, which may be minimal or substantial, can only come to an end with the disappearance of the state itself, which in turn depends on the disappearance of class divisions and class struggles; and most likely a lot else as well.

I noted earlier that Marx and Engels discussed the state's relative independence mainly in connection with regimes where the executive power was exceptionally strong. This makes it appear that it is only in such regimes that they thought the state was relatively independent. More important, the way they discussed that relative independence in the regimes they did consider is somewhat confusing, in so far as it involves the use, particularly by Engels, of a concept of 'equilibrium' between contending social forces, which 'equilibrium' is supposedly provided by the state.

In *The Eighteenth Brumaire*, Marx contrasts as follows Bonapartism and the regimes which had preceded it: 'Under the Restoration, Louis Philippe and the parliamentary republic', what Marx called 'the bureaucracy', and which here stands for the state, 'was the instrument of the ruling class, however much it strove for power in its own right'. 'Only under the second Bonaparte', Marx goes on, 'does the state seem to have attained a completely autonomous position. The state machine has established itself so firmly *vis-à-vis* civil society that the only leader it needs is the head of the Society of December 10 . . .' (i.e. Bonaparte).[29]

This would appear to suggest the *complete* independence of the state power from all social forces in civil society. But Marx goes on to say that 'the state power does not hover in mid-air', and that Bonaparte 'represents a class, indeed he represents the most numerous class of French society, the *small peasant proprietors*'.[30] What the notion of 'representation' means here is not at all clear, and the discussion of the nature and status of Bonapartism which follows is very weak: on the one hand, Bonaparte is described as 'the executive authority which has attained power in its own right, and as such he feels it to be his mission to safeguard "bourgeois order".[31] But the strength of this bourgeois order lies in the middle class. He therefore sees himself as the representative of the middle class and he issues decrees in this sense'.[32] On the other hand, Marx also writes that 'the contradictory task facing the man explains the contradictions of his government, the confused and fumbling attempts to win and then to humiliate first one class and then another, the result being to array them all in uniform opposition to him'.[33] This obviously understates and indeed obscures the quite specific class role which Bonaparte and his regime were called upon to play.

Twenty years later, in *The Civil War in France*, the significance of Bonapartism is much more clearly articulated. Marx describes the Second Republic which was overthrown by the *coup d'état* of 2 December 1851, as a 'regime of avowed terrorism and deliberate insult toward the "vile multitude"'; and he then goes on to describe how the 'party of Order' paved the way for the Bonapartist dictatorship:

The restraints by which their own divisions had under former regimes still checked the state power were removed by their union; and in view of the threatening upheaval of the proletariat, they now used that state power mercilessly and ostentatiously as the national war-engine of capital against labour. In their uninterrupted crusade against the producing masses they were, however, bound not only to invest the executive with continually increased powers of repression, but at the same time to divest their own parliamentary stronghold—the National Assembly—one by one, of all its own means of defence against the executive. The executive, in the person of Louis Bonaparte, turned them out. The natural offspring of the 'party-of-Order' republic was the Second Empire.[34]

Marx described the Empire as 'the only form of government possible at a time when the bourgeoisie had already lost, and the working class had not yet acquired, the faculty of ruling the nation'.[35] We may leave aside the notion that the French bourgeoisie had, in 1851, lost the faculty of ruling the nation. Also, the formulation lends itself to the view that the state somehow comes 'in between' the contending classes. But the context makes it absolutely clear that Marx meant precisely the opposite.[36]'Imperialism', he wrote, here meaning the type of regime represented by the Second Empire, 'is, at the same time, the most prostitute, and the ultimate form of the state power which nascent middle-class society had commenced to elaborate as a means of its own emancipation from feudalism, and which full-grown bourgeois society had finally transformed into a means for the enslavement of labour by capital'.

There is here no doubt about the class nature and the class function of the Napoleonic regime. On the other hand, the notion of the state as serving to maintain (or to bring about) a certain 'equilibrium' between warring classes occurs in the observations of Marx and Engels on the subject of Absolutism,[37] and was also used by Engels to describe both the Second Empire and the Bismarckian state.

In his *The Origin of the Family, Private Property and the State* (1884), Engels wrote of the state that: 'it is, as a rule, the state of the most powerful, economically dominant class, which, through the medium of the state, becomes also the politically dominant class, and thus acquires new means of holding down and exploiting the oppressed class.'[38]

Having given the state of antiquity, the feudal state and the 'modern representative state' as examples of the class state, he then goes on:

By way of exception, however, periods occur in which the warring classes balance each other so nearly that the state power, as ostensible mediator, acquires, for the moment, a certain degree of independence of both. Such was the absolute monarchy of the seventeenth and eighteenth centuries, which held the balance between the nobility and the class of burghers; such was the Bonapartism of the First, and still more of the Second French Empire, which played off the proletariat against the bourgeoisie and the bourgeoisie against the proletariat. The latest performance of this kind . . . is the new German Empire of the Bismarck nation: here capitalists and workers are balanced against each other and equally cheated for the benefit of the impoverished Prussian cabbage junkers.[39]

The point here is not that the characterization is historically erroneous, but that it departs considerably from the classical theory of the state associated with Marx and Engels. In the formulation above, the state not only acquires a very high degree of independence, albeit 'by way of exception', but this independence appears to free it from its character as a class state: it seems to have become what might be described as a 'state for itself'. In a famous letter written in 1890, Engels strengthens this impression in his reference to 'the interaction of two unequal forces': 'On the one hand, the economic movement, on the other, the new political power, which strives for as much independence as possible, and which, having been once established, is endowed with a movement of its own.'[40]

In the same passage, Engels explicitly retains the primacy of the 'economic movement': but his formulations do not point to the class identity of the relatively independent state. Engels never did in fact suggest that the state was a 'state for itself', or that it could be. But his theorization of the relative autonomy of the state is, in class terms, nevertheless evidently inadequate and indeed fairly misleading. As was already noted earlier, the relative independence of the state does not reduce its class character: on the contrary, its relative independence makes it *possible* for the state to play its class role in an appropriately flexible manner. If it really was the simple 'instrument' of the 'ruling class', it would be fatally inhibited in the performance of its role. Its agents absolutely need a measure of freedom in deciding how best to serve the existing social order.

This 'problematic' has the major advantage of helping to explain a crucial attribute of the state in capitalist society, namely its capacity to act as an agency of reform.

Reform has been a major characteristic of capitalist regimes—not surprisingly since reform has been a *sine qua non* of their perpetuation. What is perhaps less obvious is that it is the state upon which has fallen the prime responsibility for the *organization* of reform. Power-holders inside the state system have been well aware of the responsibility, and have acted upon that awareness, not because they were opposed to capitalism, but because they wanted to maintain it.

But to act as the organizers of reform, power-holders have needed some elbow room, an area of political manoeuvre in which *statecraft* in its literal sense could be exercised. What to concede and when to concede—the two being closely related—are matters of some delicacy, which a ruling class, with its eyes fixed on immediate interests and demands, cannot be expected to handle properly. Power-holders themselves may fail but their chances are better and in this respect at least—the defence of the capitalist economic and social order—their record has been fairly successful, though account must here also be taken of the various weaknesses, errors, and difficulties of their opponents.

Still, the point needs to be stressed that much, if not most, of the reform which power-holders have organized in capitalist societies has generally been strongly and even bitterly opposed by one or other fraction of the 'ruling class', or by most of it. Nor is that opposition to reform altogether 'irrational'. No doubt, the resistance to reform on the part of an economically and socially dominant and privileged class is in the long run all but certain to lead to great trouble, instability, revolt, and possibly overthrow. In this sense, such resistance is 'irrational'; and a systematic and comprehensive resistance on principle to all reform is in any case stupid and eccentric. But from the point of view of the class or classes concerned, resistance to reforms organized by power-holders, in so far as that resistance is selective and flexible, cannot be taken as being necessarily 'irrational'. After all, power-holders may well miscalculate and statecraft can go wrong. It is, for instance, possible to argue that there are occasions and circumstances where reform, far from stilling discontent, will encourage demands for more, and further raise expectations: the phenomenon is familiar. Also, even if the general point holds that reform must in the long run be accepted if a social order is to have any chance to perpetuate itself, the price to be paid in the short run is often real and unpalatable. It is nonsense to say, as is often said on some parts of the Marxist left, that reform does not 'really' affect the 'ruling class'. The latter's members squeal much more than is usually warranted. But the squealing is on the other hand rather more than mere sham: the *sense* of being adversely affected and constrained is real; and this is quite often an accurate reflection of the concrete impact of this or that measure and action of the state.

The fact that the state is the organizer of reform, often against the wishes of large sections of the 'ruling class' is one reason why the bourgeoisie as a whole has not, in 'normal' circumstances, shown any great craving for dictatorship of the Fascist or authoritarian type. Its members want a state which is strong enough to impose 'law and order', to contain challenge, and to ensure stability. But the authoritarian or Fascist form of state has, from the point of view of an economically and socially privileged class, the great disadvantage not only of placing a vast amount of power in executive hands to the detriment of other elements in the state, but also of making it much more difficult for hitherto powerful bourgeois elements to exercise a restraining and controlling influence on the people now in charge of the state power. In such situations, the exercise of state power can become dangerously unpredictable and much too 'individualized'.

Undoubtedly, there are circumstances when the bourgeoisie, or large sections of it, will choose this option, notwithstanding its disadvantages. In *The Eighteenth Brumaire* Marx noted that 'once the bourgeoisie saw "tranquillity" endangered by every sign of life in society, how could it want to retain a *regime of unrest*, its own *parliamentary regime*, at the head of society? . . . The parliamentary regime leaves everything to the decision of majorities, why then should the great majority outside parliament not want to make the decisions';[41] and he went on to say that

by branding as 'socialist' what it had previously celebrated as 'liberal', the bourgeoisie confesses that its own interest requires its deliverance from the peril of its own self-government; that to establish peace and quiet in the country its bourgeois parliament must first of all be laid to rest; that *its political power must be broken in order to preserve its social power intact; that the individual bourgeois can only continue to exploit the other classes and remain in undisturbed enjoyment of property, family, religion and order on condition that his class is condemned to political insignificance along with the other classes . . .*[42]

This is very well said. But it is precisely because authoritarian and Fascist regimes entail at least the danger of 'political insignificance' for people who do have a strong sense of their own significance that they must hesitate to opt for this alternative. In a letter to Marx on 13 April 1866, Engels wrote that 'Bonapartism is after all the real religion of the modern bourgeoisie.'* But this

---

* K. Marx–F. Engels, *Werke* (Berlin, 1965), vol. 31, p. 208. 'I see ever more clearly', Engels goes on, 'that the bourgeoisie is not capable of ruling directly, and that where there is no oligarchy, as there is in England, to take on the task of leading the state and society in the interests of the bourgeoisie for a proper remuneration, a Bonapartist semi-dictatorshp is the normal form; it takes in

was not the case when he wrote these words, nor did it become the case later: the authoritarian option is not 'the religion' of the bourgeoisie: it is its last resort (assuming it is an available resort, which is itself a large and interesting question)[43] when constitutional rule and a limited form of state appear to be inadequate to meet the challenge from below and to ensure the continuance of the existing system of domination.

3

The main points concerning the forms of the capitalist state and its relative autonomy may be illustrated by reference to the functions which it performs. Briefly, four such functions may be distinguished, even though there is much overlap in practice between them: (a) the maintenance of 'law and order' in the territorial area or areas over which the state is formally invested with sovereignty—the repressive function; (b) the fostering of consensus in regard to the existing social order, which also involves the discouragement of 'dissensus'—the ideological-cultural function; (c) the economic function in the broad sense of the term; and (d) the advancement, so far as is possible, of what is held to be the 'national interest' in relation to external affairs—the international function.

All states perform these functions. But they perform them differently, depending on the kind of society which they serve; and the state in capitalist society also performs them in different ways, depending on a variety of factors and circumstances. The present context, it should be stressed, is that of advanced capitalism: the question of the state in different contexts requires separate treatment.

The repressive function is the most immediately visible one, in a literal sense, in so far as it is embodied in the policeman, the soldier, the judge, the jailer, and the executioner. But whether immediately visible or not, the state is a major participant in the class struggles of capitalist society. In one way or another, it is permanently and pervasively present in the encounter between conflicting groups and classes—these never meet, so to speak, on their own. The state is always involved, even where it is not

---

hand the big material interests of the bourgeoisie even against the bourgeoisie, but leaves it with no part in the process of governing. On the other hand, this dictatorship is itself compelled to adopt against its will the material interests of the bourgeoisie' (ibid., p. 208).

invoked, if only because it defines the terms on which the encounter occurs by way of legal norms and sanctions.

In the Marxist perspective, and for the reasons which have been advanced in this chapter, the intervention of the state is always and necessarily partisan: as a class state, it always intervenes for the purpose of maintaining the existing system of domination, even where it intervenes to mitigate the harshness of that system of domination.

But the *ways* in which it intervenes in the affairs of civil society constitute precisely one of the major defining differences between the forms which the capitalist state assumes. Thus the bourgeois democratic state is so designated because its powers of intervention, among other things, are variously circumscribed and its police powers variously constrained. In the same vein, the authoritarian state has as one of its distinguishing traits the fact that its powers of intervention are far less constrained and its police powers much larger, much less regulated than is the case for the bourgeois democratic state; and the point applies with even greater emphasis to the Fascist-type state proper.

The limits within which the bourgeois democratic state wields its powers of intervention are not rigidly fixed. Police powers, for instance, vary greatly from period to period, and in the same period depending on what and who is involved. The scope and severity of the repressive power of capitalist regimes cannot be overestimated, notwithstanding long traditions of constitutionalism and a hallowed rhetoric of civic freedom. In periods of serious social conflict, this repressive aspect of the bourgeois democratic state is very quickly deployed; and there are large sections of people to whom this aspect of the bourgeois democratic state is very familiar at all times, including times of relative social peace. To these people—the poor, the unemployed, the migrant workers, the non-whites, and large parts of the working class in general—the bourgeois democratic state does not appear in anything like the same guise as it appears to the well-established and the well-to-do.

Even so, there are qualitative differences between such regimes and authoritarian ones. One crucial such difference is that the latter always make it their first task to destroy the defence organizations of the working class—trade unions, parties, co-operatives, associations, and so on. Bourgeois democratic regimes on the other hand have to accept such organizations as part of their political existence, and are also significantly defined in terms of that acceptance. Such regimes curtail, and are forever seeking to curtail further, the rights and prerogatives which the defence organizations of the working class, and notably trade unions, have managed to acquire over the years. Such attempts at curtailment and erosion are a 'normal' part of the class conflict in which the bourgeois democratic state itself is engaged. So are its constant attempts to integrate, absorb, buy off and seduce the leadership of the defence organizations of the working class. But all this is a very different thing from the actual destruction of independent working-class organizations, which is the hallmark of authoritarian and Fascist regimes (but also of Communist ones, for different reasons which also require separate treatment).

In a somewhat different perspective, the repressive function performed by the capitalist state involves the assurance of 'law and order'. The reason why 'law and order' usually appear in Marxist writing on the subject in inverted commas is not, obviously, because the notions of law and of order are here spurious, but that they are shot through in their conception and in their application with the class connotations imposed upon them by the fact that they are the law and order of particular class societies, applied by particular class states. The 'bias' may be much less visible and specific than is expressed in the popular saying that 'there is a law for the rich and there is a law for the poor'—though the truth that saying contains should not be overlooked. The point, however, is that a general, pervasive, and powerful set of *class* premises and practices affects every aspect of law and order.

This is of more general application. Engels noted that the state performs a number of 'common' services and functions. This is indeed the case. But it performs these 'common' functions in ways which are deeply and inherently affected and even shaped by the character and 'climate' of the class societies in question. Such matters as law and order, health, education, housing, the environment, and 'welfare' in general are, as all else, not only responsive to but determined, or at least powerfully affected, by the 'rationality' of the system.

This 'problematic' is of exceptional and direct importance in relation to the 'economic' function which the state performs in capitalist society. State intervention in economic life has always been a central, decisive feature in the history of capitalism, so much so that its history cannot begin to be understood without reference to state action, in all capitalist countries and not only those, such as Japan, where the state was most visibly involved in the development of capitalism.

The state and those who were acting on its behalf did not always intervene for the specific purpose of helping capitalism, much less of helping capitalists, for whom power-holders, notably those drawn from a different social class, say the landowning aristocracy, have often had much contempt and dislike. The question is not one of purpose or attitude but of 'structural constraints'; or rather that purposes and attitudes, which can make some difference, and in special circumstances a considerable difference, must nevertheless take careful account of the socio-economic system which forms the context of the political system and of state action. Moreover, purposes and attitudes, values and aims, judgements and perspectives, are themselves generally shaped or at least greatly affected by that socio-economic context, so that what appears 'reasonable' by way of state action (or non-action) to power-holders will normally be in tune with the 'rationality' and requirements of the socio-economic system itself: external and antithetical criteria, in so far as they offend that 'rationality', are by definition 'unreasonable'.

These considerations acquire added significance by virtue of the fact that state intervention has become an ever more pronounced feature of the economic life of capitalism in the last hundred years—and even this formulation runs the risk of greatly understating the extreme acceleration of the process in recent decades, as does the notion of 'intervention' which understates the pervasive and permanent presence of the state, in a multitude of forms, in the economic life of advanced capitalism.

The constantly increasing importance which the state must assume under capitalism is well recognized in classical Marxist writing, and was linked to the accurate prognosis of the ways in which capitalist production would develop. In *Capital*, Marx had shown that centralization and monopoly were part of 'the immanent laws of capitalistic production itself';[44] and some ten years after the publication of *Capital*, Engels had forecast in

Anti-Dühring (1878) that, as a culmination of this process of centralization and monopoly, 'the official representative of capitalist society—the state—will ultimately have to undertake the direction of production.'[45] However far this might be carried, he also intimated, it would not transform the nature of the state:

> The modern state, no matter what its form, is essentially a capitalist machine, the state of the capitalists, the ideal personification of the total national capital. The more it proceeds to the taking over of the productive forces, the more does it actually become the national capitalist, the more citizens does it exploit. The workers remain wage-workers—proletarians. The capitalist relation is not done away with. It is rather brought to a head. [46]

Engels seems to have had in mind a situation not dissimilar to that created by the growth of joint-stock companies, where 'all the social functions of the capitalist are now performed by salaried employees', and where 'the capitalist has no further social function than that of pocketing dividends, tearing off coupons, and gambling on the Stock Exchange, where the different capitalists despoil one another of their capital'.[47] On the other hand, the continued existence of 'capitalists' would only be compatible with state ownership of the means of production if these 'capitalists' were assured of dividends to pocket and coupons to tear off. Engels did not pursue the question, save to say that state ownership could provide no solution to the contradictions of capitalist production, and that 'the harmonizing of the modes of production, appropriation, and exchange with the socialized character of the means of production' could only be brought about 'by society openly and directly taking possession of the production forces which have outgrown all control except that of society as a whole'.[48]

This formulation obviously raises problems. But it is at any rate clear that for Marx and Engels as well as for a later Marxist tradition, the notion of state intervention in the capitalist process of production is an intrinsic part of the analysis of that process of production itself. Indeed, so concerned were Marxist thinkers after Engels to underline the role of the state in twentieth-century capitalism that they came to speak not only of 'monopoly capitalism' but of 'state capitalism' and of 'state monopoly capitalism', the latter form being the 'official' designation of present-day capitalism by all Communist parties.

'State capitalism' was used by Lenin to denote two different situations: firstly, that already described by Engels, in which the state plays an ever greater role in the productive process of advanced capitalism. Germany, he wrote in *'Left-Wing' Childishness and the Petty-Bourgeois Mentality* of 1918, was '"the last word" in modern large-scale capitalist engineering and planned organisation, *subordinated to Junker-bourgeois imperialism'*.[49] The second situation was an altogether different one, in which 'state capitalism' is used by Lenin in a much more imprecise and blurred sense, namely the post-revolutionary situation in Russia, when he wanted the Soviet government to foster the growth of capitalist enterprise under the strict supervision of the Soviet government and in accordance with 'national accounting and control'.[50] State capitalism in this case is characterized by the detailed control which a revolutionary workers' state exercises over capitalist production.

Both these usages seem to me arbitrary and misleading. In the first, 'German', usage, the notion that state intervention in capitalist production amounts to the state 'taking over' capitalism, which is the connotation that 'state capitalism' tends to convey, is clearly mistaken. In this sense, the closest that capitalism has ever been to 'state capitalism' was in Nazi Germany, which answers well Lenin's (and Bukharin's) description of the process of state intervention, regulation, control, and even dictation: but even here, capitalism under the Nazis did not turn into 'state capitalism': it remained what it had always been, namely a system of production mainly carried on by way of private ownership and control of the predominant part of the means of production, distribution, and exchange, with a much greater apparatus of state direction than hitherto imposed upon that system, though it is also worth remembering that much of that apparatus of direction was itself manned and controlled by people who were part of the traditional German capitalist class.

Nor is there much to be said for the second meaning given to 'state capitalism' in Lenin's usage. Even if the assumption is made that a *predominantly* capitalist economy can co-exist with and be directed by a revolutionary regime—and it is a very large and to my mind an unwarranted assumption—there would still be no ground for describing such an economic system as 'state capitalism': at most, it could be described as 'state-directed capitalism', or some such. In fact, it would be a capitalist economic system which a revolutionary government would seek to develop, direct, and plan, and into which it might seek to inject some 'socialist' modes of behaviour.

'State capitalism' has also been used in some Marxist quarters, and by the Chinese Communists, to designate collectivist regimes of the Soviet type, and notably the Soviet Union, mainly as a term of abuse intended to suggest the gap between achievement and promise. But however great the gap may be, and however justified the view that these regimes are not 'socialist', there is no theoretical or practical justification for designating as 'state capitalist' regimes in which private ownership and control of the whole or of the largest and most important part of the means of economic activity has been abolished—save as a term of abuse, in which case there is no problem.

As for 'state monopoly capitalism', the designation is misleading inasmuch as it tends to suggest something like a symbiotic relation between the contemporary capitalist state and monopoly capitalism. This is inaccurate and opens the way to an over-simplified and reductionist view of the capitalist state as the 'instrument' of the monopolies. In reality, there is the capitalist state on the one hand and 'monopoly capitalism' on the other. The relation between them is close and getting ever closer, but there is nothing to be gained, and much by way of insight to be lost, by a reductionist over-simplification of that relation. 'State monopoly capitalism' does not leave enough space, so to speak, in the relation between the two sides to make the concept a useful one: in so reducing this space, it renders the relation too unproblematic, at any level.

Nevertheless, the state does of course 'intervene' massively in the life of advanced capitalism, and sustains it in a multitude of different ways which cannot all by any means be labelled 'economic'.[51] It mainly does so in accordance with the 'rationality' of the capitalist mode of production, and within the constraints imposed upon it by that mode of production. But this is not a simple process either, least of all in a bourgeois democratic and constitutional setting. For in such a setting, the political system allows pressures to be generated and expressed against and in the state, and may turn the state itself into an arena of conflict, with different parts of the state system at odds with each other, and thereby reducing greatly the coherence which the state requires to fulfil its functions, 'economic' or otherwise. From this point of view, the authoritarian alternative is also intended to restore coherence to a state system which has come to reflect rather than subdue the class conflicts and the socio-economic contradictions of civil society. In the conditions of late twentieth-century capitalism, the state in bourgeois democratic regimes is under constant pressure to meet the expectations and demands of the subordinate classes. What is wanted from it is that it should provide and manage—as it alone can—a vast range of collective and public services whose level largely defines the conditions of life for the overwhelming majority of the populations of advanced capitalist countries, who depend upon these services. But against the expectations and demands emanating 'from below' must be set the requirements of capitalist enterprise; and whatever the state does by way of provision and management of services and economic intervention has to run the gauntlet of the economic imperatives dictated by the requirements of the system—and what emerges as a result is always very battered. Hence the contradictory pulls within the state itself, and the need, somehow, to restore its coherence and its capacity to fulfil what is expected of it.

The authoritarian alternative I have referred to is in its extreme forms the *ultimate* resort of dominant classes, or rather it *may* be such a resort: the assumption has generally been much too easily made in Marxist writing that dominant classes could simply 'choose' whether to adopt the authoritarian alternative or not. The matter is a lot more complicated than this. But in any case, the bourgeois democratic state is perfectly capable of deploying a vast apparatus of repression, and of resorting to considerable police powers within the constitutional framework in existence. What is involved is the further restriction of civic rights and of the opportunities of organized protest and challenge, and the attempts by the bourgeois state to achieve these restrictions, particularly in times of crisis, is a 'normal', unsurprising part of the civic history of capitalism.

On the other hand, success in this field partly depends on the degree of consent and legitimacy which the state and the social order enjoy, particularly among the subordinate classes themselves; and this links up with a third function of the state that was mentioned earlier, namely its ideological-cultural or persuasive function.

I have already noted that this persuasive function is not primarily carried out by the state in bourgeois democratic regimes, where much or most of it is left to a variety of agencies and institutions which are part of civil society and which largely express the class power of the dominant classes. But it was also noted there that the state is also deeply involved, in such regimes and directly or indirectly, with the business of legitimating the existing social order and with the discouragement of dissidence. This intervention assumes many different forms, which I do not propose to discuss further here, though it may be worth repeating the point that was made in Chapter III that the bourgeois state is ever more closely involved in this form of intervention in the life of civil society; and that the availability of immeasurably more efficient means of communication provides a further spur to such efforts.

Even so, the difference in this realm as in many others between the bourgeois democratic state and the various forms which authoritarianism has assumed in capitalist societies is very great. One of these differences is of course that in the latter case dissident ideas and dangerous thoughts, not only in the realm of politics but in many other realms as well, are forcibly suppressed. Some of this also occurs in bourgeois democratic regimes: but to nowhere near the same extent, nor in a systematic way. A second difference is that the authoritarian state in capitalist regimes itself assumes the main responsibility for the spread of officially approved ideas. It may do so either directly, say by the use of radio, television, and government-sponsored newspapers and other publications; or more indirectly, through Fascist-type parties and other organizations; or both. But it is in any case thoroughly involved in the propagation, effectively or not, of ideas which are deemed acceptable and 'functional'; and in the suppression of ideas which are not. The same is also true for Communist states, which have thoroughly monopolized forms of communication, through the Party and the various institutions it controls.

The fourth of the functions of the state to which I referred earlier, its international function, raises many different questions with which Marxism has in one way and another always been greatly concerned. This is discussed in the next section.

4

From the beginning, Marxism has treated the state as part of a world of states whose relations and actions are deeply influenced and even determined by the fact of capitalist development. In the international as in the national sphere, the socio-economic context is crucial, particularly because of the supra-national character of the capitalist mode of production.

In a famous passage of the *Communist Manifesto*, Marx and Engels noted the centralizing tendencies of capitalism, as a result of which 'independent, or but loosely connected provinces, with separate interests, laws, governments, and systems of taxation, became lumped together into one nation, with one government, one code of laws, one national interest, one frontier and one customs tariff'.[52] But just as it created the conditions for the centralized, concentrated nation-state, so did capitalism also set in motion powerful supra-national tendencies:

The bourgeoisie has through its exploitation of the world market given a cosmopolitan character to production and consumption in every country . . . it has drawn from under the feet of industry the national ground on which it stood . . . in place of the old local and national seclusion and self-sufficiency, we have intercourse in every direction, universal interdependence of nations . . . The bourgeoisie, by the rapid improvement of all instruments of production, by the immensely facilited means of communication, draws all, even the most barbarian, nations into civilization.[53]

The reference to 'even the most barbarian nations' has a distinctly 'Victorian' ring, but no matter: Marx and Engels were, here as so often elsewhere, accurately projecting the lines of future capitalist development. On the other hand, the processes to which they were pointing have produced intense contradictions, which have multiplied rather than diminished with the passage of time, and have presented major and unresolved problems for Marxist theory and Communist practice.

The most basic of the contradictions in the world-wide development of capitalism is that its expansion did indeed generate 'intercourse in every direction, universal interdependence of nations', and thus created 'one world' in an immeasurably more meaningful sense than had ever been the case before; but it also and simultaneously strengthened, and in many cases *engendered*, the will to sovereign statehood. On the one hand, there was the economic knitting together of one world; on the other, a heightened drive to political fragmentation by way of the sovereign state in a world of states, each seeking to maximize its power of independent action.

A paramount explanation of this contradiction is that statehood is the absolutely essential condition, though not of course a sufficient one, for the achievement of the aims which those who are able to determine or influence state action may have. It may not be possible, for whatever reason, to achieve these aims *with* statehood: but it is likely to be even more difficult to achieve them without it.

More specifically, capitalist development and expansion has meant in effect the development of particular national capitalisms, with their respective national states seeking to advance capitalist interests. Obviously, this does not mean that the people in charge of state power necessarily acted with the conscious purpose of serving these interests. What they were doing, in their own view, was to serve the 'national interest', fulfilling their country's 'manifest destiny', spreading civilization and Christianity, serving Queen or Emperor, or whatever. But none of these aims, they also thought, was incompatible with the advancement of national business interests. On the contrary, the advancement of these interests, and their defence against other national interests protected by their own states, was generally felt by power-holders to be congruent and even synonymous with whatever other purposes they had in mind.

The world which Marx and Engels knew in their later years was dominated by large states involved in various forms of rivalry with each other. Some of them, like France, Britain, Russia, and Austria, had had statehood for a long time, and only needed to concern themselves with the preservation of their national and imperial domains, or with further additions to it by way of imperialist expansion. Others, like Germany and Italy, had achieved statehood much more recently and were concerned both with consolidation and with the carving of a share in imperial expansion. One major state, the United States, had had to fight a civil war to retain unitary statehood; and another, the Ottoman Empire, barely held together disparate nationalities.

These were all 'established' states. But the logic which made them cling jealously to what they had, also impelled various national groupings inside one or other of these empires to seek their own statehood. In the nineteenth century, this mainly involved various subject nationalities everywhere. The motivation behind this drive is usually described as 'nationalism'. It is a convenient term but not an altogether adequate one. For it suggests a specific *ideological* commitment *common* to an enormously varied scatter of groups and classes (including varied groups and classes forming part of the same subject nationality), which had in fact very *different* economic, social, political, cultural aims. 'Nationalism' does not properly cover these different aims, and is too easily turned into a catch-all formula, much too diffuse and imprecise. The term cannot be dispensed with, of course, for it describes some very real drives. But these drives and many others are given much greater precision if they are seen to point, as they all do, to *statehood*: however diverse the groups and their aims, and whether based on 'nationality' or not, what they do have in common is the will to acquire their 'own' state, to be 'masters in their own house', to achieve independent statehood—often on the basis of a combination of nationalities, ethnic, linguistic, and cultural groupings, depending on particular historical and local circumstances.

So powerful has this drive to statehood been that it has resulted in the proliferation of states to the point where almost 150 of them (a majority of recent creation) are now recognized as 'sovereign' political units, each with the right to a seat in the United Nations. Nor is the power of that drive to statehood at all spent: on the contrary, it is constantly manifesting itself in new places, and has come to pose fairly serious problems to old-established states like Britain and France, where demands are heard much more loudly than for a very long time past not merely for greater autonomy but for actual independence of one or other constituent element of the existing 'national' state. There is nothing mysterious about this drive to statehood: it simply marks the recognition that 'sovereignty', however limited it may be, makes possible the fulfilment of aims which may otherwise be unattainable. Whether the aims are good or bad, reasonable or not, is not here in question.

The *appeal* which statehood has and the support it generates are not confined to any particular class or social group. 'Nationalism' in the nineteenth century and the drive to statehood had exceptional appeal to various elements of the 'national bourgeoisie' of various subject 'nations'. But it was not confined to such bourgeois elements. Nor certainly has it so been confined in the twentieth century. 'Nationalism', more or less strongly seasoned with various other ideological ingredients is available to, and where suitable seized by, any class or group aspiring to independent statehood.

With certain qualifications, classical Marxism was on the whole favourably inclined towards the achievement of independent statehood by subject peoples, though the whole question has become ever more difficult for Marxists to handle in the course of the twentieth century.

The main qualification, in regard to Marx and Engels, is that they quite rightly saw much if not most of the 'nationalism' expressed in their own times as oriented to bourgeois aims—indeed as intended, at least in part, to provide an alternative to revolutionary socialism. In this sense, the adoption by the proletariat of a 'nationalism' free from socialist and revolutionary perspectives, and designed to create supra-class allegiances, was naturally seen by them as constituting an instance of 'false consciousness'.

Marx and Engels said in the *Communist Manifesto* that 'national differences, and antagonisms between peoples, are daily more and more vanishing, owing to the development of the bourgeoisie, to freedom of commerce, to the world market, to unformity in the mode of production and in the conditions of life corresponding thereto'.[54] But however much they might hope and strive for the development of proletarian internationalism and solidarity, they continued to think of the nation-state as the basic unit of political life; and to support the right of nations, such as the Irish, the Poles, and the Italians, to national independence and statehood.

However, Marx and Engels also tended to favour larger rather than smaller national units; and it is significant, in this context, that Marx, in *The Civil War in France*, should have defended the Paris Commune against the accusation that it sought to destroy the unity of France. 'The Communal constitution', he wrote, 'has been mistaken for an attempt to break up into a federation of small states, as dreamed of by Montesquieu and the Girondins, that unity of great nations which, if originally brought about by political force, has now become a powerful coefficient of social production'.[55]

This attitude of qualified but quite strong support for the right of 'peoples' to self-determination and statehood is bound to present problems in practice, and has often done so: there are always *conflicting* considerations which intrude into the question.

Lenin reaffirmed again and again the right of subject peoples to self-determination and independent statehood: 'In the same way', he wrote, 'as mankind can arrive at the abolition of classes only through a transition period of the dictatorship of the oppressed class, it can arrive at the inevitable integration of nations only through a transition period of the complete emancipation of all oppressed nations, i.e. their freedom to secede.'[56] But this did not prevent him from freely admitting that the matter could not be treated in absolute terms. Thus, he noted in the same text that Marx was occasionally taxed with having objected to the 'national movement of certain peoples' (i.e. the Czechs in 1848), and that this was taken to refute 'the necessity of recognizing the self-determination of nations from the Marxist standpoint'. But this, Lenin claimed, was incorrect, 'for in 1848 there were historical and political grounds for drawing a distinction between "reactionary" and revolutionary-democratic nations. Marx was right to condemn the former and defend the latter. The right of self-determination is one of the demands of democracy which must naturally be subordinated to its general interests.'[57]

Irrespective of the merits of the particular argument, this too is a substantial qualification. But it remains true that Lenin and the Bolsheviks were strongly committed to the right of subject peoples to self-determination. The one major Marxist figure to reject this position was Rosa Luxemburg, who consistently denounced the 'right of self-determination' as hollow phraseology and as a diversionary, corrupting, and self-defeating slogan.

It is important not to draw false contrapositions here. The point is not that Lenin and the Bolsheviks 'believed' in national independence and statehood for subject peoples, while Rosa Luxemburg did not: to view the controversy in this light is to misunderstand its basis. The point is that Lenin and the Bolsheviks believed that Marxists could not deny the right of subject peoples to independence, and that Marxists who belonged to an oppressor nation, as they did, could do so least of all. This is not the same as 'believing' that independence was always to be encouraged. As for Rosa Luxemburg, she did not of course believe that subject peoples should be denied the right to independence; but that this could only be achieved on the basis of an international socialist struggle that must not be 'diverted' by the acceptance of such slogans as the 'right to self-determination'.

It is a little ironic in the light of experience that Rosa Luxemburg should have denounced so scathingly the Bolsheviks' 'doctrinaire obstinacy' on this issue, and their adherence to what she called 'this nationalistic slogan'.[58] In the course of 1917, she warned that acceptance of the right of secession, far from encouraging the revolutionary forces in the subject nations of the Russian Empire, 'supplied the bourgeoisie in all border states with the finest, the most desirable pretext, the very banner of the counterrevolutionary efforts . . . By this nationalistic demand they brought on the disintegration of Russia itself, pressed into the enemy's hand the knife which it was to thrust into the heart of the Russian Revolution.'[59]

In fact, the Bolsheviks themselves became aware of the force of the argument almost as soon as they came to power, and very quickly retreated from their commitment. As early as January 1918, Stalin was telling the Third All-Russia Congress of Soviets that the right of self-determination should be taken to mean 'the right to self-determination not of the bourgeoisie but of the labouring masses of the given nation. The principle of self-determination should be a means in the struggle for socialism and should be subordinated to the principles of socialism.'[60] With varying degrees of reluctance, or of enthusiasm, this was the view which the Bolsheviks came to adopt, which meant in effect that the right to secession, while formally retained, was for all practical purposes abandoned for the peoples who formed part of Soviet Russia.

On the other hand, the 'right to self-determination' for subject peoples remained a central part of Marxist and Communist thinking in relation to the national question; and it has always figured very large in the anti-colonial and anti-imperialist struggles of this century. However, the qualifications remain and no clear line has ever been established in either Marxist theory or practice to decide where the right to independent statehood is or is not 'justified'. Communist attitudes and policies were long shaped by the internal and external requirements of the Soviet Union; and the contradictory policies adopted by the U.S.S.R. and China over various independence movements—for instance Biafra and Bangla Desh—indicate well enough how much practical considerations impinge upon the determination of attitudes to self-determination.

In recent years, as already noted, the question has rapidly crept up on the agenda of 'old' states as well as forming a key problem for 'newer' ones. On the whole, Marxist attitudes to demands for statehood on the part of ethnic, linguistic, and 'national' forces such as the Scots, the Basques, the Catalans, the Corsicans, the Bretons, the Welsh, etc., have been negative to the point of opposition and hostility. Demands for regional autonomy or for a federal system present few problems to Marxists, who are in favour of it. 'National' claims, on the other hand, do present major problems, of the kind to which Rosa Luxemburg pointed. But as against this, the Leninist stress remains—there may come a point, even in 'old' states, where demands for statehood on the part of a constituent element of an existing state—e.g. Scotland *vis-à-vis* the United Kingdom—cannot be resisted on principled socialist grounds, or cannot be resisted without resort to suppression, which comes to the same thing. From this point of view, 'nationalism' has proved a much more enduring and therefore a much more difficult problem to confront than early Marxists thought likely; and its emergence as a major problem in 'old' states is a token of the strength of the drive to statehood which was noted earlier. In any case, that drive does not detract but rather reinforces the state as the key unit of political life. States may change and fragment: but *the* state, with its claims to territorial 'sovereignty' and 'independence' remains.

This fact is not, as might at first sight appear, seriously affected by economic developments in the life of capitalism which are subsumed under the rubric of the multi-national corporation. No doubt, the growth of capitalist enterprise, and the coming into being of the multi-national giants, as was noted earlier, is a major fact in the life of the state, in so far as those who hold power in it have to take the existence of these giants into careful account, to put it very modestly, when they decide upon policy. But there is nothing essentially novel about this; nor is there about the fact that *foreign* enterprises, located in any particular national state, can have an important role in the determination of its policies.

This in effect is what the multi-national corporation amounts to in regard to the capitalist state. 'Multi-national' is in any case misleading for most of the enterprises concerned: the largest number of them are United States corporations, with branches in many countries. It is this which makes them 'multi-national', *not* multi-nationality of ownership or control. Behind the corporations stand their governments: and it is the power which they are able to wield and the influence which they are able to exercise which constitute the additional and sometimes the decisive factor of constraint upon the policies and actions of the 'sovereign' nation-state.

But this does not affect the nature of that state. Whatever else in the development of capitalism may require a revision of the Marxist theory of the state, the multi-national corporation does not. On the contrary, the latter merely reinforces the argument that the capitalist state is subject to formidable capitalist constraints—in this instance with an additional international dimension.

At the same time, the point needs to be made that the multi-national corporation creates a situation in which the nation-state is seen by some elements at least of the indigenous capitalist class as a necessary instrument of defence against what amounts in effect to foreign interests; while other such elements may seek alliance with these interests rather than defence against them. But in any case, and whether this is so or not, the nature of the state is not thereby brought into question.

5

What has so far been said about the Marxist view of the state mainly refers to its nature and role in advanced capitalist societies. The question which this raises is how far if at all Marxist concepts on this subject are appropriate for the analysis of the state in different types of society, namely 'Third World' and Communist ones. Clearly, it is not possible simply to transpose the categories of analysis used for the state in advanced capitalist societies to these different economic, social, and political structures: but what else to do and in what manner to proceed either for 'Third World' societies or for Communist ones is a large problem which, as I noted in the Introduction, has so far not been adequately tackled in Marxist political theory, particularly in relation to Communist societies, where serious Marxist work on the state and politics was for many decades virtually impossible, and where it even now remains peculiarly difficult. The present section purports to do no more than offer certain suggestions about the directions which the required theorization might take.

The first and most obvious feature of the state in both 'Third

World' and Communist societies is a very pronounced inflation of state and executive power, particularly marked in Communist regimes, and with which is usually associated a very high degree of autonomy, at least from the civil society over which the state holds sway. What has been an occasional phenomenon in advanced capitalist societies by way of the extreme inflation of executive power is a common one in these other types of society, though the reasons for this are not the same, or not necessarily the same, in 'Third World' and Communist countries.

In the case of 'Third World' societies, this inflation occurs because social groups which would have an interest in limiting and controlling the power of the state do not have the power or the will to do so; while dominant classes and groups, where they do exist, find it to their advantage to have a strong and repressive state to act on their behalf.

'Third World', as I noted when I first used the term in the Introduction, covers a multitude of specific circumstances and milieux, but in the present context, the countries which are subsumed under this label may be divided into two major categories: those where economically dominant classes, well-entrenched and developed, do exist; and those where they do not. The first category would include the Latin-American continent (with nowadays the obvious exception of Cuba) and the countries of South Asia. The second category would include most countries of Africa, with the major exception of South Africa, which is an advanced capitalist country. In both categories, foreign capitalist interests constitute an important and in some cases a decisive political element as well as a crucially important economic one.

In the case of countries of the 'Third World' where an economically dominant class exists, or where there is more than one such class, the Marxist analysis of the state presented earlier only requires various adaptations and changes of emphasis rather than fundamental revision. No doubt, there are many aspects of their economic and social structure, their history and political culture, which greatly affect the character and operation of the state in each of them. Differences in economic and social structure produce considerable differences in the nature of class antagonisms and their expression, and in the manner in which the state responds to them. So does the fact of 'under-development' and 'dependence', and often of recent colonialism, affect the state's weight and role in economic, social and political life. But all these are specificities which, however important and determinant, are susceptible to an analysis that remains identifiably 'Marxist'; in other words to an analysis that is squarely and adequately derived from a Marxist problematic.

The same cannot be said with quite the same confidence about countries that belong to the second category, namely those where an economically dominant class or group, or a number of such classes or groups, did not exist before the establishment of a 'new' state in place of a colonial regime. Of course, it is perfectly possible to point in all such countries to a scatter of local entrepreneurs and traders, alongside the large foreign interests that may exist and which form pockets of large-scale enterprise in an otherwise 'under-developed' context. But the scatter of local entrepreneurs and traders cannot seriously be said to constitute an 'economically dominant class'. Nor can the foreign interests that are present be so designated. This is not to say that these interests are not important politically; or that local business interests, however small the scale of their enterprises, do not represent a point of reference for the state. The point is rather that the element which is absolutely basic in the classical Marxist view of the state, namely an economically dominant class, is not to be found here, in any meaning that makes real economic, social, and political sense. This being so, the question at issue is what the state power in these societies actually 'represents', and what its nature and role may be said to be.

The answer is that, in such societies, the state must be taken mainly to 'represent' itself, in the sense that those people who occupy the leading positions in the state system will use their power, *inter alia*, to advance their own economic interests, and the economic interests of their families, friends, and followers, or clients. A process of enrichment occurs, which assumes a great number of forms and leads to a proliferation of diverse economic ventures and activities. In this process, a genuine local bourgeoisie may come into being and grow strong, with continuing close connections to the state and its leading members, who are themselves part of that new bourgeoisie.

In such cases the relation between economic and political power has been inverted: it is not economic power which results in the wielding of political power and influence and which shapes political decision making. It is rather political power (which also means here administrative and military power) which creates the possibilities of enrichment and which provides the basis for the formation of an economically powerful class, which may in due course become an economically dominant one. The state is here the source of economic power as well as an instrument of it: state power is a major 'means of production'.

It is an instrument of economic power, not in the sense that those who hold state power serve the interests of an economically dominant class separate from these power-holders and located in society at large; but that those who hold state power *use* it for their own economic purposes and the economic purposes of whoever they choose. This use of state power assumes many different forms, including of course the suppression of any challenge to the supremacy of what turns in effect into an *economically and politically dominant class*.

No more than its counterparts anywhere else is this dominant class homogeneous and united. On the contrary, it tends to be very divided and fragmented, with power highly personalized and therefore subject to frequent and violent changes. These societies are poorly articulated in economic and social terms, and therefore in political terms as well. They are in fact depoliticized, with the state itself, often under military rule, assuming a monopoly of political activity through parties and other groupings which are seldom more than bureaucratic shells with very little living substance.

In such circumstances, the state assumes a very high degree of autonomy indeed, and does, almost, become a 'state for itself', or at least for those who command it. There are some qualifications to this, but few. One of these, which may be very considerable, is the existence of foreign interests, which need to be accommodated by the power-holders. On the other hand, the process of accommodation of these foreign interests is not, in many cases, quite as one-sided as it used to be. There are now many 'Third World' countries and states which have a greater freedom of manoeuvre *vis-à-vis* such interests than used to be the case: there are now fewer 'banana republics' than there were. But if so, it means that the degree of autonomy of the state is commensurately increased, and the area of freedom which is available to power-holders similarly enlarged. What they have to fear is not the restraint of their power, but its sudden and usually violent termination by way of a coup engineered by rival groups of people, themselves representing little except their own ambitions and interests.

The question of the state in Communist countries presents very different problems from those which arise in the 'Third World'. There are many different reasons for this, but the most important one is the fact that the economic context is fundamentally different and affects every aspect of the state's role.

In the 'Third World', what the state does is decisively affected by the fact that capitalist enterprise either exists already in one form or other and on a substantial scale, or that it exists on a small scale but can be developed further. This growth of capitalist enterprise is indeed what 'development' largely means in these countries. The 'rationality' of state action in the 'Third World' is determined by this possibility of economic development by way of state encouragement of capitalist enterprise. This state action may not be particularly effective and development may be sluggish or deformed, but that is not here relevant. For all practical purposes, and in terms of what it does, the state has, so to speak, nowhere else to go, no other 'rationality' to follow. The one qualification is that the state may come to be completely dominated by one man and his family and followers, who proceed to stifle and suppress all activity except for such activity as may be of benefit to them. Haiti under Duvalier is a case in point, but such instances are rare and of no great consequence, save for the unfortunate people who live in these countries.

The decisive fact about Communist countries is that they are *collectivist regimes* in which capitalist enterprise is for all practical purposes non-existent. What there is of it is kept to minimal levels and is positively prevented from growing. It is possible, in these countries, to accumulate a fair amount of money by saving on large salaries, and also to own some property, for instance a house and even a 'second residence'. But it is not possible to make private wealth grow by way of capitalist enterprise.

Just as the possibility of such enterprise decisively shapes state action in the 'Third World', so does its absence shape equally decisively the character and role of the state in collectivist societies. For it means that those who control state power in these societies are subject to 'structural constraints' of a most formidable kind, in so far as they cannot direct that power to private capitalist purposes. They may seek and achieve private enrichment, though the scale on which this occurs is fairly limited. And they may well act to the advantage of some classes or groups rather than to that of others—some categories of workers rather than others, or workers as against peasants, or managers as against either, and so on. But this is a very far cry indeed from the possibilities offered by the existence of a capitalist context, and imposes an altogether different 'rationality' upon those who control collectivist societies, and who are in this sense controlled by the collectivism over which they preside.

It was precisely the fear that the U.S.S.R. under Stalin was moving towards the restoration of capitalism, with the dynamic implications which this would have had, which led the Trotskyist Opposition to warn, from the twenties onwards, of the dangers of a Russian 'Thermidor': and had a capitalist sector been restored in the Soviet Union, by way of a return of a major part of the public sector to private enterprise, the chances are indeed that a 'Thermidor', in one form or other, would have occurred, and fundamentally reshaped the 'rationality' of the Soviet state.

But in fact, no such restoration occurred. On the contrary, every part of private economic activity was ruthlessly stamped out, most notably by forced collectivization of the countryside. The experience of other Communist countries has in many respects been different from that of the U.S.S.R. But as I have already noted, they are all predominantly and solidly collectivist in their mode of economic organization; and this leaves open the question of the nature and role of the state in this kind of system.

Left critics of Soviet-type regimes have pointed to the very considerable inequalities of power and reward which are to be found in them, and which are sanctioned, maintained, defended, and fostered by an exceedingly powerful state; and they have consequently argued that this state was the instrument of a 'new class', 'bureaucratic stratum', 'state bourgeoisie', whose principal purpose, like that of any other 'ruling class', was to maintain and enlarge its power and privileges.

There has over the years been much controversy among Marxist critics of these regimes over whether their rulers did constitute a class or not. The point is obviously of some importance, in so far as the answer to it may provide an initial clue to the degree of cohesion, solidarity, community of purpose, and social basis of these rulers.

However, and as should have been expected, no conclusive answer to the question has ever been returned, or can be. There are Marxists who have said that, because 'the bureaucracy' could not own capitalist property and therefore pass it on to their descendants, they did not form a class; and there are other Marxists who have argued that capitalist property was not the only criterion to be used, and that the privileges which accrued to the people concerned, and from which their descendants could derive advantages of a substantial kind, did mean that 'the bureaucracy' constituted a class.

The word matters less than the substance which it designates; and it is scarcely a matter of serious doubt that those who occupy leading positions in Soviet-type systems do enjoy advantages which are denied to the mass of the population. These advantages may be greater in some of these systems than in others; and greater efforts are made in some cases than in others to reduce such advantages and to de-institutionalize them, at least to some degree. But they clearly continue to form part of Communist life, though they are not of course peculiar to it, and are in fact significantly lower, in material terms, than in other systems. 'Bureaucrats' in collectivist systems are better off than those over whom they rule, and the higher the position a 'bureaucrat' occupies, the better off he is likely to be: but with the probable exception of those at the very top, the pickings would seem to be comparatively modest. Office is an avenue to material well-being; but not to great wealth.

This is by no means accidental. It is primarily the result of the absence of opportunities for capitalist enterprise. No doubt there are other factors which account for this aspect of political life in Communist countries, but here is the primary constraint.

This, however, is no refutation of the thesis that the state in these countries is the instrument of a 'power élite', who may be unable to derive vast material advantages from their position in the state system, yet who are able to use that position to appropriate and enjoy far from negligible such advantages; and who are also able to enjoy *power*. On this view, the notion of the state as having as its function the advancement of the power and privileges of those who control it, and the repression of those who challenge it, remains fairly well intact. The 'state bourgeoisie' or whatever it is called is not here viewed as a greatly plutocratic class or stratum: but it is nevertheless a privileged class or stratum, and privileged above all in its enjoyment of power.

There is a great deal more in this view than the propagandists of these regimes and other apologists would ever concede. Indeed, the view of Communist regimes as dominated by a 'power élite' located at the top and upper echelons of a pyramid of power seems entirely apposite and sensible. But it is nevertheless entirely inadequate to explain the nature, function, and dynamic of the state in these societies. The reason for this is that it places far too great an emphasis on the purposes and motivations of those who hold power; and it concomitantly grossly underestimates the massive fact constituted by the collectivist context in which they operate and wield their power.

In all Communist countries, the greatest possible emphasis has been placed throughout on economic growth and development, notably of the industrial sector, which was in some cases minimal when the Communists took over. But it was also taken for granted from the beginning that this economic development must occur under the auspices of the state, one of whose absolutely prime functions it was to plan and organize this enterprise and to take all necessary measures for the purpose, including in many cases the ruthless coercion of unwilling populations. No doubt, 'the state' must here be taken to include the Party, whose role in the process has been crucial. But in so far as the Party and state leaders have more or less been the same people, with the Party organization acting as the arm of the Party-state, this presents no particular problem of analysis in the present context.

The point is not that this vast process, amounting to one of the greatest upheavals in human history, and certainly the greatest *organized and engineered* upheaval of its kind, is incompatible with the 'power and privileges' thesis. There is nothing intrinsically absurd in the idea that many of those who have held power in these regimes were mainly or even wholly moved by the wish to use the state for the aggrandizement of their own power and privileges, whatever the rationalizations they used and believed: the purposes by which all people in power anywhere are moved must be reckoned to be endlessly varied and to span the whole gamut of human motivations, from the noblest to the basest. The point is rather that, whatever the particular motives of the people in power, these motives could only be fulfilled by serving larger purposes *as well*.

But this is where collectivist constraints play a determinant role in shaping the functions of the state. For in the absence of an economically dominant capitalist class, and of opportunities for capitalist enrichment by those holding state power, there only remained certain options open—in effect state-fostered economic growth in the broad sense, and including the state-fostered provision of social services and cultural developments; national defence, also of course under the responsibility of the state; and the maintenance of 'law and order', including the massive enlargement of police powers for the purpose of repressing various forms of dissidence.

The same question that was asked earlier in regard to 'Third World' countries arises here: whom and what does this state 'represent' in the discharge of these functions?

The best answer would seem to be that it 'represents' no single class or group and is the instrument of no such class or group: the collectivist character of the society precludes it from being such an instrument, for the reasons stated earlier. Instead, the state may be taken to 'represent' the collectivist society or system itself, and to have as its function the service of its needs as these are perceived and defined by those who control the state.

This answer differs fundamentally from that returned by the theorists of the 'power and privileges' thesis, according to whom the state in Communist societies must be taken to 'represent' the interests of 'the bureaucracy', the 'state bourgeoisie', the 'new class', etc.

It also differs—but not nearly as much—from the designation which was given to the Soviet state in the Khrushchev era, and which has remained the orthodox way of describing it, namely as a 'state of the whole people'. This is unacceptable because it begs too many questions: it has an intensely ideological and apologetic ring, and it assumes, among other things, a quality of 'representation' of the state, in the sense of actually 'representing' the will and wishes of the people. But this is an assumption which the nature of the political system makes it impossible to be seriously tested.

'The state' effectively means here the leaders of the Communist Party. For it is the leadership of the Party, and location at its topmost levels, which confers the power to rule and to use the power of the state for the purpose of ruling. Unlike most countries of the 'Third World' (Mexico being probably the most notable exception), Communist regimes are all distinguished by highly structured and organized mass parties, whose role in the articulation of power in these regimes is absolutely crucial. They are for the most part authentically mass parties, with a membership running, in the case of the U.S.S.R. and China, into many millions. But these mass parties are also distinguished by their pyramidal structure, with an extreme concentration of power at the top of the pyramid.

Some party leaderships may be more autocratic than others, and more personalized. But all these parties are instruments of concentrated power; and the 'democratic centralism' which they all profess has always been a figurative term for an extreme concentration of power and the narrow subordination of the lower organs to the top one. Moreover, Communist parties in these regimes have always, in practice, held a monopoly of political power, whether they were, as in the U.S.S.R., the only legal party, or whether, as in some other Communist countries, other parties were allowed to exist. The latter's existence never seriously impinged upon the 'leading role' of the Communist Party, meaning in effect its complete predominance.

On this basis, those who control the Party also control the state, which is their executive and coercive arm. Nor is the Party-state constrained by social forces—let alone political ones—which are external to it. Of course, party and state leaders must take some account of existing social classes and groupings in determining the policies which they wish to pursue: if they do not, or if they miscalculate, there may be trouble. But their ability to make autonomous decisions, without reference to anyone outside their own restricted circle, is very great indeed and has often been all but unlimited, the extreme example being that of Stalin over a period of a quarter of a century.

This autonomy is constrained, as has already been noted, by the structural context in which Communist societies operate, and this is in many ways very severe. But *this* constraint does not reduce the power-holders' autonomy *vis-à-vis* the societies over which they preside, which is the question at issue.

Similarly, Party-state leaders are constrained, save in very unusual cases of total predominance such as Stalin came to enjoy, by internal rivalries and divisions, and the existence at the top of the pyramid of factions and tendencies which may 'represent' particular interests, e.g. the army and defence apparatus, the managers, or managers of some sectors against those of others, and so on; and there may also be divisions based on ideology, differences of generations and experiences, and all the other factors which cause men of power to divide. These are very genuine constraints upon leaders, even upon leaders who have established their ascendency, but who must yet tread warily, and conciliate or disarm opposition, or crush it with the aid of allies, which itself may require concessions to these allies.

But nothing of this fundamentally affects the fact that *the state in these systems does have a very high degree of autonomy from society*: nowhere is that autonomy substantially constrained by institutions and agencies, either inside the state system or outside, which are in any real sense independent of executive power. 'Freedom', Marx said in the *Critique of the Gotha Programme* of 1875, 'consists in converting the state from an organ superimposed on society into one thoroughly subordinate to it; and even today state forms are more or less free depending on the degree to which they restrict the "freedom of the state".'[61] There is a vast programme of political construction which these formulations propose; and it is a programme to which Communist regimes have not so far seriously addressed themselves.

NOTES

1 *Revs.*, p. 69.
2 *SE*, p. 282.
3 Loc. cit.
4 G. Dimitrov, *The United Front* (London, 1938), pp. 12, 110. Quoted in M. Johnstone, 'Trotsky and the Popular Front' in *Marxism Today*, October 1975, p. 311.
5 See L. Trotsky, *The Struggle Against Fascism in Germany* (New York, 1971).
6 *SE*, p. 89.
7 Ibid., p. 61.
8 *FI*, p. 226. My italics.
9 *SE*, p. 237.
10 Ibid., p. 236.
11 Ibid., p. 71.
12 Ibid., p. 127.
13 Ibid., p. 127.
14 Ibid., p. 134.
15 *FI*, p. 251. The quotation is from a first draft of *The Civil War in France*.
16 Ibid., p. 324. The Congress was held in The Hague and the speech was delivered in Amsterdam.

17 *SW* 1950, I, p.109, fn. 1.
18 Ibid., p. 124; p. 665 in *SW* 1968.
19 Ibid., p. 124; p. 665 in *SW* 1968.
20 Ibid., p. 125; p. 665 in *SW* 1968.
21 See Rosa Luxemburg's comment, below, p. 161.
22 *Two Tactics of Social-Democracy in the Democratic Revolution*, in *SWL*, p. 76.
23 Ibid., p. 79.
24 'Inflammable Material in World Politics', in *CWL* (1963), vol. 15, p. 186.
25 'The Working Class and the National Question', ibid., vol. 19, p. 91.
26 *The State and Revolution*, in *SWL*, p. 264.
27 Ibid., p. 290.
28 Ibid., p. 264.
29 *SE*, p. 238.
30 Ibid., p. 238.
31 Ibid., p. 245.
32 Ibid., p. 246.
33 Ibid., p. 246.
34 *FI*, p. 207.
35 Ibid., p. 208.
36 Ibid., p. 208.
37 See P. Anderson, *Lineages of the Absolutist State* (London, 1974).
38 *SW* 1968, p. 587.
39 Ibid., p. 588.
40 F. Engels to C. Schmidt, 27 October 1890, ibid., p. 696.
41 *SE*, p. 190.
42 Ibid., p. 190. My italics. See also pp. 224–5.
43 See below, pp. 175–6.
44 K. Marx, *Capital*, I, p. 763.
45 F. Engels, *Anti-Dühring*, p. 380.
46 Ibid., p. 382.
47 Ibid., p. 381.
48 Ibid., p. 382.
49 *SWL*, p. 443. This text, which was published in *Pravda* in May 1918, is not to be confused with *'Left-Wing' Communism—An Infantile Disorder*, which was published in 1920.
50 Ibid., p. 445.
51 For instance the cultural realm.
52 *Revs.*, p. 72.
53 Ibid., p. 71.
54 Ibid., p. 85.
55 *FI*, p. 211.
56 V. I. Lenin, *The Socialist Revolution and the Right of Nations to Self-Determination*, in *SWL*, p. 163.
57 Ibid., p. 163, fn. 1.
58 R. Luxemburg, *The Russian Revolution*, in *Rosa Luxemburg Speaks* (New York, 1970), p. 380.
59 Ibid., p. 382.
60 M. Liebman, *Leninism under Lenin* (London, 1975), p. 273.
61 *FI*, p. 354.

V. Class and Party

1

Ruling classes have at their disposal a formidable range of weapons for the maintenance of their domination and the defence of their power and privileges. How then are these ruling classes to be undone, and how is a new social order to be established?

That this *can* be achieved is an essential theme of the Marxist message: but a no less essential theme of that message is that it does have to be *achieved*. No doubt, the desired transformation must largely depend upon, or at least be linked with, the deepening of the contradictions of capitalism and their consequent and manifold impact upon the superstructure. But even so, the transformation will have to be brought about by human intervention and practice, and will be the result of growing class conflict and confrontation, in which the working class must play a predominant role.

In order that it may play that role effectively, there must be organization: against the vast array of powerful forces which the ruling class is able to deploy in the waging of class struggle, the working class and its allies cannot hope to succeed unless they are organized.

The question is what this means; and there have on this score been very wide divergences within the spectrum of Marxist political thought. These divergences must not be translated into a simplistic and misleading contraposition of 'organization' and 'spontaneity'. There is no Marxist thinker, of any sort, who has ever advocated pure spontaneity as a way of revolutionary practice. The notion is evidently absurd: even a *levée en masse* requires to be organized if it is to get anywhere.

Nor, at the other extreme, has anyone within the Marxist tradition ever advocated that a revolution should be made by an organized group or party without any measure of popular support. This *has* at one time or other been put forward as a means of revolutionary action and change; but it does not form part of any variety of Marxism, and has in fact been consistently rejected and denounced by Marxists as mere 'putschism'.

The question then is not, in Marxist terms, of a 'choice' between organization and spontaneity, or between the party and the class. There is in reality no such choice; and Marxists have quite rightly insisted that this was for them a false dichotomy. But the divergences have nevertheless been very real, and have centred round different views of the relation of the working class to the organization, and of the relative weight to be attributed to either. The differences may be matters of emphasis; but emphasis in this realm is not a matter of detail.

These divergences point to a permanent tension in Marxist thought and practice in regard to the relation of class and party, not surprisingly since the issues which that relation raises are crucial, not only to the advancement of the revolutionary process but to the shape and character of the Marxist project itself. The attempt has often been made to blur and negate this tension by reference, here as in other questions, to the 'dialectical' interrelation which must be established between class and party. This is no doubt desirable, but to say so is not to resolve anything; it merely restates the problem in different words.

Given the wide spectrum of views and attitudes on the question of class and party, it is as well to note first that Marx himself stands at one end of the spectrum, in so far as his own emphasis falls very heavily on the action of the class. His concern throughout his political life was not simply with the emancipation of the working class: this could be said to be the avowed purpose of all revolutionaries. His concern is with the emancipation of the working class *by its own efforts*. He expressed this most succintly in the Preamble to the Provisional Rules of the First International in 1864. 'That the emancipation of the working classes must be conquered by the working classes themselves'.[1]

Neither this nor anything else Marx said on the subject precludes organization in the form of a party of the working class; and there are in his work innumerable references to the need for the working class to organize itself. On the other hand, he was not particularly concerned with the form which the political organization of the proletariat should assume, and was content to leave workers in different countries to determine this according to their own circumstances.[2] The one definite prescription was that the party should not be a sect, isolated from the working class, and composed of the 'professional conspirators' whom he savagely denounced as the 'alchemists of revolution' in 1850.*

---

* 'It goes without saying', Marx wrote ironically, 'that it is not enough for them to engage in the organisation of the revolutionary proletariat. Their business

Whatever the form of the party, it is the working class, its developing consciousness and its struggles for self-emancipation which really matter to Marx: the party is only the political expression and the instrument of the class. Even this formulation may go further than is warranted in Marx's case and it may be more accurate to interpret him, in this connection, as seeing the working class itself performing its political role, with the political party helping it to do so. The formulation is rather ambiguous—but so are Marx's pronouncements on this issue.

What is not at all ambiguous is the faith which Marx and Engels had in the capacity of the working class to achieve self-emancipation. In a Circular Letter to the leadership of the German Social-Democratic Workers' Party, written in 1879, they angrily rejected any flirtation with the idea that 'the working class is incapable of liberating itself by its own efforts' and that 'for this purpose it must first accept the leadership of "educated and propertied" bourgeois, who also have "opportunity and time" to acquaint themselves with what is good for the workers.'[3] They reminded the leaders of the party that 'when the International was formed, we expressly formulated the battle-cry: the emancipation of the working class must be the work of the working class itself', and that 'we cannot ally ourselves, therefore, with people who openly declare that the workers are too uneducated to free themselves and must first be liberated from above by philanthropic big bourgeois and petty bourgeois.'[4] The point they were making is clearly of wider application; what they were concerned to stress was their general belief in the self-emancipating capacities of the working class. The question here is not whether they were right or wrong, and what are the problems they were overlooking. The fact is that for them, the class always came first, the party a long way behind. This cuts very deep, and has a direct bearing on the wider question of the direct and indirect exercise of popular power, and on the meaning of socialist democracy.[5]

By the time Engels died in 1895, German Social Democracy was well on the way to becoming an authentic mass organiza-

consists precisely in the anticipation of revolutionary development, in artificially bringing it to a crisis, in making a revolution by improvisation without the conditions of a revolution. For them, the only condition for a revolution is the proper organisation of their conspiracy. They are the alchemists of revolution and are quite like the earlier alchemists in their narrowness of mind and fixed prejudices' (*Werke*, (Berlin, 1960), op. cit. VII, p. 273).

tion, and it continued thereafter to make great progress. As one writer has noted, the German Social Democratic Party had by 1914 'become a vast institution that was staffed by more than 4,000 paid functionaries and 11,000 salaried employees, had 20,000,000 marks invested in business and published over 4,000 periodicals'.[6] It also had a very substantial parliamentary representation and was a force in provincial and local government. To a greater or lesser extent, much the same was coming to be true of other European Social Democratic parties; and it was more or less taken for granted that the parties of the working class would be, and indeed must be, mass parties, deeply involved in the political life of their respective countries, though loosely linked in the Second International. With this growth of working-class parties, and the expectation of their further implantation and progress, there also went a very general, though not of course unanimous, acceptance that the transformation of capitalist society must be envisaged as a strictly constitutional process, which must on no account be endangered by an ill-conceived activism and adventurist policies. How widespread this acceptance was, inside German Social Democracy but also elsewhere, was somewhat masked by the opposition which Bernstein aroused by his explicit 'revisionism'. But in more accentuated forms or less, with variations that were less important than rhetoric was intended to suggest, 'revisionism' was the perspective which dominated all but a small part of European Social Democracy: the great 'betrayal' of 1914—and of the years of war—was a natural manifestation of it.

In the present context, what is important about this perspective is that it inevitably led to the exaltation of the party as the accredited and ever more influential representative in national life of the working class, as the expression of its political presence at all levels, but also as its guardian against those who pressed upon the working class actions and policies which the leadership of the party judged and proclaimed to be irresponsible and dangerous. The exaltation of the party also meant the enhancement of the status and position of the party leaders, the men who were in charge of that complex and delicate machinery whereby the locomotive of socialism was to be driven, at safe speed, through capitalist society.

This is not to endorse Robert Michels's 'iron law of oligarchy', which was formulated in his *Political Parties* (1915) with the German Social Democratic Party as a main point of reference. But we must note here that there was, in the notion and practice of the working-class mass party, integrated in the constitutional framework of bourgeois society, a powerful logic driving towards the concentration of power in the hands of leaders claiming to be the representatives and spokesmen of the working class, and occupying a privileged position in the determination of policy. It was not Lenin who started it all.

Lenin had in fact an extraordinarily strong sense of the need *both* to build a party of a special kind, given the conditions of Czarist Russia, *and* to maintain as close a link as possible with the working class. Without the constant reinvigoration of the party by the working class, it would go stale and bureaucratic, and 'lag behind' the masses—one of Lenin's constant fears. He had conceived from his earliest days in the revolutionary movement of a party of 'professional revolutionaries', adapted to the struggle against a despotic regime by a highly centralized command structure, which came to be called 'democratic centralism'. He did not suggest, before 1914, that the party he wanted for Russia was suitable for what he called 'countries where political liberty exists'.[7] The important point for him—indeed the essence of Lenin's contribution to Marxism—was that there must be *organization* and *direction* if the revolutionary process was to be advanced.

Lenin did not fear the passivity of the working class, but that its struggles would lack political effectiveness and revolutionary purpose. It was to *this* end that the party was essential: without its guidance and leadership the working class would be a social force capable of spasmodic and incoherent actions, but incapable of turning itself into the disciplined army that was required to overthrow Czarism and to advance towards the conquest of socialist power.

Even so, it needs to be stressed that Lenin knew well that the party could not fulfil its tasks without being steeped and involved in the experiences of the masses; and whenever opportunity offered for the party to 'open up'—as in 1905 and 1917 and after—he seized the chance and mercilessly castigated the 'party bureaucrats' steeped in their routine.[8] Even in those of his writings which most insistently focus on the need for organization, centralism, discipline, etc., and of which *What is to be Done?* is

Whatever the form of the party, it is the working class, its developing consciousness and its struggles for self-emancipation which really matter to Marx: the party is only the political expression and the instrument of the class. Even this formulation may go further than is warranted in Marx's case and it may be more accurate to interpret him, in this connection, as seeing the working class itself performing its political role, with the political party helping it to do so. The formulation is rather ambiguous—but so are Marx's pronouncements on this issue.

What is not at all ambiguous is the faith which Marx and Engels had in the capacity of the working class to achieve self-emancipation. In a Circular Letter to the leadership of the German Social-Democratic Workers' Party, written in 1879, they angrily rejected any flirtation with the idea that 'the working class is incapable of liberating itself by its own efforts' and that 'for this purpose it must first accept the leadership of "educated and propertied" bourgeois, who also have "opportunity and time" to acquaint themselves with what is good for the workers.'[3] They reminded the leaders of the party that 'when the International was formed, we expressly formulated the battle-cry: the emancipation of the working class must be the work of the working class itself', and that 'we cannot ally ourselves, therefore, with people who openly declare that the workers are too uneducated to free themselves and must first be liberated from above by philanthropic big bourgeois and petty bourgeois.'[4] The point they were making is clearly of wider application; what they were concerned to stress was their general belief in the self-emancipating capacities of the working class. The question here is not whether they were right or wrong, and what are the problems they were overlooking. The fact is that for them, the class always came first, the party a long way behind. This cuts very deep, and has a direct bearing on the wider question of the direct and indirect exercise of popular power, and on the meaning of socialist democracy.[5]

By the time Engels died in 1895, German Social Democracy was well on the way to becoming an authentic mass organiza-

consists precisely in the anticipation of revolutionary development, in artificially bringing it to a crisis, in making a revolution by improvisation without the conditions of a revolution. For them, the only condition for a revolution is the proper organisation of their conspiracy. They are the alchemists of revolution and are quite like the earlier alchemists in their narrowness of mind and fixed prejudices' (*Werke*, (Berlin, 1960), op. cit. VII, p. 273).

tion, and it continued thereafter to make great progr writer has noted, the German Social Democratic Pa 1914 'become a vast institution that was staffed by 4,000 paid functionaries and 11,000 salaried empl 20,000,000 marks invested in business and publishec periodicals'.[6] It also had a very substantial parliam resentation and was a force in provincial and local g To a greater or lesser extent, much the same was c true of other European Social Democratic parties; more or less taken for granted that the parties of 1 class would be, and indeed must be, mass par involved in the political life of their respectiv though loosely linked in the Second Internationa growth of working-class parties, and the expecta further implantation and progress, there also general, though not of course unanimous, accepta transformation of capitalist society must be en strictly constitutional process, which must on n endangered by an ill-conceived activism and policies. How widespread this acceptance was, ir Social Democracy but also elsewhere, was somewl the opposition which Bernstein aroused by 'revisionism'. But in more accentuated forms or le tions that were less important than rhetoric wa suggest, 'revisionism' was the perspective which but a small part of European Social Democracy: rayal' of 1914—and of the years of war—was a nat tion of it.

In the present context, what is important abou tive is that it inevitably led to the exaltation of t accredited and ever more influential representat life of the working class, as the expression of it: ence at all levels, but also as its guardian aga pressed upon the working class actions and pol leadership of the party judged and proclaimed sible and dangerous. The exaltation of the party enhancement of the status and position of the p men who were in charge of that complex and del whereby the locomotive of socialism was to b speed, through capitalist society.

This is not to endorse Robert Michels's 'iron l

which was formulated in his *Political Parties* (1915) with the German Social Democratic Party as a main point of reference. But we must note here that there was, in the notion and practice of the working-class mass party, integrated in the constitutional framework of bourgeois society, a powerful logic driving towards the concentration of power in the hands of leaders claiming to be the representatives and spokesmen of the working class, and occupying a privileged position in the determination of policy. It was not Lenin who started it all.

Lenin had in fact an extraordinarily strong sense of the need both to build a party of a special kind, given the conditions of Czarist Russia, and to maintain as close a link as possible with the working class. Without the constant reinvigoration of the party by the working class, it would go stale and bureaucratic, and 'lag behind' the masses—one of Lenin's constant fears. He had conceived from his earliest days in the revolutionary movement of a party of 'professional revolutionaries', adapted to the struggle against a despotic regime by a highly centralized command structure, which came to be called 'democratic centralism'. He did not suggest, before 1914, that the party he wanted for Russia was suitable for what he called 'countries where political liberty exists'.[7] The important point for him—indeed the essence of Lenin's contribution to Marxism—was that there must be *organization* and *direction* if the revolutionary process was to be advanced.

Lenin did not fear the passivity of the working class, but that struggles would lack political effectiveness and revolutionary purpose. It was to *this* end that the party was essential: without its guidance and leadership the working class would be a social force capable of spasmodic and incoherent actions, but incapable of turning itself into the disciplined army that was required to overthrow Czarism and to advance towards the conquest of socialist power.

Even so, it needs to be stressed that Lenin knew well that the party could not fulfil its tasks without being steeped and involved in the experiences of the masses; and whenever opportunity offered for the party to 'open up'—as in 1905 and 1917 and —he seized the chance and mercilessly castigated the 'party bureaucrats' steeped in their routine.[8] Even in those of his writings which most insistently focus on the need for organization, centralism, discipline, etc., and of which *What is to be Done?* is

tween organization and spontaneity, or between the party and the class. There is in reality no such choice; and Marxists have quite rightly insisted that this was for them a false dichotomy. But the divergences have nevertheless been very real, and have centred round different views of the relation of the working class to the organization, and of the relative weight to be attributed to either. The differences may be matters of emphasis; but emphasis in this realm is not a matter of detail.

These divergences point to a permanent tension in Marxist thought and practice in regard to the relation of class and party, not surprisingly since the issues which that relation raises are crucial, not only to the advancement of the revolutionary process but to the shape and character of the Marxist project itself. The attempt has often been made to blur and negate this tension by reference, here as in other questions, to the 'dialectical' inter-relation which must be established between class and party. This is no doubt desirable, but to say so is not to resolve anything; it merely restates the problem in different words.

Given the wide spectrum of views and attitudes on the question of class and party, it is as well to note first that Marx himself stands at one end of the spectrum, in so far as his own emphasis falls very heavily on the action of the class. His concern throughout his political life was not simply with the emancipation of the working class: this could be said to be the avowed purpose of all revolutionaries. His concern is with the emancipation of the working class *by its own efforts*. He expressed this most succinctly in the Preamble to the Provisional Rules of the First International in 1864. 'That the emancipation of the working classes must be conquered by the working classes themselves'.[1]

Neither this nor anything else Marx said on the subject precludes organization in the form of a party of the working class; and there are in his work innumerable references to the need for the working class to organize itself. On the other hand, he was not particularly concerned with the form which the political organization of the proletariat should assume, and was content to leave workers in different countries to determine this according to their own circumstances.[2] The one definite prescription was that the party should not be a sect, isolated from the working class, and composed of the 'professional conspirators' whom he savagely denounced as the 'alchemists of revolution' in 1850.*

* 'It goes without saying', Marx wrote ironically, 'that it is not enough for them to engage in the organisation of the revolutionary proletariat. Their business

an extreme example,* the need for an organic connection with the working class is never ignored. And it was also Lenin who wrote the following in 1920:

History as a whole, and the history of revolutions in particular, is always richer in content, more varied, more multiform, more lively and ingenious than is imagined by even the best parties, the most class-conscious vanguards of the most advanced classes. This can readily be understood, because even the finest of vanguards express the class-consciousness, will, passion and imagination of tens of thousands, whereas at moments of great upsurge and the exertion of all human capacities, revolutions are made by the class-consciousness, will, passion and imagination of tens of millions, spurred on by a most acute struggle of classes.[9]

This, however, did not in the least lead him to decry the crucial importance of the party in the revolutionary process, and to devalue its role in relation to the working class. He could never have said, as Rosa Luxemburg said in 1904, that 'historically, the errors committed by a truly revolutionary movement are infinitely more fruitful than the infallibility of the cleverest Central Committee.'[10] He did not believe in the 'infallibility' of any Central Committee or party organ. But neither did he believe that a 'truly revolutionary movement' was conceivable that did not include a well-structured organization. It was in the same work from which the earlier quotation is taken that Lenin observed, in answer to those in the German Communist movement who counterposed 'dictatorship of the party or dictatorship of the class; dictatorship (party) of the leaders, or dictatorship (party) of the masses', that '. . . as a rule and in most cases—at least in present-day civilized countries—classes are led by political parties . . . political parties, as a general rule, are run by more or less stable groups composed of the most authoritative, influential and experienced members, who are elected to the most responsible positions, and are called leaders'.[11]

In saying this, Lenin was pointing to the obvious but essential (and to many the rather uncomfortable and disagreeable) fact that any 'model' of the revolutionary process, or for that matter

* Lenin noted some years after the publication of his pamphlet that, in the circumstances in which it was written, he had had to 'bend the stick' somewhat, and that some of his formulations had been deliberately polemical. This however was no repudiation of the basic themes of the argument.

of working-class politics in general, would have to include an organized political formation, which also meant that there would be a leadership and a structure of command. Lenin's whole emphasis in this respect was different from that of Marx and Engels. As was noted earlier, they too had a concept of the party: yet the shift of emphasis is unmistakable. But this, to a greater or lesser extent, was true of all strands of Marxist thought: well before 1914, the international Marxist movement, West as well as East, had developed 'models' of the party, both of which attributed much greater importance to the party than Marx and Engels had ever thought necessary, though the point is less certain in relation to Engels in his last years, when he was closely involved in the affairs of the German Social Democratic Party.

It was not of course on the issue of the party itself that Lenin's opponents attacked him, but on the dictatorial centralism which they accused him of advocating, and for seeking, as they suspected and alleged, his own personal dictatorship through the centralized and subordinate party. In 1904, after the great split of 1903 between Bolsheviks and Mensheviks and the subsequent publication of Lenin's ultra-centralist *One Step Forward, Two Steps Back*, Trotsky published *Our Political Tasks*, in which he warned against the dangers of 'substitutism' and issued the prophecy to which much later events were to give an exceptional resonance: 'Lenin's methods lead to this: the party organization at first substitutes itself for the party as a whole; then the Central Committee substitutes itself for the organisation; and finally a single "dictator" substitutes himself for the Central Committee.'[12] Like Lenin's Menshevik opponents, he wanted a 'broadly based party' and insisted that 'the party must seek the guarantee of its stability in its own base, in an active and self-reliant proletariat, and not in its top caucus . . .'[13]

There was a great deal in this, as in the whole debate, which was rhetorical and illusory , in so far as many of the participants tended to exaggerate very considerably what really separated them from Lenin and the 'centralists'. This was certainly true of Trotsky, who was in his years of power to exhibit even more 'centralist' tendencies than Lenin had done or was later to do. Lenin would hardly have demurred from the view that there was need for an 'active' proletariat: he never ceased to make the point himself. But what did 'self-reliant' exactly mean? Surely not, for

Trotsky, that the proletariat could do without the party. As for the need to have a 'broadly based' party, this too would depend on the meaning of the concept: as Lenin showed within a year of the publication of Trotsky's pamphlet, that is to say in the course of the Russian Revolution of 1905, he had no wish whatever to create a party that was small, self-contained and inward-looking. When 1905 appeared to open new possibilities, he seized them eagerly; and so too in 1917.

In her own contribution to the debate after the split of 1903, namely *Organizational Question of Social Democracy*, which was also published in 1904, Rosa Luxemburg attacked Lenin for his 'ultra-centralism' and argued that 'social democratic centralism cannot be based on the mechanical subordination and blind obedience of the party membership to the leading party centre'.[14] Lenin would of course have denied that this is what he wanted. But more important than the accusation was Rosa Luxemburg's own acceptance of a certain kind of centralism—what she called 'social democratic centralism', which she opposed to 'unqualified centralism'. But save for her insistence that the party must on no account stifle the activity of the movement, she was unable to define what her centralism would entail, particularly for a regime like the Russian, and she indeed noted that 'the general ideas we have presented on the question of socialist centralism are not by themselves sufficient for the formulation of a constitutional plan suiting the Russian party';[15] 'In the last instance', she added, 'a statute of this kind can only be determined by the conditions under which the activity of the organization takes place in a given epoch.'* At the time, Lenin would hardly have disagreed with that.

However, there was much more to the debate on party and class than the question of centralism. What was in fact at stake was the very nature of Marxist politics in relation to the class or classes whose emancipation was its whole purpose. The issues involved acquired an entirely new dimension with the Bolshevik seizure of power in 1917; and they have remained central to Marxist politics right to the present day.

---

* Ibid., p. 122. It may also be noted that her celebration of the mass strike, based on the experience of the Russian Revolution of 1905, was intended to incorporate this means of struggle into the political strategy of Marxism, and to dissociate it from anarchism. See R. Luxemburg, *The Mass Strike, The Political Party and the Trade Unions*, ibid., p. 158.

2

The first of these issues concerns the representativeness of working-class parties. The early debate which opposed Luxemburg to Lenin had largely turned on the role of the party in relation to the working class. Lenin did not believe that the latter would, without proper leadership, become a truly revolutionary force; while Luxemburg feared that the party, if it came to control the working class, would stifle its militant and creative impulses.* *Both*, however, assumed—and so did everybody else who took part in the debate—that given the right form of organization and sufficient time, there was a point in the spectrum where class and party could form a genuinely harmonious and organic unity, with the party as the true expression of a class-conscious and revolutionary working class. People might differ greatly over the question of how this could be achieved, and where the point on the spectrum was located: but they did not differ in the belief that there was such a point, and that it was their business to get to it. In other words, 'substitutism' was a danger, and might become a reality. But it was in no way ineluctable.

This failed to take into account the fact that *some* degree of 'substitutism' is bound to form part of any kind of representative organization and of representative politics at all levels. Of course, the degree matters very greatly, and can be very considerably affected, one way or the other, by various means and devices as well as by objective circumstances. But the notion of the party achieving an organic and perfectly harmonious representation of the class is nothing but a more or less edifying myth. Marx mostly avoided the problem by focusing on the class rather than the party, but the problem is there all the same. It is there, it may be noted, for the best of reasons, namely that Marxists have a commitment to thorough political democratization and to what may be called the dis-alienation of politics. Parties and movements which have no such commitment, or for whom it has much less importance, naturally have in this respect an easier time of it.

The problem of 'substitutism' arises in various forms and

* Ibid., p. 121. 'The tendency is for the directing organs of the socialist party to play a conservative role.'

degrees because the working class, as was noted and discussed in Chapter II, is not a homogeneous entity, and that the 'unity of the working class', which the party seeks or claims to embody, must be taken as an exceedingly dubious notion, which may well come to have some definite meaning in very special and unusual circumstances, but which normally obscures the permanent and intractable differences and divisions which exist in this as in any other social aggregate.

On this view, a united party of the working class, speaking with one voice, must be a distorting mirror of the class; and the greater the 'unity', the greater the distortion, which reaches its extreme form in the 'monolithic' party.

Yet, political parties of the working class are not debating societies, to use a consecrated formula; and they do need some degree of unity in what is a permanent and often bitter class struggle. A genuinely 'representative' party, in which all the divisions of the working class find full expression by way of factions and tendencies and endless debate, may thereby find itself unable to cope with the very responsibilities which are the reason for its existence; and this is likely to be exceptionally true in periods of acute conflict and crisis. The demands of representatives on the one hand, and of effectiveness on the other, are not altogether irreconcilable, in that a more representative party may be more effective than one which lives by imposed and spurious 'unity'. But it is an illusion to think that the contradiction is not a genuine one. It is genuine; and although it may be capable of attenuation by democratic compromise and toleration, it is very unlikely to be fully resolved in any foreseeable future.

In any case, it is unrealistic to speak of 'the party' as if it could be taken for granted that there was one natural political organ of the working class, with the unique mission to represent it politically (and for that matter in many other ways as well).

It was perhaps inevitable that the concept of 'the party' should have come to be enshrined or at least accepted very early in the Marxist perspective of working-class politics. It will be recalled that in the *Communist Manifesto*, Marx and Engels claimed as the distinctive mark of 'the Communists' that 'in the national struggles of the proletarians of the different countries, they point out and bring to the front the common interests of the entire proletariat, independently of all nationality'; and that 'they always and everywhere represent the interests of the movement as a whole'. This being the case, they added, the Communists were 'practically, the most advanced and resolute section of the working-class parties of every country'; and they were also those who had the advantage over the great mass of the proletariat 'of clearly understanding the line of march, the conditions, and the ultimate general results of the proletarian movement'.[16] Although these formulations left open the question of the form of organization which the Communists should adopt,* it is obvious that Marx and Engels were here talking of a definite vanguard; and the notion of more than one vanguard is absurd.

From the notion of a vanguard to that of a *vanguard party*, there was only a short step, which Russian revolutionaries in particular, given their specific circumstances, found it easy to take, and which they had very little option but to take. Moreover, the solidification of Marxism into 'scientific socialism' further helped to strengthen the view that there could only be one true party of the working class, namely the one which was the bearer of the 'truth' of the movement. This might not prevent the existence of other parties, but it made much more difficult the acceptance of the notion that there might be more than one Marxist working-class party. Indeed, it made that notion virtually unacceptable.

From a very different political tradition, German Social Democracy, as it developed in the last decades of the nineteenth century, was also driven towards the concept of the *unified* party of the working class, which would bring together not only different sections of the working class into a coherent political formation, but which would also be capable of bringing under its own banner other classes and strata, and thus become the party of all those who wanted a radical reorganization of the social order.

Nor, given the relative looseness in ideology and organization of this mass party, and the fact that it did attract a very large measure of working-class support, was there much encouragement, for those who found the party inadequate or worse, to cut loose and form their own party. It is highly significant in this

---

* 'The Communists do not form a separate party opposed to other working class parties', ibid., p. 79. The formulations which appear in the *Manifesto* are in this context by no means unambiguous—nor of course do they represent the authors' last word on the subject.

connection that the German Social Democratic Party should have held together until well into the First World War, despite the intense alienation felt by a substantial fraction of its left-wing members. Even Rosa Luxemburg took it that 'the party', i.e. the existing German Social Democratic Party, was her only possible political home, notwithstanding her disagreements with it. By the time she and others changed their minds, or had their minds changed for them by the circumstances of war, it was too late: the massive bulwark of the existing social order which the German Social Democratic Party effectively represented was intact, and the leaders of the party were both able and ready to sustain that social order in its hour of greatest need, in the winter of 1918/19.

The encouragement to retain a unified party is further strengthened by the hope of changing its policies; by the fear that splitting off must mean isolation, marginality, and ineffectiveness; and by even greater fear of acting as a divisive agent and thereby (so it is thought) weakening the working-class movement. These are very strong pressures, which clearly work in favour of the leadership and apparatus of the mass party, and strengthen their appeal to unite, close ranks, show loyalty and so forth.

Even so, the working-class movement in capitalist countries has not normally found its political expression in one single party. In some cases, one party has been able to establish a quasi-monopoly as the party of organized labour—the Labour Party in Britain being a case in point. But even in such cases, the labour movement has produced more than one party; and the quasi-monolistic party has had to fight very hard to maintain its position. It is clear that more-than-one-party is in fact the 'natural' expression of the politics of labour. 'The party' as the single legitimate expression of the labour movement is an invention which postdates the Bolshevik Revolution. There is nothing in classical Marxism which stipulates such singularity.

Given the heterogeneity of the working class and of the working-class movement, it would be very remarkable if one party did constitute its natural expression; and the point is reinforced by the extension of the notion of the working class which is required by the evolution of capitalism. It may be assumed that the more-than-one-party form constitutes a more accurate representation of the movement's reality than the one-party alternative. But the point made earlier about the potentially contradictory demands of representativity and effectiveness also applies here: a more-than-one-party situation in all likelihood produces greater representativity; but it may also make for less effectiveness. However, this is to say no more than that differences between people and groups make it more difficult than would otherwise be the case for them to take decisions. That is so. But there is a limit to what can be done about it, except by constraint and imposition.

Whether it makes for lesser political effectiveness or not—and the answer will vary according to different circumstances and factors—the more-than-one-party situation does not resolve the problem of 'substitutism', and it may not even greatly affect it one way or another. This is because two parties or more, purporting to represent the working class and the labour movement, may well take decisions that belong to the politics of leadership rather than the politics of the party as a whole. Indeed, it is likely that the more-than-one-party situation enhances the politics of leadership, in so far as it requires an often complex set of negotiations between allies or potential allies, and such negotiations emphatically form part of the politics of leadership.

So, from another angle, do most forms of revolutionary transformation, and notably revolutionary transformation by way of an insurrectionary seizure of power. A revolutionary movement launched on such a venture may well enjoy the support of a majority, even of an overwhelming majority, which may for instance be yearning to be freed from a hated regime. But this is by definition a matter of surmise; and revolutions, even in the best of circumstances, are not *made* by majorities, least of all revolutions which are made by way of insurrection. There may be no other way. But revolutions are made by minorities, and have usually been the work of relatively small minorities. At the very least, some element of 'substitutism' is here inevitable; and the refusal to engage in it may be fatal. Rosa Luxemburg is a good case in point. Her draft programme adopted by the founding congress of the German Communist Party in December 1918 included the following declaration: 'The Spartacus Union will never take over the power of government otherwise than by a clear manifestation of the unquestionable will of the great majority of the proletarian mass of Germany. It will only take over the power of government by the conscious approval of the mass of the workers of the principles, aims, and tactics of the Spartacus Union.'[17]

This indeed is a rejection of 'substitutism'. We do not know what would have happened in Germany if Luxemburg and her comrades, in a period of extreme political and social crisis, had viewed matters differently, and been less oppressed by the fear of usurping the popular will. But we do know that one month after she drafted the programme, she and Liebknecht were dead, and the old order was safe. Too great a propensity to 'substitutism' may turn into 'Blanquism' and lead to catastrophe. But so, in certain circumstances, may the rejection of 'substitutism' lead to defeat and catastrophe. In any case, Rosa Luxemburg's conditions, as set out in the above quotation, are most probably incapable of ever being met to the letter. In other words, revolutions are not only bound to include a certain element of 'substitutism' but actually to require it. This too weighs upon the Marxist project, and must at least to some extent affect the exercise of post-revolutionary power, and may affect it very greatly.

The discussion of class and party has so far proceeded as if the working class could only express itself politically by way of a party or parties. But this of course is not the case: although parties are its most important means of expression, there are other forms of working-class organization which have a direct bearing on political issues and struggles. One of these forms is trade unionism; another is 'conciliar' forms of organization—workers' councils, soviets, councils of action, and the like. These forms of organization also affect the whole question of the relation of class and party.

As far as trade unions are concerned, Marx and Engels saw them as performing a dual role, which they wanted to see linked. They believed that trade unions were the natural and indispensable product of the permanent struggle of labour against capital over all aspects of the work situation; and they also wanted them to be instruments in the political battle that had to be waged for the victory of labour over capital.

In his Instructions for Delegates to the Geneva Congress of the First International in September 1866, Marx expressed this duality by stating that 'if the trade unions are required for the guerilla fights between capital and labour, they are still more important as *organized agencies for superseding the very system of wage labour and capital rule'.*[18] This formulation did no more than recognize a fact which was very familiar to Marx, given his knowledge of English trade unions, namely that unions might well seek to improve the conditions of labour within capitalism without being and without seeking to become 'organized agencies for superseding the very system of wage labour and capital rule'.

'Too exclusively bent upon the local and immediate struggles with capital', Marx also wrote in the same Instructions, 'the trade unions have not yet fully understood their power of acting against the system of wage slavery itself'; and he urged that 'apart from their original purposes, they must now learn to act deliberately as organizing centres of the working class in the broad interest of its *complete emancipation*. They must aid every social and political movement tending in that direction.'[19]

What is particularly notable about these and many other such formulations is not only that they show the crucial importance which Marx attached to the trade unions as *political* organizations; but also that he consistently failed to relegate the unions to the somewhat secondary and limited role, as compared to the party, which was assigned to them in later Marxist thinking. However this may be judged, it follows from the fact that neither Marx nor Engels had a particularly exalted view of 'the party' as the privileged expression of the political purposes and demands of the working class; and they did not therefore find it difficult to ascribe to trade unions a politically expressive role only a little less significant than that of 'the party'. This is not to suggest any kind of 'syndicalist' streak in Marx, but only to note yet again that his emphasis on the working class itself and on the role which it must play in its own emancipation led him—whether rightly or wrongly—to be much less concerned than were later Marxists with the assignment of a towering role to the party as compared with that of the trade unions.*

* In a speech to a delegation of German trade unionists in 1869, Marx said that 'if they wish to accomplish their task, trade unions ought never to be attached to a political association or place themselves under its tutelage; to do so would be to deal them a mortal blow. Trade unions are the schools of socialism. It is in trade unions that workers educate themselves and become socialists because under their very eyes and every day the struggle with capital is taking place. Any political party, whatever its nature and without exception, can only hold the enthusiasm of the masses for a short time, momentarily; unions, on the

The relative devaluation of trade unions as political agencies—and it is no more than a *relative* devaluation—is quite marked in Lenin. I have already noted in a previous chapter Lenin's famous remark in *What is to be Done?* that 'the working class, exclusively by its own effort, is able to develop only trade-union consciousness'.[20] The designation is intended to suggest, as Lenin makes perfectly clear, a predominant concern of trade unions with immediate and limited economic demands associated with 'wages, hours and conditions'. This for Lenin did *not* mean that such concerns and demands would not have a political charge. On the contrary, he believed, as did Marx and Engels,* that all struggles for economic improvements and reforms had and could not but have a certain political dimension; but also that the political aspects of such struggles would remain confined to its specific economic purposes. 'Trade-union consciousness' does not mean the absence of politics: it means the absence of *revolutionary* politics. For the latter to be present and for the transcendence of 'trade-union consciousness', what was required was an agency other than trade unions, namely the revolutionary party. Trade unions in the Leninist perspective are of very great importance; but nothing like as important, in terms of revolutionary politics, as the party.

One of the party's tasks is, in fact, to combat 'trade-union conciousness' in the trade unions themselves, and to treat them as arenas in which revolutionaries must struggle against trade-union leaders and a 'labour aristocracy' determined to prevent the transcendence of 'trade-union consciousness'. One of the sections of Lenin's *'Left-Wing' Communism—An Infantile Disorder* was entitled 'Should Revolutionaries Work in Reactionary Trade Unions?', and his answer was an unqualifies yes. 'We are waging a struggle against the "labour aristocracy"', he wrote, 'in the name of the masses of the workers and in order to win them over to our side . . . To refuse to work in the reactionary trade unions means leaving the insufficiently developed or backward masses of workers under the influence of the reac-

---

other hand, lay hold on the masses in a more enduring way; they alone are capable of representing a true working-class party and opposing a bulwark to the power of capital.' (D. McLellan, *The Thought of Karl Marx* (London, 1971) p. 175).

* 'Every class struggle is a political struggle' (*Manifesto of the Communist Party*, in *Revs.*, p. 76).

tionary leaders, the agents of the bourgeoisie, the labour aristo-
crats, or "workers who have become completely bourgeois".'*

In the same text, written, it will be recalled, in 1920, Lenin also
noted that 'the trade unions were a tremendous step forward for
the working class in the early days of capitalist development';
but that 'when the *revolutionary party of the proletariat, the
highest* form of proletarian class organisation, began to take
shape ... the trade unions inevitably began to reveal *certain*
reactionary features, a certain craft narrow-mindedness, a certain tendency to be non-political, a certain inertness, etc.' But he
also went on to say that 'however, the development of the proletariat did not, and could not, proceed anywhere in the world
otherwise than through the trade unions, through reciprocal
action between them and the party of the working class'.[21] These
formulations express clearly enough the basic Leninist view of
trade unions as an indispensable element of class struggle, but
also as an inevitably inadequate one, whose inadequacy must be
remedied by the party. What this meant for the exercise of
Bolshevik power is also spelt out very clearly by Lenin in
'*Left-Wing*' *Communism* (and elsewhere), and will be considered presently. But it may be noted here that, while Lenin
speaks of 'reciprocal action' between trade unions and the party,
he also very firmly asserts the primacy of the party, 'the highest
form of proletarian class organisation'. In so far as the party is
involved in some degree of 'substitutism', the trade unions can
only help, at best, to reduce its extent, provided 'reciprocal
action' can be given effective meaning.

The question of soviets, workers' councils, and 'conciliar'
forms of organization in general, poses an even more direct
challenge to Marxist political theory and practice in relation to
class and party than does the question of trade unions. The
challenge lies in the fact that councils are in one form or another
a recurring and spontaneous manifestation of popular power in
history; and that such forms of power come up, at least in
twentieth-century revolutionary history, against the form of
power represented by the workers' party or parties.

There is no 'guidance' at all to be had here from Marx, since
the key text from him on the issue of popular power, namely

* *SWL*, p. 541. Lenin's quotation, he noted, was taken from a letter of Engels to
Marx about British workers in 1858.

The Civil War in France is entirely free of any reference to political parties of the working class. This text, written in the last weeks of the Paris Commune, is a glowing celebration of the form of popular power which he presented the Commune as having inaugurated or at least foreshadowed—'the political form at last discovered under which to work out the economical emancipation of labour'.[22]

Instead of deciding once in three or six years which member of the ruling class was to misrepresent the people in parliament, universal suffrage was to serve the people, constituted in communes, as individual suffrage serves every other employer in the search for the workmen and managers in his business. And it is well known that companies, like individuals, in matters of real business know how to put the right man in the right place, and, if they for once make a mistake, to redress it promptly.[23]

There is much else about this 'political form' which will need to be considered later, but the important point in the present context is that 'the people' is not, to all appearances, organized by anybody, nor is its relation with its representatives mediated, directed, or guided by a political party.

Nor, incidentally, did the passage of time cause Marx to place greater emphasis than he had done in *The Civil War in France* on the question of the lack of adequate organization and leadership from which the Commune obviously suffered. In a letter of 1881 he noted that the Commune 'was merely the rising of a city under exceptional conditions', and that its majority 'was in no wise socialist, nor could it be'.[24] Obviously (and rightly), he held that conditions were not right for the Commune's success: 'With a modicum of common sense', he wrote in the same letter, 'it could have reached a compromise with Versailles useful to the whole mass of the people—the only thing that could be reached at the time.'[25] But nowhere does he suggest that a different and more favourable outcome could have been achieved had the Communards been better organized, or even that any such venture imperatively requires organization, parties, leadership, etc. He did say in a letter written in April 1871, at the time when *The Civil War in France* was being composed, that the Central Committee of the National Guard 'surrendered its power too soon, to make way for the Commune';[26] and he would undoubtedly have welcomed a better organization of the Commune's endeavours. But it also appears that the absence of organization is not what mainly preoccupied him, or even that it greatly concerned him at all. This shows the dramatic shift of emphasis which occurred on this question in subsequent years.*

The idea of workers' concils and of 'communal' or 'conciliar' power formed no significant part of Marxist thought after the Paris Commune,† until it suddenly forced itself upon the attention of Marxists in the form of the soviets in the Russian Revolution of 1905. In the light of later Bolshevik proclamations of their crucial importance, it may seem surprising that their emergence should have owed nothing to Marxist initiative, but it is nevertheless so.

In fact, there was much Bolshevik suspicion and even hostility to the Petersburg Soviet when it was set up in October 1905.‡ In essence, this attitude was a reflection of a dilemma which was at the heart of Bolshevik perspectives—on the one hand, the stress on the absolutely central role of the party in the revolutionary movement and of its *guidance* of the movement; on the other, the emergence of popular movements and institutions which owed nothing to the party and which could not be expected to be brought easily—or at all—under its guidance and control.

In 1905, Lenin responded differently from most Bolsheviks to the eruption of the Soviets on the political scene. In a letter to the Editor of the Party paper *Novaya Zhizn* (who did not publish it), Lenin, writing from Stockholm on his way back to Russia,

---

* It is instructive, in this context, to compare Marx with Trotsky, who expressed here a commonly accepted view: 'The Commune', he wrote, 'shows us the heroism of the working masses, their capacity to unite in a single bloc, their willingness to sacrifice themselves in the name of the future, but it also shows us at the same time the incapacity of the masses to choose their way, their indecision in the direction of the movement, their fatal inclination to stop after the first success, thus enabling the enemy to get hold of himself, to restore his position'. 'The Parisian proletariat', he went on, 'had no party, no leaders, to whom it would have been closely linked by previous struggles'; and again, 'it is only with the help of the party, which anticipates theoretically the paths of development and all its stages and extracts from this the formula of necessary action, that the proletariat frees itself from the necessity of ever beginning its history anew: its hesitations, its lack of decision, its errors' (Preface to C. Talès, *La Commune de 1871* (Paris, 1921), pp. viii–ix).

† This is not to forget Engels's Introduction of 1891 to *The Civil War in France* but neither this nor the pamphlet itself affected the movement *away* from notions of 'conciliar' power.

‡ See e.g. M. Liebman, *Leninism under Lenin*, pp. 86 ff. The Petersburg Soviet represented 250,000 workers.

denied that the question facing the Party was 'the Soviet of Workers' Deputies or the Party?'. On the contrary, he said, 'the decision must *certainly* be: *both* the Soviet of Workers' Deputies *and* the Party'; and he added that 'the only question—and a highly important one—is how to divide, and how to combine, the tasks of the Soviet and those of the Russian Social-Democratic Labour Party'.[27]

This was indeed the question. But the reflux of the revolutionary movement removed it from the Marxist agenda until 1917, when new Soviets again confronted the Bolsheviks with the same question, but this time with much greater insistence and urgency. It was then, in the months immediately preceding the October Revolution, that Lenin took up the question of the Soviets in his *The State and Revolution*. But it is precisely one of the most remarkable features of that extraordinary document that it not only fails to answer the question of the relation between the Soviets and the Party, but that it barely addresses itself to it.

The State and Revolution is an apotheosis of popular revolutionary power exercised through the Soviets of Workers' and Soldiers' Deputies. But these deputies would be subject to recall at any time, and they would operate within very strict limits, imposed upon them by the fact that they, in common with all other organs of power, would be subordinate to the proletariat. This and other aspects of *The State and Revolution* will be discussed later; but the crucial point here is that the party barely makes an appearance anywhere in the text. In fact, the only relevant reference to the party occurs in the following passage:

By educating the workers' party, Marxism educates the vanguard of the proletariat, capable of assuming power and *leading the whole people* to socialism, of directing and organising the new system, of being the teacher, the guide, the leader of all the working and exploited people in organising their social life without the bourgeoisie and against the bourgeoisie.[28]

But even though the party only makes a fleeting appearance in *The State and Revolution*, there is no doubt that Lenin did intend 'the vanguard' to lead the people. In an article written even more closely to the time of the Bolshevik seizure of power, and in anticipation of it, he spoke glowingly of the Soviets as an entirely new form of state apparatus, immeasurably more democratic than any previous one, and he also noted that one of its advantages was that

> it provides an organisational form for the vanguard, i.e. for the most class-conscious, most energetic and most progressive section of the oppressed classes, the workers and peasants, and so constitutes an apparatus by means of which the vanguard of the oppressed classes can elevate, train, educate, and lead the *entire vast mass* of these classes, which has up to now stood completely outside of political life and history.[29]

What is missing from these and other such texts is any indication of how 'the vanguard', which must either be taken to be the party, or of which the party must be taken to be the core, would relate to those whom it wished to lead; and there is no indication either of what mechanisms would resolve the possible—indeed the inevitable—divergences between them. In other words, *The State and Revolution* did not answer what Lenin had in 1905 called 'the highly important' question of 'how to divide, and how to combine, the tasks of the Soviet and those of the Russian Social-Democratic Party'. The reason for that failure was that Lenin in 1917 was carried ahead by an extreme revolutionary optimism, fostered by the advance of the popular movement, and which led him to ignore the question he had posed in 1905. His optimism was of course unwarranted; and the Bolsheviks were soon compelled by the circumstances which they confronted to answer the question in very different ways from those which Lenin had envisaged when he hailed the 'new state apparatus' which he believed to be foreshadowed by the Soviets.

3

The State and Revolution is the most authoritative text in Marxist political writing on the dictatorship of the proletariat—a concept to which Marx attached supreme importance but which he never defined in any detail.* In the *Critique of the Gotha Programme* (1875), Marx had written that 'between

---

* In his Introduction of 1891 to *The Civil War in France*, Engels, addressing the 'Social-Democratic philistine' who was 'filled with wholesome terror at the words: Dictatorship of the Proletariat', had said: 'Do you want to know what this dictatorship looks like? Look at the Paris Commune. That was the Dictatorship of the Proletariat' (SW 1968, p. 262). Marx himself never said this, though it is reasonable to assume that his description of the Commune's organization was a close approximation to the main features of the dictatorship of the proletariat, as he conceived it.

capitalist and communist society lies a period of revolutionary transformation from one to the other. There is a corresponding period of transition in the political sphere and in this period the state can only take the form of a *revolutionary dictatorship of the proletariat*.'[30] Lenin quite rightly emphasized again and again that its basic premise was, as Marx had said in *The Civil War in France*, that 'the working class cannot simply lay hold of the ready-made state machinery, and wield it for its own purposes'.* In the letter to Kugelmann to which I have already referred, Marx also reminded his correspondent that in the *Eighteenth Brumaire*, 'I declare that the next attempt of the French Revolution will be no longer, as before, to transfer the bureaucratic-military machine from one hand to another, but to *smash* it, and this is the preliminary condition for every real people's revolution on the Continent. And this is what our heroic Party comrades in Paris are attempting'.† It was this 'smashing' of the existing state which Lenin, following Marx, took as the first and absolutely essential task of a genuinely revolutionary movement and party.

What would follow, he explained, was 'a gigantic replacement of certain institutions by other institutions of a fundamentally different type'.[31] Here too, Lenin was faithfully following Marx's pronouncements on the Commune in *The Civil War in France*. 'The first decree of the Commune', Marx had said, 'was the suppression of the standing army, and the substitution for it of the armed people';[32] and he then went on to list other major features of the Commune's organization:

The Commune was formed of the municipal councillors, chosen by universal suffrage in the various wards of the town, responsible and revocable at short terms. The majority of its members were naturally working men, or acknowledged representatives of the working class. The Commune was to be a working, not a parliamentary body, executive and legislative at the same time. Instead of continuing to be the agent of the central government, the police was at once stripped of its political attributes, and turned into the responsible and at all times revocable agent of the Commune. So were the officials of all other branches of the administration. From the members of the Commune

* FI, p. 206. He and Engels thought the point sufficiently important to single out the quotation and reproduce it in their 1872 Preface to the German Edition of the Communist Manifesto (SW 1968, p. 32); and Engels reproduced it once again in his Preface to the English Edition of 1888 (SW 1950, I, p. 29).

† SC, p. 318. In the *Eighteenth Brumaire*, Marx had said that 'all political upheavals perfected this machine instead of smashing it' (K. Marx, SE, p. 238).

downwards, the public service had to be done at *workmen's wages*. The vested interests and the representation allowances of the high dignitaries of state disappeared along with the high dignitaries themselves.[33]

It was *this* which for Lenin constituted a whole programme, precisely the 'gigantic replacement of certain institutions by other institutions of a fundamentally different type', these other institutions being the Soviets, which provided 'a bond with the people, with the majority of the people, so intimate, so indissoluble, so easily verifiable and renewable, that nothing remotely like it existed in the previous state apparatus'.[34] Moreover, the Soviets made it possible 'to combine the advantages of the parliamentary system with those of immediate and direct democracy, i.e. to vest in the people's elected representatives both legislative *and executive functions*'.[35]

There can be no doubt that Lenin believed that the Soviet system, once in operation, would represent the most democratic and popular regime that could be achieved before the advent of a fully socialist society. 'Compared with the bourgeois parliamentary system', he also wrote, 'this is an advance in democracy's development which is of world-wide, historic significance'.[36] A few weeks after this was written, the Bolsheviks had taken power, and the Soviet system continued to spread all over Russia. At the Third All-Russia Congress of Soviets which assembled in January 1918, Lenin felt able to say to the delegates: 'Look wherever there are working people, look among the masses, and you will see organizational, creative work in full swing, you will see the stir of a life that is being renewed and hallowed by the revolution.'[37]

This conviction that a new political order of an unprecedented popular and democratic kind was actually being born was obviously not the only or even the main reason for the momentous decision which Lenin and the other Bolshevik leaders took to dissolve the Constituent Assembly as soon as it had met at the beginning of January 1918. But the belief that there was a genuinely Soviet-type alternative to the Constituent Assembly undoubtedly helped to reinforce the political and ideological considerations which led to that decision.* Lenin

* The most important of these considerations was obviously the fact that the elections to the Constituent Assembly, which had been held in November 1917, had returned a majority of opponents of the Bolsheviks. Whatever view

did speak in the first months after the October Revolution as if he believed that it had inaugurated a regime of popular and democratic power such as he had outlined in *The State and Revolution*, in which the problem of class and party would be resolved in a sort of symbiotic relation between them. On this basis, it was obviously possible to think not only that the Constituent Assembly would place a dangerous brake—at the least—upon a still developing revolutionary movement but that, from the point of view of democracy itself, it was also an unnecessary encumbrance and a regression to parliamentarism at a time when new and immensely more democratic forms of political power had come into being and were spreading.

In fact, the faith which Lenin had placed in the Soviets was rendered altogether illusory by the circumstances of revolution and civil war. Whether they could have fulfilled even some of his expectations had circumstances been more favourable is an open question. But even if they had, the relation between the Party and the Soviets would still have posed the question which Lenin had asked in 1905. As it was, the disintegration of the Soviets and the terrible dangers to which the revolution was exposed from within and from without vastly favoured the 'substitutism' which some revolutionaries had previously feared and which some in the Bolshevik ranks virulently attacked after 1917.

Lenin responded to such attacks by denying that the party was usurping the place of the proletariat and by pleading exceptional conditions. His change of perspective from the period preceding and following the Bolshevik seizure of power is well indicated by his claim in 1919 that 'the dictatorship of the working class is carried into effect by the party of the Bolsheviks which since 1905 has been united with the whole revolutionary proletariat'.[38] It was also the same view of the special character of the Bolshevik Party which led him defiantly to accept the charge of 'dictatorship of one party': 'Yes, the dictatorship of one party! We stand upon it and cannot depart from this ground, since this is the party which in the course of decades has won for itself the position of vanguard of the whole factory and industrial proletariat.'[39]

---

is taken of the Assembly's dissolution, the Bolsheviks were obviously right to think that their rule was incompatible with the Assembly's continued existence.

It is true that Lenin and the Bolsheviks were alone capable of saving what was after all their revolution; and there was no real possibility of alliance with any other group or party.[40] But what this situation entailed was the dictatorship of the Bolshevik Party over the proletariat as well as over all other classes, by means of the repressive power of the state which the party controlled. Lenin might well deny that it was appropriate to speak of a stark dichotomy between 'dictatorship of the party or dictatorship of the class',[41] but the fact remained that the party *had* 'substituted' itself for a ravaged and exhausted working class, in a country gripped by civil war, foreign intervention and economic collapse.

But the growing concentration of power which these circumstances encouraged very quickly came to affect the party itself. E. H. Carr notes that 'the seventh party congress of March 1918 which voted for the ratification of Brest-Litovsk was the last to decide a vital issue of policy by a majority vote . . . Already in October 1917 it was the central committee which had taken the vital decision to seize power; and it was the central committee which succeeded to the authority of the congress.'[42] But this too, as he also notes, was soon followed by the exercise of power by more restricted and secretive organs.

The changes that were occurring in the nature and spirit of the party found formal expression in the decision taken at the Tenth Party Congress in March 1921 at the instigation of Lenin to forbid all groups and factions within the party and to give to the Central Committee full powers to punish, if need be by expulsion, 'any breach of discipline or revival or toleration of fractionalism'.[43] The previous three years, although full of crises and dangers, had been marked by considerable controversy in the ranks of Bolshevism, or at least among its leading personnel. The polemics had ranged over many issues, notably over the proper application of 'democratic centralism' and the role of the trade unions in the new Soviet state.* In the debate on the trade unions one faction, led by Trotsky, wanted the thorough subordination of the unions to the state; another, the 'workers' opposition', wanted much greater independence for them and their assumption of far larger powers in the running of economic and

---

* The first major issue had been whether to accept the peace terms of Brest-Litovsk.

industrial life.* Lenin occupied a middle position, and rejected both the 'militarization' of the unions which Trotsky advocated, and also an independence for them that would have threatened the new regime with a 'syndicalist' deformation. But by the beginning of 1921, the 'Workers' Opposition' had emerged as a distinctive group, with a substantial measure of support, and with a programme sufficiently loose to attract a great deal more support at a time of acute economic stress and political crisis (the Tenth Party Congress met as the Kronstadt rising was being crushed). It was in these circumstances that the decision was ratified by that Congress to enforce 'unity' upon the party.

There is no question that it was Lenin who bore the prime responsibility for this major step forward in the direction of what I have referred to earlier as 'dictatorial centralism'. But it is of interest that he was by no means the most extreme advocate of that decision and that he did not try to make a virtue of what he believed to be required by dire circumstances ('We need no opposition, comrades, now is not the time').[44] Ironically, Trotsky who had so virulently denounced Lenin's 'substitutism' in 1903 unequivocally claimed in 1921 the party's right 'to assert its dictatorship even if that dictatorship temporarily clashed with the passing moods of the workers' democracy ... The party is obliged to maintain its dictatorship, regardless of temporary wavering in the spontaneous moods of the masses, regardless of the temporary vacillations even in the working class.'†

However, it was also Trotsky who, in a new Preface to his book *1905*, dated 12 January 1922, came closest to the heart of the problem which had confronted the Bolsheviks. Referring to the period from March to October 1917, he wrote that 'although having inscribed on our banner: "All power to the Soviets", we were still formally supporting the slogans of democracy, unable as yet to give the masses (or even ourselves) a definite answer as to what would happen if the cogs of the wheels of formal democracy failed to mesh with the cogs of the Soviet system'; and he then went on:

* For the debate on the trade unions, see e.g. I. Deutscher, *Soviet Trade Unions (Their Place in Labour Soviet Policy)* (London, 1952).

† Deutscher, *The Prophet Armed*, op. cit., p. 509. Note, however, Trotsky's further remark that 'the dictatorship does not base itself at every given moment on the formal principle of a workers' democracy, although the workers' democracy is, of course, the only method by which the masses can be drawn more and more into the political life' (ibid.). The strain in thought is here evident.

The dispersal of the Constituent Assembly was a crudely revolutionary fulfilment of an aim which might also have been reached by means of a postponement or by the preparation of elections. But it was precisely this peremptory attitude towards the legalistic aspects of the means of struggle that made the problem of revolutionary power inescapably acute; and in its turn, the dispersal of the Constituent Assembly by the armed forces of the proletariat necessitated a complete reconsideration of the interrelationship between democracy and dictatorship.*

It was precisely this 'complete reconsideration' which the Russian Communists were unable to undertake in Lenin's lifetime, and which they were forbidden to undertake after his death. By the Twelfth Party Congress in 1923, which Lenin's illness prevented him from attending, Zinoviev was already proclaiming that 'we need a single strong, powerful central committee which is leader of everything',[45] and it was, of all people, Stalin who demurred, since he did not want power concentrated in the Central Committee at the expense of the Secretariat and other working organs of the Party.[46]

This evolution from October 1917 until 1923—the years of Leninism in power—has inevitably been considered, particularly since 1956, in the light of the grim experience of Stalinism; and it has become a familiar argument that Leninism 'paved the way' for Stalinism, and that the latter was only the 'natural' successor of the former.

The argument turns on the meaning which is given to Stalinism. If it is merely taken to mean a further centralization of power than had already occurred and a greater use of the repressive and arbitrary power than was already the case in the Leninist years, then the continuity is indeed established.

But Stalinism had characteristics and dimensions which were lacking under Leninism, and which turned it into a regime much more accurately seen as marking a dramatic break with anything that had gone before. The most important of these must be briefly noted here.

To begin with, it was a regime in which one man did hold absolute power of a kind which Lenin never remotely had (or ever gave the slightest sign of wanting to achieve); and Stalin used that power to the full, not least for the herding into camps

* L. Trotsky, 1905 (London, 1971), pp. 21–2. Trotsky added that 'In the final analysis, this represented both a theoretical and a practical gain for the Workers' International', which is obviously absurd.

of millions upon millions of people and the 'liquidation' of countless others, including vast numbers of people who were part of the upper and upmost layers of Soviet society—this devastation of all ranks of the regime's officialdom, which was a recurring phenomenon, is unique as an historical event. The sheer *scale* of the repression is a second feature of Stalinism which distinguishes it most sharply from Leninism. The Soviet Marxist (and 'dissident') historian Roy Medvedev put the point in a striking formulation by saying that 'the NKVD arrested and killed, within two years, more Communists than had been lost in all the years of the underground struggle, the three revolutions and the Civil War';[47] and he also quotes figures which suggest that for three years of the Civil War, 1918–20, fewer than 13,000 people were shot by the Cheka.[48] Even if the figures are contested as being far too low, the difference in scale between the repression that occurred in the years of revolution, civil war, and foreign intervention on the one hand, and the holocaust of Stalinism on the other, is so vast as to discredit the notion of continuity. Moreover, repression on such a scale required a gigantic police apparatus that reached out to every corner of Soviet life, not only to arrest, deport, and execute, but to maintain detailed surveillance over Soviet citizens who were not imprisoned and to guard those who were. This was an exceedingly elaborate system which was quite deliberately woven into the tissue of the larger social system and that decisively affected the latter's total pattern.

This points to a third characteristic of Stalinism, namely that it required from the people a positive and even enthusiastic acceptance of whatever 'line', policy, position and attitude was dictated from on high, however much it might contradict the immediately preceding one. This applied not only to major aspects of policy, or even to minor ones, but to every conceivable aspect of life and thought. Conformity was demanded over literature and music as well as over foreign policy and Five-Year plans, not to speak of the interpretation of Marxism-Leninism and of history, particularly the history of the Russian Revolution; and every vestige of opposition was ruthlessly stamped out. Indeed, Stalinism was a regime which stamped out opposition in anticipation, and constantly struck at people who were perfectly willing to conform, on suspicion that they might eventually cease to be willing. No such conformity was demanded in the first years of the revolution; and it formed no part of Leninism.

This Stalinist requirement of total conformity to all Soviet policies and actions was also extended to the world Communist movement. Whenever the regime could, it physically stamped out opposition or suspected opposition among foreign Communists; and it demanded the same rigid endorsement of every single aspect of Russian internal and external policy that it was able to exact inside the Soviet Union. (That it recieved this ensorsement is of course one of the most remarkable and still very poorly charted phenomena of the twentieth century.) What happened was the total Stalinization of every single Communist Party throughout the world, in the name of the sacred duty imposed upon every Communist to defend the U.S.S.R.; and defending the U.S.S.R. rapidly came to be interpreted as including the defence of every twist and turn in Soviet internal as well as external policy; the endorsement of whatever Stalinist 'line' might be current on literature, biology, linguistics, or whatever; the denunciation as traitors, renegades, and foreign agents of anyone who was so labelled by the Soviet leadership, including all but a few of those who had been the leading figures of Bolshevism; and the complete and vehement rejection as bourgeois (or Fascist) lies of any charge levelled at the rulers of 'the socialist sixth of the world'. This kind of automatic submission to Russian requirements formed no part of Leninism either.

In the perspective of the present chapter, another characteristic of Stalinism must be stressed: this is the apotheosis of 'the Party'. In so far as 'the Party' meant in fact its leadership, and above all its supreme leader, this could be taken as part of the 'cult of personality'. But the distinction between the latter and what might be called the cult of the party nevertheless needs to be made. For it became habitual and indeed necessary after Lenin's death to speak of 'the Party' in quasi-religious terms and to invoke its 'unity' as a quality that must on no account be infringed, and whose infringement warranted the direst penalties. This was not only of the utmost value to those who controlled the Party: it was also a paralysing constraint on those who opposed them. As early as the Thirteenth Party Congress in May 1924, the first after Lenin's death, Trotsky, who had belatedly identified himself with the cause of inner-party democracy, nevertheless still spoke of the Party in terms which were of greater comfort to his enemies in power than to his allies in opposition: 'Comrades', he said, 'none of us wishes to be or can be right against the party. In the last instance the party is always right, because it is *the only historic instrument which the working class possesses for the solution of its fundamental tasks.*'[49]

He refused to recant, as he had been required to do by Zinoviev, who was then allied to Stalin; and he said that he did not believe that all the criticisms and warnings of those who opposed the leadership were wrong 'from beginning to end'. But he also said 'I know that one ought not to be right against the party. One can be right only with the party and through the party because history has created no other way for the realization of one's rightness.'[50]

Trotksy soon changed his mind. But in one form or another, such debilitating notions continued to help disarm generation after generation of revolutionaries in all Communist parties, and must be taken as part of the explanation for the extreme weakness of the Marxist opposition to Stalinism in subsequent years. A conviction was deeply implanted—and Stalinist propaganda did all it could to strengthen it—that outside the party, there could be no effective action; and inside the party, there was total control from the top. This was the case for all Communist parties. Opponents in these parties were either subdued or expelled, and in a number of cases physically destroyed.

Lenin had never made a cult of the party. He had in the stress of crisis identified the dictatorship of the proletariat with the dictatorship of the party; and his name is indissolubly linked with the idea that no revolutionary movement is conceivable without a revolutionary party to lead it. But he never invested 'the Party' with the kind of quasi-mystical attributes that became habitual after his death, and which had hitherto been more properly associated with religious than with secular institutions—but then a religious frame of mind did come to dominate the world Communist movement in the years of Stalinism, with 'Marxism-Leninism' as its catechism, 'dialectical materialism' as its mystery, 'the Party' as its Church, and Stalin as its prophet.

This frame of mind also made it easy to suppress the question of 'substitutism'; and it was indeed one of the hallmarks of Stalinism to turn this into a non-question. It was taken for granted that 'the Party' and the working class formed a perfect unity, and that the former by definition 'represented' the latter;

and since there was no problem of 'substitutism', neither was there any need to look seriously for remedies or answers to it.

On the other hand, Lenin's anguished awareness in his last years that the problem was real and growing did not lead him to propose any adequate solution to it, either in the short term or the long.[51] In truth, he had no such solution to offer. Nor was there one to be had within the confines of a system that combined the monopoly of one party with dictatorial centralism.

The difficulties presented by the relation of party to class were enormously compounded by the specific and desperately unfavourable conditions of post-revolutionary Russia: but they did not stem from these conditions. The point is underlined by reference to the attempt which Gramsci made, quite independently of Russian experience or circumstances, to resolve the question theoretically, and by the fact that he was only able to restate it.

In an article, 'The Problem of Power', in L'Ordine Nuove, which appeared in November 1919, Gramsci wrote that this was

the problem of the modes and forms which will make it possible to organise the whole mass of Italian workers in a hierarchy which organically culminates in the party. It is the problem of the construction of a state apparatus which, internally, will function democratically, that is, will guarantee freedom to all anti-capitalist tendencies, the possibility of becoming parties of proletarian government, but externally, will be like an implacable machine which crushes the organisations of the industrial and political power of capitalism.[52]

Commenting on this, Gwyn Williams suggests that 'the relationship between party and masses in this, as in other projects of a similar temper (Rosa Luxemburg's concept of leadership, for example) reads like an attempt to square the circle'.[53] Whether so or not, it is clear that these formulations do not point to any solution of the question. The same has to be said of Gramsci's later Prison Notebooks. These include some illuminating reflections on the proletarian party's role as the 'modern Prince', the 'collective intellectual' of the working class and as its essential form of political organization. But they do not provide the theoretical material for the resolution of the tension between class and party. Nor, as I have suggested earlier, is it likely that such a resolution is wholly possible: what can be achieved is the attenuation of this tension; and the degree to which it is attenuated is a matter of crucial importance. But this requires severe and effective limitations on the powers of leaders, which is no small undertaking and which is itself dependent on the existence or the achievement of a cluster of favourable circumstances.

The Chinese experience, which some people on the left have tended to regard as a demonstration of how the problem can be solved, is in fact an instructive example of its gravity. Not very paradoxically, this is so precisely because no Communist leader has been more explicitly and more consistently concerned than Chairman Mao with the relation of leaders to led and with the meaningful application of the principle of 'democratic centralism': yet the Chinese record, in this realm at least, is far from impressive. It may well be argued that it is better than the Russian one; but this is not saying much.

One of the most distinctive features of Maoism has been its constant stress on the danger that leaders and cadres would become isolated, rigid, and remote from the masses; and a related distinctive feature has been the conviction that the remedy lay not only in the acceptance but in the encouragement and fostering of criticism and challenge 'from below'. The following quotation from a talk by Chairman Mao in 1962 to a Conference of 7,000 cadres from various levels may serve as a typical instance of his approach to this issue:

If there is no democracy, if ideas are not coming from the masses, it is impossible to establish a good line, good general and specific policies and methods. Our leading organs merely play the role of a processing plant in the establishment of a good line and good general and specific policies and methods. Everyone knows that if a factory has no raw material it cannot do any processing. If the raw material is not adequate in quantity and quality it cannot produce good finished products. Without democracy, you have no understanding of what is happening down below; the situation will be unclear; you will be unable to collect sufficient opinions from all sides; there can be no communication between top and bottom; top-level organs of leadership will depend on one-sided and incorrect material to decide issues, thus you will find it difficult to avoid being subjectivist; it will be impossible to achieve unity of understanding and unity of action, and impossible to achieve true centralism.[54]

The first thing to note about this text is that the argument for 'democracy' is primarily a 'functional' one: cadres will be better informed and will reach better decisions if they listen and pay heed to what the masses are saying. What the masses are saying is the 'raw material' which cadres have to process. The stress is always on 'letting the masses speak out' in order to improve the work of the Party. But there is no question that the Party must always remain in command and be the final arbiter of what is to be done.

Chairman Mao was willing to go very far in trying to compel the Party to 'listen to the masses' and to 'apply the mass line'—how far is best shown by the Cultural Revolution which was directed against 'persons in authority who had taken the capitalist road', and most of which were obviously Party cadres and Party members. One of the slogans put forward at the beginning of the Cultural Revolution, under the inspiration of the Chairman, namely 'Bombard Party Headquarters', is indicative of the spirit of challenge which was being generated at the time. (The argument, incidentally, that the whole operation was designed by the Chairman and his acolytes to get rid of his opponents or at least to subdue them, is of no great relevance here—the methods employed are what matters.)

On the other hand, it is equally significant that the Chairman never gave any indication that he had the slightest intention of surrendering or even reducing the 'leading role' of the Party; or of bringing about major institutional reforms in its mode of being. Whenever the movement that he had generated or encouraged gave any sign of really getting out of hand and of engulfing the Party, he and his partisans firmly reasserted the crucial importance of maintaining its directing character. Other organizations—the People's Liberation Army and revolutionary committees—could and did play a major role. But it was never suggested that they or any other organization could conceivably replace the Party or assume a co-equal role with it. Nor indeed *was* this conceivable in the circumstances of the Chinese Revolution.

It is rather more interesting that Chairman Mao never gave any sign that he was concerned to give an institutional and solidly constructed basis to the process of involvement of the masses which he consistently advocated; and that he never suggested that such involvement required the creation of institutions *independent* from Party control.

Popular involvement is not the same thing as democratic participation and control; and it is perfectly possible to have a very large measure of the one without having much (or even any) of the other. Millions upon millions of people have been involved in great and tumultuous movements in China; and their involvement has included the (officially encouraged) criticism of cadres and 'persons in authority'. Many of these have been swept from their offices and positions, either temporarily or for good. But however fruitful such movements of criticism and challenge may be judged to be, they are by no means the same as democratic participation and popular control and do not, in any serious meaning of the word, have much to do with either.

The kind of 'purges' which have been part of Maoism, notably in the Cultural Revolution, have generally speaking been a great improvement on the 'purges' of Stalinism: but they have not changed the system which made the 'purges' necessary in the first place. Chairman Mao spoke of the need to have a whole series of Cultural Revolutions stretching into the indefinite future. The trouble is that, in so far as such Revolutions do not greatly affect structures and institutions, they are not an adequate means of dealing with the degenerative processes with which the Chairman was rightly concerned.

Much may be claimed for the Chinese experience. But what cannot be claimed for it, on the evidence, is that it has really begun to create the institutional basis for the kind of socialist democracy that would effectively reduce the distance between those who determine policy and those on whose behalf it is determined. Nor for that matter has Maoism made any notable contribution to the theoretical attack of the question.

In terms of Marxist politics in general, the question remains open; and its discussion is best pursued by considering the Marxist view of the revolutionary process, with which the discussion of socialist democracy is intertwined.

NOTES

1 *FI*, p. 82.
2 See, e.g., Marx's insistence on this point in an interview in *The World* in July 1871, in *Werke* (Berlin, 1964), op. cit. XVII, p. 641. See also M. Johnstone, 'Marx and Engels and the Concept of the Party' in *The Socialist Register 1967* (London, 1967).
3 *FI*, p. 370.
4 Ibid., p. 375.
5 See below, pp. 138 ff.

6 H. Gruber, *International Communism in the Era of Lenin* (New York, 1972), p. 12.

7 V. I. Lenin, *What is to be done?* p. 106.

8 See, e.g., Liebman, *Leninism under Lenin.*

9 *'Left-Wing' Communism—An Infantile Disorder*, in SWL, p. 574.

10 R. Luxemburg, *Organizational Question of Social Democracy*, in *Rosa Luxemburg Speaks*, p. 130.

11 Lenin, op. cit., p. 532.

12 I. Deutscher, *The Prophet Armed. Trotsky: 1879–1921* (London, 1954) p. 90.

13 Ibid., p. 90.

14 R. Luxemburg, *Organizational Question of Social Democracy*, in *Rosa Luxemburg Speaks*, p. 118.

15 Ibid., p. 122.

16 *Revs.*, pp. 79–80.

17 H. Gruber, *International Communism in the Era of Lenin*, p. 114.

18 *FI*, p. 91.

19 Ibid., pp. 91–2.

20 V. I. Lenin, *What is to be Done?*, p. 375.

21 SWL, p. 539.

22 FI, p. 212.

23 Ibid., p. 210.

24 SC, p. 410.

25 Ibid., p. 410.

26 K. Marx to L. Kugelmann, 12 April 1971, in SC, p. 319.

27 V. I. Lenin, 'Our Tasks and the Soviet of Workers' Deputies', in CWL, vol. 10 (1962), p. 19.

28 *The State and Revolution*, in SWL, p. 281.

29 V. I. Lenin, *Can the Bolsheviks Retain State Power?*, ibid., p. 373. Notwithstanding its title, this *was* written on the eve of October.

30 FI, p. 355.

31 V. I. Lenin, *The State and Revolution*, SWL, p. 293.

32 FI, p. 209.

33 Ibid., p. 209.

34 *Can the Bolsheviks Retain State Power?*, SWL, p. 373.

35 Ibid., p. 374.

36 Ibid., p. 374.

37 Liebman, op. cit., p. 219.

38 E. H. Carr, *The Bolshevik Revolution, 1917–1923* (London, 1950) p. 230.

39 Ibid., p. 230.

40 For Lenin's attitude to other parties and groups, and vice versa, see Liebman, op. cit., pp. 238 ff.

41 See the reference to *'Left-Wing' Communism—An Infantile Disorder*, p. 123 above.

42 Carr, op. cit., p. 193.

43 Ibid., p. 201.

44 Ibid., p. 199.

45 Ibid., p. 231.

46 Ibid., p. 231.

47 R. Medvedev, *Let History Judge: The Origins and Consequences of Stalinism* (London, 1972), p. 234.

48 Ibid., p. 390.

49 I. Deutscher, *The Prophet Unarmed. Trotsky: 1921–1929* (London, 1959), p. 139.

50 Ibid., p. 139.

51 See, e.g., M. Lewin, *Lenin's Last Struggle* (London, 1969).

52 *L'Ordine Nuove*, 29 November 1919, in *New Edinburgh Review. Gramsci*, II, p. 73. The article is one of a number reproduced in the Review in a Section entitled 'Proletarian Forms' and edited by Gwyn Williams.

53 Ibid., p. 73.

54 *Mao Tse-tung Unrehearsed. Talks and Letters: 1956–71* (London, 1974), p. 164.

VI. Reform and Revolution

1

At Marx's graveside on 17 March 1883, Engels said of him that he was 'before all else a revolutionist' and that 'his real mission in life was to contribute, in one way or another, to the overthrow of capitalist society and of the state institutions which it had brought into being, to contribute to the liberation of the modern proletariat . . .'[1] Commonplace though this may be, it is very much worth stressing that this was indeed Marx's fundamental and unwavering purpose; and that Marxism as a political doctrine has above all been about the making of socialist revolution.

But what *strategy* does the making of socialist revolution require? A hundred years of debate have shown well enough that however unambiguous the Marxist purpose may be, its advancement has been by far the most contentious of all issues within the ranks of Marxism. Nor has the debate grown less intense with the years and with the accumulated experience they have provided. The lines of division have remained as deep as ever on this central issue of strategy, and will undoubtedly remain so for a long time to come.

The reason for the endurance and intractability of these divisions is that they represent two very different paths of advance, and the differences also concern the meaning which is to be attached to the notion of socialist 'revolution' and the 'overthrow' of capitalist regimes. Each of these different paths have appeared to their respective champions as the only reasonable and realistic one, by which token the alternative one has been condemned as unrealistic, self-defeating and a betrayal or deformation of Marxism; and it has also been possible for the respective antagonists to defend their chosen positions, with varying degrees of plausibility, as representing authentic Marxist positions, or as representing the only possible Marxist position in the circumstances, or some such argument.

It is not pointless or impossible to determine fairly precisely what Marx's position on this issue of strategy was at any given time, or Engels's, or Lenin's. But this never settles anything; and the more important requirement, in the present context, is to try and clarify what the *real* lines of division are on the subject of revolutionary strategy within the Marxist perspective. It is particularly necessary to try and do this because the inevitable acerbity and virulence of the controversies have greatly obscured what these lines of division actually are; and also what they are not.

The two paths in question are in essence those which have commonly been designated as the 'reformist' and the 'revolutionary'. For reasons which will be discussed presently, these terms are rather misleading and fail to provide a proper contraposition of the alternatives. Those Marxists who have been called 'reformists' by their 'revolutionary' Marxist opponents have vehemently repudiated the label as an insult to their own revolutionary integrity and purpose; and they have in turn denounced their opponents as 'adventurist', 'ultra-left', etc. All the designations which have formed part of this Marxist debate on strategies of advance have been greatly overloaded with question-begging connotations, and no label in this controversy is altogether 'innocent'. 'Constitutionalist' and 'insurrectionary' probably come nearest to an accurate description of the alternative positions; but there are problems here too. I have continued to use the term 'reformist', in a sense that will be specified, and without pejorative intent.

Before proceeding with the discussion of the alternative strategies, there is one source of confusion which must be cleared up. This is the fact that there has always existed a trend in working-class movements—and for that matter outside—towards *social reform*; and this is a trend which, in so far as it has no thought of achieving the wholesale transformation of capitalist society into an entirely different social order, must be sharply distinguished from the 'reformist' strategy, which has insisted that this was precisely its purpose.

As was noted earlier, social reform has been an intrinsic part of the politics of capitalism, and those who have supported it have not only *not* been concerned to advance towards socialism but have on the contrary seen in social reform an essential prophylactic against it. It was this which Marx and Engels called in the *Communist Manifesto* 'Conservative or Bourgeois Socialism' and which they attributed to 'a part of the bourgeoisie . . . desirous of redressing social grievances, in order to secure the continued existence of bourgeois society'.[2] 'The socialistic bourgeois', they also wrote, 'want all the advantages of modern social conditions without the struggles and dangers necessarily resulting therefrom. They desire the existing state of society minus its revolutionary and disintegrating elements. They wish for a bourgeoisie without a proletariat'; and the reforms that such people wanted by no means involved the 'abolition of the bourgeois relations of production', which required a revolution, and 'in no respect affect the relations between capital and labour'.[3]

The last statement is obviously an exaggeration, since reforms can affect and have affected in some respects the relations between capital and labour; and both Marx and Engels worked very hard to achieve reforms to that end, for instance inside the First International.[4] But the characterization of 'Conservative or Bourgeois Socialism' remains generally speaking extraordinarily modern, notwithstanding the passage of 130 years; and it encompasses much more than 'part of the bourgeoisie'. Marx and Engels themselves saw the same limited and prophylactic intentions in the reforms of straightforward conservative figures such as Louis Bonaparte (whose 'Imperial Socialism' Marx mocked), Bismarck and Disraeli; and they also applied it, in the aftermath of the 1848 revolutions, to what they called the 'republican petty bourgeois', 'who now call themselves Red and social-democratic because they cherish the pious wish of abolishing the pressure of big capital on small capital, of the big bourgeois on the small bourgeois'. Such people, they said, 'far from desiring to revolutionize all society for the revolutionary proletarians . . . strive for a change in social conditions by means of which existing society will be made as tolerable and comfortable as possible for them'.[5]

But Marx and Engels also saw develop in their lifetime movements and associations of workers whose aims did not go beyond the achievement of specific and limited reforms: British trade unionism is a case in point, and Marx and Engels frequently deplored its narrow and firmly un-revolutionary consciousness and purposes,[6] which did not however stop them from working with British trade unionists when they found this useful to their own purposes, as in the First International.[7] It is also this concern with limited amelioration which Lenin described as 'trade union consciousness', and which he wanted the revolutionary party to extend to larger anti-capitalist purposes. Of course trade unions, however limited their horizons, have seldom been able to concern themselves exclusively with 'hours, wages and conditions' if only because these tend to bring other issues into focus. But this need not go beyond improvements of various kinds for the working class within the capitalist system, and with no thought of superseding that system; and this 'trade union consciousness' has been and remains an important and in some instances a dominant trend inside organized labour under capitalism.

In the twentieth century this trend has not only been present in the trade unions: it has also come to dominate large (and in some cases the largest) working-class parties in capitalist countries. Britain, Germany, and Sweden are obvious instances. No doubt most such parties have a formal and explicit commitment to the achievement of a different social order; and they also include many people who deeply believe in the reality and meaningfulness of that commitment on the part of their parties—or who believe at least that their parties can eventually be made to take that commitment seriously.

Whatever may be thought of that hope, it must be obvious that the parties concerned are in fact parties of social reform, whose leaders and leading personnel are in their overwhelming majority solidly and comfortably established in the existing social order, and who have absolutely no intention of embarking on anything resembling its wholesale transformation, in however piecemeal and pacific a perspective. Their purpose is reform, very often conceived, in more or less the same way as it is by their conservative counterparts, as a necessary insurance against pressure for reforms of a too radical and rapid kind. The 'socialism' which these leaders proclaim, where they do proclaim it, is a rhetorical device and a synonym for various improvements that a necessarily imperfect society requires. These reforms do not form part of a coherent and comprehensive strategy of change, least of all socialist change.

'Reformism', on the contrary, is such a strategy, at least theoretically. Indeed, not only is it one of the two main strategies of the Marxist tradition: for good or ill, it is also the one which, notwithstanding a deceptive rhetoric, has always found most favour and support within that tradition. This strategy naturally includes the pursuit of reforms of every kind—economic, social, and political—within the framework of capitalism. But unlike parties of social reform, parties which are guided by this particular Marxist tradition do not consider such reforms as being their ultimate purpose: these are at best steps and partial means towards a much larger purpose, which is declared to be the 'overthrow' of capitalism and the achievement of an altogether different, that is socialist, society.

I have already noted in Chapter IV how easily Marx and Engels accepted the idea that bourgeois democratic regimes afforded the most promising ground for the development of the proletarian revolutionary movement; and also how easy they found it to envisage a strategy for the revolutionary movement which entailed thorough involvement in 'ordinary' political life and the pursuit of reform, *allied* to a constant concern for the advancement of a revolutionary purpose that naturally went far beyond anything that reformers of one sort or another could envisage.

The distinctiveness of that Marxist revolutionary purpose was emphasized again and again by Marx and Engels. In *The Class Struggles in France*, Marx thus identifies it as

the *declaration of the permanence of the revolution*, the *class dictatorship* of the proletariat as a necessary intermediate point on the path towards the *abolition of class differences in general*, the abolition of all social relations which correspond to these relations of production, and the revolutionizing of all ideas which stem from these social relations.[8]

Similarly in the Address to the Central Committee to the Communist League to which reference was made earlier, Marx and Engels insisted that the limited demands of the 'democratic petty bourgeois' could in no way suffice 'for the party of the proletariat':

It is our interest and our task to make the revolution permanent, until all more or less possessing classes have been forced out of their position of dominance, until the proletariat has conquered state power, and the association of proletarians, not only in one country but in all the dominant countries of the world, has advanced so far that competition among the proletarians of these countries has ceased and that at least the decisive productive forces are concentrated in the hands of the proletarians. For us the issue cannot be the alteration of private property but only its annihilation, not the smoothing over of class antagonisms but the abolition of classes, not the improvement of existing society but the foundation of a new one.[9]

'Making the revolution permanent', in this context, clearly

means striving for the advancement of these aims within the framework of capitalism and a bourgeois democratic regime; and this striving obviously included pressure for reforms of every sort. Indeed, Lenin in 1905 made the achievement of a bourgeois democratic republic the immediate aim of the revolutionary movement. In *Two Tactics of Social Democracy in the Democratic Revolution*, he said that 'we cannot get out of the bourgeois-democratic boundaries of the Russian revolution, but we can vastly extend these boundaries, and within these boundaries we can and must fight for the interests of the proletariat, for its immediate needs and for conditions that will make it possible to prepare its forces for the future complete victory.'[10]

This perspective entails a *combination* of two concepts which have often been erroneously contraposed in Marxist thinking on strategies of revolutionary advance, namely the concept of 'two stages' and that of 'permanent revolution'. The 'two stages' concept means in effect the struggle for the achievement of a bourgeois democratic regime where such a regime does not exist, and where conditions for a socialist revolution are deemed not to exist either. The concept of 'permanent revolution', at least in Marx's usage, involves the application of continuous pressure for pushing the process further and creating the conditions for a revolutionary break with the bourgeois democratic regime itself.* In 1905, Lenin was arguing not only that Marxists should struggle for the achievement of such a regime, but that they must assume the leadership of that struggle by way of the 'revolutionary-democratic dictatorship of the proletariat and the peasantry'.[11] For all its vast significance, he also said, 'the democratic revolution will not immediately overstep the bounds of bourgeois social and economic relations.' But its success would 'mark the utter limit of the revolutionism of the bourgeoisie, and even that of the petty bourgeoisie, and the beginning of the proletariat's real struggle for socialism'.[12]

Whatever may be thought of this 'scenario' (and the notion of a 'revolutionary-democratic dictatorship of the proletariat and

* As envisaged by Trotsky, with whom the notion of 'permanent revolution' is most closely associated, it entailed a much more dramatic belief in the need and possibility to by-pass in Russia the bourgeois revolution and move directly to the dictatorship of the proletariat; and 'permanent revolution' also meant for him the fostering of revolution abroad as an essential part of the process. (See Deutscher, *The Prophet Armed*, op. cit., Ch. VI.)

the peasantry' carefully refusing to overstep the bounds of bourgeois social and economic relations is certainly strange),* it is clearly the case that the struggle for reforms in a bourgeois democratic regime was never taken by classical Marxism to be incompatible with the advancement of revolutionary aims and purposes. On the contrary such a struggle is an intrinsic part of the Marxist tradition. *Within* that tradition, there is undoubtedly room for much controversy and debate as to the kind of reforms to be pursued, the importance that should be attached to them, and the manner in which they should be pursued. Thus supporters of a 'revolutionary' as opposed to a 'reformist' strategy have generally tended to place relatively less emphasis and value on reforms, and to press for reforms which they did not believe to be attainable, as part of a 'politics of exposure' of capitalism—and also of 'reformist' labour leaders. But there are limits to this kind of politics, which are imposed *inter alia* by the working-class movement itself: if the 'politics of exposure' are pushed too far, all that they are likely to expose are the people who practice them, and leave such people in a state of ineffectual sectarian isolation. In any case, and notwithstanding the undoubted differences of emphasis within the Marxist tradition on the degree of importance to be attached to reforms, it is not this which essentially distinguishes the two contrasting strategies within that tradition. It is not, in other words, the pursuit of reforms which defines 'reformism'.

Nor is 'reformism', in its Marxist version, to be defined as 'gradualism', according to which the achievement of a socialist society is conceived as a slow but sure advance by way of a long sequence of reforms, at the end of which (or for that matter in the course of which) capitalism would be found to have been transcended. This is what Sidney Webb and the original Fabians roughly had in mind when they thought of socialism. But they were not Marxists, and loudly proclaimed that they were not; and their version of socialism had much more to do with piecemeal collectivist social engineering, inspired, directed, and administered from on high than with any version of the Marxism which they opposed. (It was not simply an aberration which led the Webbs to be so deeply attracted to the Soviet

---

* With the outbreak of revolution in Russia in 1917, Lenin abandoned this schema and his views as to what could and should be done moved much closer to those of Trotsky in 1905.

Union in the early thirties—there was much about it which matched their vision of socialism as state-imposed collectivism.) Whatever else may be said about 'reformist' Marxism, it never at any time envisaged the 'transition to socialism' in such a smoothly gradualist perspective, with so marked a stress as in the case of Fabianism on the conversion of members of the middle (and upper) classes to state intervention and collectivist measures.

Marxist 'reformism' does have a long-term view of the advance towards socialism, and that view does include a belief in the need to chip away at the structures of capitalism. But 'reformism' envisages this process in terms of struggle and more specifically class struggle on many different fronts and at many different levels: in this sense, it remains quite definitely a politics of conflict.

The really important point, however, is that this is a politics of conflict envisaged as being conducted within the limits of constitutionalism defined by bourgeois democracy, with a strong emphasis on electoral success at municipal, regional and national levels, and with the hope of achieving majority or at least strong representation in local councils, regional assemblies, and national parliaments. Where relevant, this would also include competition in presidential elections, with the hope of either winning outright, or at least of being able to achieve a favourable bargaining position for this or that purpose: there are obviously many possible permutations.

This emphasis on constitutionalism, electoralism, and representation is certainly crucial in the definition of 'reformism'. But it is often caricatured by its opponents on the far left as a necessarily exclusive concern with electoral success and increased representation. In fact, 'reformism' is also compatible, both theoretically and practically, with forms of struggle which, though carried on within the given constitutional framework, are not related to elections and representation—for instance industrial struggles, strikes, sit-ins, work-ins, demonstrations, marches, campaigns, etc., designed to advance specific or general demands, oppose governmental policies, protest against given measures, and so on.* No doubt, such activities and the

* There is an interesting discussion of this strategy, and of its problems, in an article of 1904 by Rosa Luxemburg, entitled 'Social Democracy and Parliamentarism': Parliamentarism, she wrote, 'is for the rising working class one of the

manner or moment in which they are conducted may be influenced by electoral preoccupations, even of a fairly distant kind. But this is not always the case, and may not be the case at all.

This having been said, it is nevertheless right to stress the constitutionalism, electoral concerns, and representative ambitions of 'reformist' Marxist parties; and also to note the very large fact that it is parties of this kind and with these characteristics which have dominated working-class movements throughout the history of the bourgeois constitutional regimes of advanced capitalism—the main alternative being social reform parties like the British Labour Party. The reasons for this predominance are central to the nature of working-class politics and highlight some of the major problems which confront Marxist parties in this kind of political system.

The basic point is that bourgeois democracy and constitutionalism generate considerable constraints for revolutionary movements and lead them towards what might be termed reciprocal constitutionalism. Working-class movements in the shape of trade unions and parties which grew up in the shadow of capitalism and gained legal recognition and political acceptance could truthfully declare that their purpose was the achievement of a socialist society; and they could also proclaim their allegiance to Marxism. But they were nevertheless part of a functioning political system and their political mode of operation had to be legal and constitutional; or rather it was so, since Marxist parties do not, in such regimes and under 'normal' circumstances, *choose* illegality, un-constitutionalism, and clandestinity.*

Legality and constitutionality do not in themselves, at least in

---

most powerful and indispensable means of carrying on the class struggle. To save bourgeois parliamentarism from the bourgeoisie and use it against the bourgeoisie is one of Social Democracy's most urgent political tasks'. However, she categorically rejected any abandonment of the extra-parliamentary class struggle: 'The real way is not to conceal and abandon the proletarian class struggle, but the very reverse: to emphasize strongly and develop this struggle both within and without parliament. This includes strengthening the extra-parliamentary action of the proletariat as well as a certain organization of the parliamentary action of our deputies' (*Rosa Luxemburg. Selected Political Writings*, R. Looker, Ed. (London, 1972), pp. 110, 113.) See also *The Mass Strike, The Political Party and the Trade Unions*, in *Rosa Luxemburg Speaks*, op. cit., p. 158.

* This needs some slight qualification for the history of Western Communist parties in the first years of their existence, for which see below.

non-revolutionary circumstances, mean an abandonment of revolutionary purposes or need not necessarily do so. After all, there are in all capitalist countries with bourgeois democratic regimes parties and groupings which claim Marxist credentials and which advocate revolutionary policies, yet which operate within the framework of bourgeois legality. With greater or lesser enthusiasm, and with occasional confrontations with the forces of law and order, they work within the system: in this respect, the difference between 'reformist' parties and their opponents on the left is a matter of emphasis and perspective rather than of fundamental and immediate choice. Much more important is the difference created between them by the electoral ambitions of 'reformist' parties, and what this entails in terms of policies, programmes, and political behaviour.

Parties with serious electoral ambitions, however genuine their ultimate intention to form and transcend capitalist structures, are inevitably tempted to try and widen their appeal by emphasizing the relative moderation of their immediate (and not so immediate) aims. It was all very well for Engels, in his 1895 Introduction to Marx's *Class Struggles in France* which I have already quoted earlier, to say that the way things were going for German Social Democracy, 'we shall conquer the greater part of the middle strata of society, petty bourgeois and small peasants', as well as the bulk of the working-class vote.[13] One thing this ignored was that such a 'conquest' might have to be bought or achieved at a substantial cost to both ideology and political programme. Engels appeared to take it for granted on the contrary that the party's programme need not be diluted in order eventually to appeal to a majority of the German voters, working class and non-working class. But this was at best a very dubious assumption, which might come to be warranted but which party leaders would themselves regard as very dubious. This being the case, they would find all but irresistible the temptation to dilute their programmes in the direction of moderation and reassurance.

Secondly, Engels's perspective also ignored the temptation to which the leaders of mass working-class parties such as the German Social Democratic Party would be exposed, namely to see themselves as the custodians of vast organizations whose effectiveness and future prospects must not be put at risk by 'extreme' policies. He had warned against the frittering away of the 'shock force' constituted by the Party in what he called 'vanguard skirmishes', and insisted that their main task was to keep the party 'intact until the decisive day'.[14] But this could easily be translated (and *was* translated) into a considerable reluctance to 'fritter away' potential electoral support by policies and attitudes which might frighten voters off—and this of course meant blunting the edges of the Party's commitments. As for the 'decisive day', it was still sufficiently far off, and blurred enough in its meaning, to constitute no embarrassing point of reference to Party leaders.

On the basis of what has been said so far, Marxist 'reformism' entails first a concern with the day-to-day defence of working-class interests and the advancement of reforms of every kind; and secondly a thorough involvement in the politics of bourgeois democracy, with the intention of achieving the greatest possible degree of electoral support, and participation in parliamentary and other representative institutions—local council, regional assemblies, and the like.

If this was all that was meant by 'reformism', the debates and feuds which it has engendered in the ranks of Marxism would not have been nearly so bitter and irreconcilable. Undoubtedly, there would still have been much to argue about, and very sharply, but more in terms of strategy and tactics in relation to specific episodes, in terms of emphasis and attitudes, than of radically different over-all positions and general strategies. Indeed, this is precisely how matters stood in the great controversies between Marxists before 1914; and one of the features of Stalinism in the intellectual and historical fields was to read later events, positions, and attitudes backward in time, and to transpose the sharpness of the divisions of a later period into a previous one, when these divisions were of a much less accented character.

Thus much had already come to separate Lenin from Kautsky and other leaders of German Social-Democracy before 1914. But Kautsky, to take him as the most obvious example of the point, had nevertheless been emphatically opposed to Bernstein's 'revisionism' at the turn of the century; and even though his opposition was not nearly as fundamental as then appeared, Kautsky remained part of a European Marxist spectrum and was indeed one of the most eminent and respected figures of European Marxism, which of course included Russian Marxism. In no way was he then in Lenin's eyes the 'renegade Kautsky' of later years. On the contrary, Lenin had in 1902 quoted Kautsky in *What is to be Done?* with much deference; and in 1905, he had rhetorically asked 'what and where did I ever claim to have created any sort of special trend in International Social-Democracy *not identical* with the trend of Bebel and Kautsky? When and where have there been brought to light differences between me, on the one hand, and Bebel and Kautsky, on the other ...?' 'The complete unanimity of international revolutionary Social-Democracy on all major questions of programme and tactics', he had himself answered, 'is a most incontrovertible fact'. Lenin rather exaggerated 'the complete unanimity' of the international revolutionary movement even then; but the denial of fundamental differences between himself and his later enemies is nevertheless worth noting.*

Leninism was not a revolutionary strategy hostile to parliamentary participation as such, either before 1914 or after. One of Lenin's most famous and influential pamphlets, *'Left-Wing' Communism—An Infantile Disorder*, written in 1920, was in part directed against what he viewed as a sectarian and ultra-left deformation among Communists in Germany and other Western countries. In effect, Lenin was attacking the obverse of what Marx had called 'parliamentary cretinism', namely anti-parliamentary cretinism, which would prevent revolutionaries from making such usage for their own purposes as bourgeois parliaments did offer. Marx's own quarrels with the anarchists in the First International had had to do among other things with the contempt that many of them had for 'ordinary' politics and their rejection of sustained and disciplined organization by revolutionaries for the purpose of involvement in such politics.

---

* V. I. Lenin, *Two Tactics* . . . , in SWL, pp. 89–90. However, Lenin sharply reproved Kautsky in the same work for the latter's rather superior attitude to the quarrels of Russian revolutionaries on the position they shold adopt in regard to an eventual provisional revolutionary government. 'Although Kautsky, for instance', Lenin wrote, 'now tries to wax ironical and says that our dispute about a provisional revolutionary government is like sharing out the meat before the bear is killed, this irony only proves that even clever and revolutionary Social-Democrats are liable to put their foot in it when they talk about something they know only about by hearsay' (ibid., p. 122). The point is sharply made, but there is none of the bitter enmity of later controversies. Nor was there reason to be—Lenin was criticising people whom he considered 'revolutionary Social-Democrats'.

Marx himself had no qualms whatever in being thus involved. Nor had Lenin.

The fundamental contraposition between 'reformism' and its alternative within Marxism, which may properly be called Leninism, concerned altogether different issues, of crucial and enduring importance.

For a start, the point needs to be made that Leninism after 1914 did become that 'sort of special trend' which Lenin, in 1905, denied having created in International Social Democracy. With the war, the collapse of the Second International and the endorsement by all of its principal constituents of the 'national interest', International Social Democracy as a more or less unified movement, or at least as one movement that could accommodate many great differences, was irreparably shattered. Lenin believed that the war had opened the era of intensified class conflict and placed proletarian revolution on the agenda; and that a new and very different organization from the previous one must bring together revolutionary parties of a very different sort from those that had dominated the Second International. In effect, what Lenin did as a result of the war was to place *insurrectionary politics* on the agenda, first for Russia, and then, with the immense prestige conferred upon him and the Bolsheviks by their conquest of power, for the international revolutionary movement.

2

'Insurrectionary politics' (the term is used here because 'revolutionary politics' is too loose) is not intended to suggest that Lenin wanted revolutionaries everywhere to prepare for immediate insurrection; and, as I have just noted, he did not believe that Communists could, even at this time, neglect politics of a different sort. It is true that he vastly exaggerated the revolutionary possibilities which existed in the aftermath of the war, and was no doubt greatly encouraged to do so by the revolutionary eruptions which had occurred in Germany, Hungary, and Austria, as well as by the very marked radical temper which had gripped large sections of the working class everywhere in 1918–20 and led to great industrial strikes and social agitation. But his misjudgements, which had very many negative consequences, nevertheless did not lead him to believe in instant revolution, made by will and proclamation. What he did believe was that the time was ripe for preparing as a matter of extreme urgency for a seizure of power which might not immediately be possible in all capitalist countries but whose appearance on the revolutionary agenda could not be long delayed in many if not most of them.

What this meant is perhaps best illustrated by extensive quotation from the famous Twenty-One Conditions of admission to the Communist International, which were adopted at the Second World Congress of the International in Moscow in July–August 1920.

The first such condition was that the daily propaganda and agitation of every party (now to be called 'Communist Party')

must bear a truly communist character and correspond to the programme and all the decisions of the Third International. All the organs of the press that are in the hands of the party must be edited by reliable communists who have proved their loyalty to the cause of the proletarian revolution. The dictatorship of the proletariat should not be spoken of simply as a current hackneyed formula; it should be advocated in such a way that its necessity should be apparent to every rank-and-file working man and woman, each soldier and peasant, and should emanate from the facts of everyday life systematically recorded by our press day after day.

The second condition required the removal from all 'responsible' posts 'in the labour movement, in the party organization, editorial boards, trade unions, parliamentary fractions, co-operative societies, municipalities, etc., all reformists and followers of the "center", and have them replaced by Communists . . .'

The third condition declared that 'the class struggle in almost all countries of Europe and America is entering the phase of civil war'. Under such conditions, it went on,

the communists can have no confidence in bourgeois law. They must everywhere create a parallel illegal apparatus, which at the decisive moment could assist the party in performing its duty to the revolution. In all countries where, in consequence of martial law or exceptional laws, the communists are unable to perform their work legally, a combination of legal and illegal work is absolutely necessary.

Subsequent conditions stipulated the duty of Communists to spread their propaganda in the countryside, to engage in unremitting struggle against reformists and 'half-reformists' everywhere, and to denounce imperialism and colonialism, this duty being particularly imperative for Communists in imperialist countries.

Condition 11 required Communist parties to

overhaul the membership of their parliamentary fractions, eliminate all unreliable elements from them, to control these fractions, not only verbally but in reality, to subordinate them to the central committee of the party, and demand from every communist member of parliament that he devote his entire activities to the interests of really revolutionary propaganda and agitation.

Condition 12 stipulated that parties belonging to the Third International 'must be built up on the principle of democratic *centralism*':

At the present time of acute civil war, the communist party will only be able fully to do its duty when it is organized in the most centralized manner, if it has iron discipline, bordering on military discipline, and if the party center is a powerful, authoritative organ, with wide powers, possessing the general trust of the party membership.

Condition 14 laid down that Communist parties 'must give every possible support to the Soviet Republics in their struggle against all counterrevolutionary forces', and that they should carry on propaganda to induce workers to refuse 'to transport munitions of war intended for enemies of the Soviet Republic'; and carry on 'legal and illegal propaganda among the troops which are sent to crush the workers' republic'.

The document made it absolutely clear that the new International would be organized on very different lines from its predecessors (and, it might be added, from the one before that—Marx's First International):

All decisions of the congresses of the Communist International [Condition 16 stated] as well as the decisions of its Executive Committee, are binding on all parties affiliated to the Communist International. The Communist International, operating in the midst of a most acute civil war, must have a far more centralized form of organisation than that of the Second International.

As for the required change of name to 'Communist Party' (Condition 17), the document declared that this was not merely a formal question, but 'a political one of great importance':

The Communist International has declared a decisive war against the entire bourgeois world and all the yellow, social democratic parties. Every rank-and-file worker must clearly understand the difference between the communist parties and the old official 'social democratic' or 'socialist' parties which have betrayed the cause of the working class.

The last of the Twenty-One Conditions perhaps best typifies the spirit of the whole document: 'Members of the party who reject the conditions and theses of the Communist International, on principle, must be expelled from the party.'[15]

In so far as the Twenty-One Conditions made any sense at all, they did so as the battle orders of an international army, organized into a number of national units under a supreme command, and being prepared for an assault that could not be long delayed on the citadels of world capitalism; and that army was therefore having its ranks cleared of those tainted and untrustworthy elements who refused to purge their past mistakes and fall in line with the strategy presented to them by the leadership of the victorious Russian Revolution.

But the tide was already ebbing by 1920. Such international army as there had been was already beginning to disband by the time the Twenty-One Conditions were issued; and some of its main units had recently been decisively defeated. The new Communist parties, far from gaining a commanding position in their respective labour movements, were finding it difficult to implant themselves solidly and seemed condemned to lead a very marginal and precarious existence in many countries and for many years to come. But the Twenty-One Conditions remained the fundamental text of the Third International throughout its history and was used to serve the inquisitorial and arbitrary purposes of its centralized leadership in Moscow: the cost that was paid for this by the international working-class movement in the next twenty years and more is incalculable.

Leninism was a political *style* adapted—or at least intended to be adapted—to a particular political *strategy*—the political strategy that I have called 'insurrectionary politics'. Stalinism, which soon after Lenin's incapacitation and death came to dominate Russia and the international Communist movement, made a frightful caricature of the style, and made of the strategy what it willed, depending on what Stalin wanted to achieve at any particular time and in any particular place. In fact, Leninism as a coherent strategy of insurrectionary politics was never seriously pursued by the Third International, which means of course that it was never seriously pursued by its constituent Communist parties.

Nor was it pursued by Communist parties in the countries of advanced capitalism after the dissolution of the Comintern in 1943. Of course, the leadership of these parties remained wholly subservient to Stalin's command after its dissolution. But it is not really plausible to attribute these parties' renunciation of insurrectionary politics—for this is in effect what occurred—to Stalin and Stalinism. The renunciation was no doubt greatly encouraged by Moscow. But the reasons for it have much deeper roots than this, as is testified by the weakness of the opposition to this renunciation, inside the Communist parties and out. If it had not corresponded to very powerful and compelling tendencies in the countries concerned, the abandonment of the strategy of insurrectionary politics would have encountered much greater resistance in revolutionary movements, notwithstanding Moscow's prestige and pressure and repression. Much more than this was here at work, which condemned left opposition to Moscow to extremely marginal significance, and which is crucially important for the understanding of the life and character of the labour movements of advanced capitalism.

The essential starting-point is not only that the revolution which the Bolsheviks so confidently expected did not occur in advanced capitalist countries at the end of the First World War and that is was never even much of a realistic prospect; but that the old leaderships which the Third International and its constituent national units wanted to supplant and destroy remained in command of a large and in most cases the largest part by far of their labour movements, industrial as well as political. It is true that these leaderships had to make certain verbal and programmatic concessions to the radical temper that had been generated by the war and its aftermath. But this really amounted to very little in practical terms.

In fact, 'reformist' leaderships, now confronted with a Bolshevik and Communist presence which they hated and feared as much as their bourgeois and conservative counterparts, became even more 'reformist' than they had been. For all practical purposes, the old parties of the now defunct Second International were, even more strongly after 1918 than before, parties of social reform—and parties of government as well. All in all, the leaderships of these parties withstood the Communist challenge with remarkable and significant success. Another way of putting this is to say that, in the sense in which the term has been used here, the politics of Leninism, insurrectionary politics, failed in the countries of advanced capitalism. What was left in these countries from the upheaval of war and revolution was, on the one hand, parties of social reform whose leaderships had absolutely no thought of revolution of any kind, and who indeed saw themselves and their parties as bulwarks against it; and, on the other hand, Communist parties formally dedicated to revolution yet pursuing at the behest of the Comintern opportunistic and wayward policies, with more or less catastrophic consequences. Nowhere was a socialist 'third force', distinct from the other two, able to achieve any substantial support. Indeed, this is putting it too strongly: it is more accurate to say that nowhere was a Marxist left, independent from both the parties of the old Second International and of those of the new Third International able to play more than a very marginal role in the life of their labour movements. The point is particularly relevant and significant in relation to the Trotskyist opposition which, from the second half of the twenties onwards, could plausibly lay claim to being the heir of Leninist insurrectionary politics. Trotskyism had an illustrious leader and small groups of dedicated and talented adherents in many capitalist countries. But these groups remained utterly isolated from their working-class movements and were never able to mount a serious challenge to their respective Communist parties.

Many different reasons have been advanced from within Marxism to account for the disappointments and defeats which soon came to mock the high hopes of 1917 and after. These reasons have to do with the unexpected capacity of capitalism to take the strain of economic dislocation and slump; the equally unexpected capacity of conservative forces to defend their regimes by ideological manipulation and, when necessary, by physical repression, with Fascism and Nazism as the most extreme forms of that defence; and also the capacity of capitalism to respond to crisis and pressure with cautious and piecemeal reforms dressed up in a rhetoric of wholesale renewal—for instance the New Deal in the United States. And Marxists also pointed to the role of social democratic leaders as, in effect, the defenders of capitalism and the agents of social stabilization—although Communists ceased to make as much of this in the thirties, when the Comintern adopted the Popular Front strategy, as they had done earlier.

Any such list of explanations why Leninist politics failed to make more headway—for this is the question—needs however to include one other factor of the greatest importance: this is the extremely strong attraction which legality, constitutionalism, electoralism, and representative institutions of the parliamentary type have had for the overwhelming majority of people in the working-class movements of capitalist societies.

Lenin himself, as it happens, was very concerned to stress the importance of this in his polemic against left Communists in 1920. 'In Western Europe and America', he wrote, 'parliament has become most odious to the revolutionary vanguard of the working class'. But this, he went on to warn, was not true of the mass of the population of capitalist countries: '. . . in Western Europe', he also wrote, 'the backward masses of the workers and —to an even greater degree—of the small peasants are much more imbued with bourgeois-democratic and parliamentary prejudices than they were in Russia . . .'[16]

Even this, however, grossly underestimated the extent and tenacity of what Lenin called 'bourgeois-democratic and parliamentary prejudices'; which is no doubt why he was led to make such absurd pronouncements as that 'in *all* civilised and advanced countries . . . civil war between the proletariat and the bourgeoisie is maturing and is imminent.'[17]

Marxism and revolutionary politics had to adapt—or at least did adapt—to the fact that Lenin was absolutely wrong. One form which that adaptation took was a new stress on 'socialism in one country', which soon became part of Stalinist dogmatics. In a wider perspective, Marxist politics continued to have not only one meaning but two. This perpetuated the situation which had existed when Leninism as insurrectionary politics had affirmed itself as an alternative strategy to the 'reformism' of the Second International: but it was now the Third International and its Communist parties which adopted the 'reformist' strategy.

What occurred in the early thirties, after the Comintern's catastrophic 'Third Period' and with the adoption of the Popular Front policies, was the barely acknowledged and theoretically still unformulated abandonment by international Communism of insurrectionary politics. This, as I have argued earlier in discussing the meaning of 'reformism', did not involve the abandonment of a programme of wholesale transformation of capitalism, of class struggle on different fronts, of the possibility that conservative violence would have to be met with violence, and least of all the abandonment of unconditional support for the Soviet Union. In fact, this unconditional support gave to Communist parties a stamp of particularity which helped to further the impression that they remained committed to insurrectionary politics long after this had ceased to be the case.* Nor did Communist 'reformism' require the formal and explicit abandonment by Communist parties of their doctrinal commitment to Marxism, or for that matter to Marxism-Leninism.†

But it did involve a progressively more definite acceptance of constitutionalism and electoralism as a possible and desirable 'road to socialism' for Communist parties, and the rejection of any notion of a 'seizure of power', at least in circumstances where legality and constitutionalism were so to speak available, or had come to be available—and even in many cases where it was not.

This strategy was developed and formulated over a fairly protracted period of time. It was not pursued with full explicitness in its earlier stages and there were cases where Stalin decided that it should not be pursued at all—thus in Eastern Europe, but under obviously exceptional conditions. In the liberated countries of Western Europe at the end of the Second World War, and already in Italy in 1943, it was pursued very faithfully.‡ The French and Italian Communist leaderships, which then acted only with the accord of the Russian leaders, opted decisively and overwhelmingly for constitutionalism and electoralism. They entered coalition governments in an essentially subsidiary capacity so far as actual policy-making was concerned, but played a critical role in the stabilization of their capitalist regimes at a time of great crisis for these regimes.

Whether a different strategy, of a more 'revolutionary' kind, would then have been realistic and capable of yielding better

---

* This unconditional support of the Soviet Union even thrust some Communist parties into illegality at certain times, for instance the French Communist Party which came under proscription at the beginning of the Second World War for its active opposition to the war.

† Thus it is only in 1976 that the French Communist Party explicitly abandoned the concept of the dictatorship of the proletariat, which it had in fact long abandoned implicitly. For the meaning and significance of this abandonment, see below.

‡ In a very different situation and for different reasons, the strategy had already been applied by the Spanish Communist Party in the Spanish Civil War, under Russian direction.

results has long been argued over and cannot obviously be settled conclusively. More important is the fact that the strategy that was then pursued, and which was the logical continuation of a process which the war had only partially suspended, was continued and further developed in the following years, notwithstanding all rebuffs, vicissitudes, and disappointments.*
The French Communist Party was suddenly offered the opportunity to move in the direction of insurrectionary politics in May 1968 and rejected it with little if any hesitation. Here too, there has been endless argument as to whether a chance of revolution was then missed. But whichever view may be taken of this, there is at least no question that the P.C.F. very firmly acted on the conviction that any resort to insurrectionary politics would have been an utterly irresponsible form of 'ultra-left' adventurism which would have been crushed and would have set the working-class movement back for decades.

The spelling out of this 'reformist' strategy gathered quickening pace in the following years, particularly in Italy and then France, and is now thoroughly articulated: advance by way of electoral gains at all levels and notably at the national level; alliance with other left-wing or radically-inclined parties (though not usually with the 'ultra-left' parties and groupings) for the purpose of obtaining an electoral and parliamentary —and where appropriate a presidential—majority; the formation of a coalition left-wing government in which the Communists must play an important and possibly predominant role; and the accomplishment of a vast programme of social and economic reforms designed to begin the structural transformation of capitalist society and the eventual achievement of a socialist society. In the course of this process—and what is involved is a process, which is seen as stretching over a number of years and more—a plurality of parties would be maintained, and this would include anti-socialist parties; civic freedoms—of speech, association, movement, etc.— would not only be preserved but enhanced; representative institutions would not only continue to function but would be reformed so that they might function more democratically and responsively; and the executive power, owing its legitimacy to universal suffrage, would

* The first Communist Party to give explicit articulation to this 'road to socialism' was the British, whose programme, The British Road to Socialism, was first published in 1951, with the full approval of Stalin.

only seek to retain it on the same basis, by way of free and unfettered elections.

Another and major ingredient of this strategy concerns foreign policy, and particularly relations with the U.S.S.R. The stress has been increasingly on complete national independence and freedom from any kind of subservience to Soviet Communism. At most, Western Communist parties envisage that a government of which they were part, and even one of which they were the major part, would have no more than a friendly relation with the Soviet Union—but not to the detriment of friendly relations with other countries or even to the detriment of existing alliances such as NATO. A government in which Communists were involved might seek to end the system of alliances created at the time of the Cold War—NATO and the Warsaw Pact. But this is a very different matter from seeking a unilateral withdrawal from NATO. Whatever else 'proletarian internationalism' may mean for these Communist parties nowadays, it means neither automatic support for the Soviet Union's external policies, nor abstention from criticism of its internal policies, notably for its derelictions in the realm of civic and democratic freedoms.

The fact that Communist parties in capitalist countries, with varying qualifications that do not affect the main drift, should have come to adopt so definite a 'reformist' strategy is obviously a matter of vast importance in general political terms as well as being important in relation to Marxist political theory; and this must be examined further.

In essence, two main questions are raised by the 'reformist' strategy; the first, and by now the less important one, is whether the achievement of executive power by electoral means is possible. The second, which is of a different order altogether, is what happens when such power has been achieved by Communists, or by Communists in a left coalition. Clearly, these are central questions in modern Marxist politics.

3

It was at one time fairly common for Marxists to argue that, if it ever looked as if a left-wing party or parties pledged to radical anti-capitalist policies might win an electoral majority, the ruling class would not allow this to happen. Something like a pre-emptive 'strike', it was argued, would be launched, most probably from within the state system and by way of a military coup. The elections would not be held; and the constitutional regime which had brought about the electoral threat would be abrogated in favour of one form or other of right-wing dictatorship.

It was very reasonable for Marxists to treat this as one possibility, and not only in cases where universal suffrage appeared to pose a threat of fundamental change: the same might also happen where elections threatened to produce a government pledged to carry out reforms which, though not actually subversive of the existing social order, were judged dangerous by people in power. After all, this is precisely what happened in Greece in 1967, when the Colonels took over in anticipation of a general election which the Right feared it would lose and which would then have brought to power a mildly reforming government. The propensity of the Right to try and mount pre-emptive 'strikes' of this kind must vary from one country to another, and depend on many different factors: but it is reasonable (and prudent) to see it always and anywhere as one possibility—and the greater the danger, from the point of view of the Right, the greater the possibility.

It is clearly *not* reasonable, on the other hand, to treat the possibility as a certainty. For there are many circumstances which may well and in some cases almost certainly will render a pre-emptive *coup* impossible, or turn it into a gamble too desperate to be actively considered by serious people. Particularly in countries with strong electoral traditions, and with well-implanted labour movements, the chances are that, in more or less normal conditions, 'dangerous' elections *will* be held, and may bring to office left-wing governments in which Communists would have a substantial representation and possibly a preponderant one, and whose announced intention was to bring about the fundamental transformation of capitalist society.

It is at this point, however, that there occurs a crucial theoretical split in Marxism between 'reformism' on the one hand and its Leninist alternative on the other. The question at issue is the 'dictatorship of the proletariat' and its *institutional* meaning.

In the last chapter, I stressed the importance which Marx (and Engels) had attached to the notion that 'the working class cannot simply lay hold of the ready-made state machinery, and wield it for its own purposes'; and I also noted the reaffirmation by Lenin of the meaning of that notion after its neglect by the Second International, in terms of the 'smashing' of the existing state power and its replacement by 'other institutions of a fundamentally different type'.[18]

In *The State and Revolution*, Lenin appeared to mean by this phrase popular power expressed directly or through the Soviets or Workers' and Soldiers' Deputies. Another and more specific example of this search for new institutional forms was provided by Rosa Luxemburg in the draft programme which she wrote for the new German Communist Party and which appeared as an article in *Die Rote Fahne* on 14 December 1918, under the title 'What Does the Spartacus Union Want?'

The main feature of the socialist society is to be found in the fact that the great mass of the workers will cease to be a governed mass, but, on the contrary, will itself live the full political and economic life and direct that life in conscious and free self-determination.

Therefore, she went on,

the proletarian mass must substitute its own class organs—the workers' and soldiers' councils—for the inherited organs of capitalist class rule—the federal councils, municipal councils, parliaments—applying this principle from the highest authority in the state to the smallest community. The proletarian mass must fill all governmental positions, must control all functions, must test all requirements of the state on the touchstone of socialist aims and the interests of its own class;[19]

and the programme also specified that workers' councils would be elected all over Germany, as well as soldiers' councils, and that these would in turn elect delegates to the Central Council of the workers' and soldiers' councils; and the Central Council would elect the Executive Council as the highest organ of legislative and executive power.[20]

The economic and social points of this programme were of an equally far-reaching nature;* and the split between 'reformism' and what I have called its Leninist alternative undoubtedly

---

* Thus the programme of economic demands included the expropriation of the land held by all large and medium-sized agricultural concerns and the 'establishment of socialist agricultural cooperatives under a uniform central administration all over the country'; the nationalization by the Republic of Councils of all banks, ore mines, coal mines, as well as all large industrial and commercial establishments; the confiscation of all property exceeding a certain limit; the take over of all public means of transport and communication; the election of administrative councils in all enterprises, 'to regulate the internal affairs of the enterprises in agreement with the workers' councils'; etc.

includes very considerable differences in the scale and extent of the immediate economic and social transformations which each strategy tends to propose. But the crucial theoretical difference consists in the acceptance on the one hand of the notion that the existing bourgeois state must be 'smashed' and replaced by an altogether different type of state embodying and expressing the 'dictatorship of the proletariat'; and on the other hand, the more or less explicit rejection of any such notion.

It might seem as if the difference stemmed from a perspective of peaceful and constitutional transition as opposed to a violent one, the first type occurring on the basis of a left-wing victory at the polls and the second on the basis of a seizure of power made possible by a regime's defeat in war, or extreme economic crisis and dislocation, or political breakdown, or some combination of any of these possibilities. But this is not in fact where the opposition necessarily lies: a constitutional accession to power might be followed by a wholesale recasting of state institutions; and a seizure of power need not involve such a recasting at all. Indeed, in so far as the intention is to extend popular power, a peaceful transition might be more favourable to such a project than a violent one. [21]

But in any case, the essential theoretical difference is between a project which envisages the carrying through of a socialist transformation by way of the main political institutions—notably parliament—inherited from bourgeois democracy, even though these might be to a greater or lesser extent reformed in more democratic directions; and a project which envisages the total transformation of the existing *political* institutions (i.e. the 'smashing' of the state) as an integral and essential part of a socialist revolution. The classical Marxist text for this contraposition is Lenin's *The Proletarian Revolution and the Renegade Kautsky*, which he wrote in 1918 in reply to Kautsky's *The Dictatorship of the Proletariat* (itself a critique of Lenin's *The State and Revolution*).

These two 'scenarios' or 'models'—'reformism' on the one hand and its Leninist alternative on the other—have constituted the two poles of a debate which has been at the centre of Marxist politics for the best part of this century; and the 'reformist' strategy to which Communist parties now firmly subscribe ensures that this debate will be sustained for a long while yet, given the bitter opposition which that strategy evokes from various other tendencies of the Marxist left. It may well be, however, that the terms of the contraposition are mistaken, in so far as neither 'model' represents realistic perspectives and projections. I believe, on a number of different grounds, that this is indeed the case: whatever the real differences between the two strategies, they cannot be as stated, because the stated positions do not correspond to any possible situation that may be envisaged.

To begin with the Leninist strategy, it is by now clear (or should be) that the 'smashing' of the existing bourgeois state does not open the way for the achievement of the 'dictatorship of the proletariat'. A revolutionary situation produced by successful insurrectionary politics as a result of which the existing state is 'smashed' requires, if the revolution is to succeed and be defended and consolidated, a new articulation of power of a kind which cannot be provided by the 'dictatorship of the proletariat'—at least not in the meaning which Marx may be taken to have given to it, or which Lenin gave to it in The State and Revolution and even in The Proletarian Revolution and the Renegade Kautsky.

In that meaning, it is always popular power which is stressed, and it is its exercise by the proletariat and its allies which is glorified. That power is exercised almost directly, and only mediated by representative institutions strictly subordinated to the people. In The State and Revolution, Lenin thus writes that the state, under these conditions, is transformed 'into something which is no longer the state proper'.[22] It is necessary to suppress the bourgeoisie and crush their resistance: 'the organ of suppression, however, is here the majority of the population, and not a minority, as was always the case under slavery, serfdom and wage slavery.[23]He then goes on:

and since the majority of the people itself suppresses its oppressors, a 'special force' for suppression is no longer necessary! In this sense, the state begins to wither away. Instead of the special institutions of a privileged minority (privileged officialdom, the chiefs of the standing army), the majority itself can directly fulfil all these functions, and the more the functions of state power are performed by the people as a whole, the less need there is for the existence of this power.[24]

True, Lenin says, 'we are not utopians, we do not "dream" of dispensing at once with all administration, with all subordination.' But this subordination 'must be to the armed vanguard of all the exploited and working people, i.e. to the proletariat'.[25]

A similar trend of thought is evident in *The Proletarian Revolution and the Renegade Kautsky*. Thus, 'the revolutionary dictatorship of the proletariat is rule won and maintained by the use of violence by the proletariat against the bourgeoisie, rule that is unrestricted by any laws';[26] and Lenin insists that 'proletarian democracy is *a million times* more democratic than any bourgeois democracy' and 'Soviet power is a million times more democratic than the most democratic bourgeois republic' because it was based on the Soviets: 'The Soviets are the direct organisation of the working and exploited people themselves, which *helps* them to organise and administer their own state in every possible way.'[27]

There is, however, an important difference between the first pamphlet and the second. By the time Lenin wrote the second one, he was leading a state that had *not* been transformed 'into something which is no longer the state proper', and would not be, and could not be.

In its proper Marxist meaning, the notion of the 'dictatorship of the proletariat' disposes much too easily, and therefore does not dispose at all, of the inevitable tension that exists between the requirement of *direction* on the one hand, and of *democracy* on the other, particularly in a revolutionary situation. As I noted in the last chapter, Lenin met the problem by affirming that the dictatorship of the party (and therefore of the state which the party controlled) *was* the dictatorship of the proletariat. But it did not take him long to realize that he had only redefined the term rather than fulfilled its original promise. In fact, it is scarcely too much to say that a time of revolution of the Leninist kind is precisely when the 'dictatorship of the proletariat' is least possible—because such a time requires the re-creation of a new and strong state, a 'state proper', on the ruins of the state which the revolution has 'smashed'. But this is not the 'dictatorship of the proletariat' of Marx, and of Lenin in *The State and Revolution*.

Nor can it be contended that the pyramid of councils, of the kind which Rosa Luxemburg projected in 1918, resolves the question of direction and democracy. For the structure which she proposed was, very reasonably, to be capped by an Executive Council 'as the highest organ of legislative and executive power';[28] and it is clear that, whatever her intentions, this organ would have been, and would have had to be, an extremely strong *state*, possibly representing the 'dictatorship of the proletariat', but not amounting to it.

Where power has been seized, revolutionaries have to create a strong state in place of the old if their revolution is to survive and begin to redeem its promise and purpose. This is bound to be an arduous task, particularly because the material circumstances in which it has to be undertaken are likely to be unfavourable and further aggravated by the hostility and opposition of the new regime's internal and external enemies. Inevitably some of its own supporters, and possibly many, will falter and turn away when the exaltation of the first phase wears off as it confronts the mundane and difficult requirements of the second.* The new regime may retain a very wide measure of popular support and find it possible to rely on continued popular involvement. It will most probably go under quite soon if it cannot. But the tension remains between state direction and popular power; and that tension cannot be resolved by invocations and slogans. Gramsci said in 1919 that

The formula 'dictatorship of the proletariat' must cease to be a formula, an occasion to parade revolutionary rhetoric. He who wills the end, must will the means. The dictatorship of the proletariat is the installation of a new State, typically proletarian, into which flow the institutional experiences of the oppressed class, in which the social life of the worker and peasant class becomes a system, universal and strongly organised.[29]

This at least acknowledges the central place which a 'state proper' must play in the new system. But in so doing, it only proposes an agenda, not a blueprint.

* Gramsci put the point about these requirements rather well: 'What is needed for the revolution', he wrote, 'are men of sober mind, men who don't cause an absence of bread in the bakeries, who make trains run, who provide the factories with raw materials and know how to turn the produce of the country into industrial produce, who ensure the safety and freedom of the people against the attacks of criminals, who enable the network of collective services to function and who do not reduce the people to despair and to a horrible carnage. Verbal enthusiasm and reckless phraseology make one laugh (or cry) when a single one of these problems has to be resolved even in a village of a hundred inhabitants' (A. Gramsci, *Ordine Nuovo, 1919–1920* (Turin, 1953), pp. 377–8) in N. Badaloni, 'Gramsci et le Problème de la Révolution' in *Dialectiques*, nos. 4–5, March 1974, p. 136. The quotation is from an article written in June 1919.

The 'reformist' strategy which is counterposed to Leninism and the 'dictatorship of the proletariat' by Communist parties (though this is not of course how they themselves put it), raises a different series of questions.

Let it be assumed that a coalition of left-wing parties, in which the Communist Party has an important or preponderant place, wins a general election on a programme of pronounced anti-capitalist policies, and 'is allowed' to come to office. What happens then?

Left critics of the 'reformist' strategy have usually argued that the answer to this was—not much. In other words, 'reformist' leaders would not seek to implement the programme on which they had been elected. No doubt there would be a good many changes in the personnel of the existing state system—not least because an hitherto excluded political army would expect to be provided with rewards, at all levels of the administrative apparatus. Some institutional and administrative reforms might be attempted. Some social reforms would be proposed and possibly implemented; and even some measures of state ownership would be introduced. But this is as much as could be expected from leaders, so the argument goes, who are by now well integrated in their bourgeois political systems, and who would act as agents of stabilization of the existing social order rather than as architects of a new one. In their role as agents of stabilization, it is further said, they would need (and would be willing) to contain and repress the militancy of the working class, which their coming to power would itself have enhanced. Thus the self-proclaimed Party of Revolution would turn into the shamefaced Party of Order—and perhaps not so shamefaced at that; and in due course, it would be thrust out of office, with the old order more or less intact.

This is a very possible 'scenario'. It might need amendment here and there; but it is certainly not unreasonable to think that some such outcome could be produced by the coming to office of a left-wing government with Communist participation. After all, Communist participation in governments in Italy and France and other countries at the end of the war and immediately after did produce precisely such an outcome. Admittedly, the governments in question were not left-wing ones but bourgeois coalitions in which the Communists accepted a subsidiary role. But while circumstances would now be different, the intervening years have also witnessed a certain 'social-democratization' of Communist parties, which is likely to be enhanced by the pressures of office, and which is unlikely to be compensated for by pressures from the left inside and outside these parties. This makes it not at all absurd for intelligent conservatives (as well as critics on the left) to believe that a left-wing government with substantial Communist participation—or even Communist-led—might not represent nearly so great a threat to capitalism and the existing social order as less intelligent conservatives believe; and that it might even turn out to be a necessary price to pay for the *maintenance* of the system.

But let it be supposed, on the other hand, that a left-wing and Communist-led government, backed by an electoral and par-liamentary majority, did decide to carry through far-reaching anti-capitalist measures, including fairly drastic measures of nationalization, imperative economic co-ordination and plan-ning, major advances in labour legislation, social welfare, edu-cation, housing, transport and the environment, all favouring the 'lower income groups' and with fiscal policies directed against the rich. This is presumably what should be expected from a government whose purpose was claimed to be the radical transformation of capitalist society in socialist directions. It might not be able to do everything at once; but it would at least be expected to make a convincing beginning. What then?

Perhaps the first thing to note about *this* 'scenario' is that there are very few precedents indeed for it. In fact, the only precedent which comes reasonably close to it is that of Salvador Allende in Chile. This is not of course to say that what happened in Chile under Allende is conclusive, though it is significant.[30] It is rather to point to the fact that, for all the controversies which have surrounded 'reformism', its strategy has hardly ever been put to the test: such 'reformist' governments as there have been have taken the first of the two options, and done nothing much—or even nothing at all—to cause concern to the powers-that-be.

The next thing to be said about the attempt to carry through the kind of measures listed above is surely that it would be bound to arouse the fiercest enmity from conservative forces defeated at the polls but obviously very far from having lost all their formidable class power.

This class power endures both inside the state system and in society at large. Of course, it must be assumed, as part of the 'scenario', and as partially demonstrated by the electoral victory of the forces of the left, that these forces of the left have deeply permeated society, that they are well implanted in most spheres of life, and that they have many friends in the state system. But to take the latter first, it is obviously realistic to expect that by far the larger part of the state personnel at the higher levels, and at least a very large number in the lower ones as well, are much more likely to be ideologically, politically, and emotionally on the side of the conservative forces than of the government. In many cases, they will only be suspicious and hesitant. But in many others, they will be firmly opposed to programmes and policies which they believe to be utterly detrimental to the 'national interest'. Many civil servants throughout the bureaucracy, many regional and local administrators and officials, and most members of the judiciary at all levels, together with the police and the officer class in general, may—and indeed must in prudence—be taken to be in varying degrees opposed to the government. The commitment need not be thought to be irrevocable: but it must be assumed to exist at the start.

No doubt new people, attuned to the government's purposes, will be brought in; and new administrative organs, staffed by such people, may be set up. But it is just as well not to underestimate the degree of administrative dislocation and even chaos that may be involved in the process, and which people of conservative disposition in the state system have no reason to try and remedy—rather the reverse. This means that a battle—in fact the class struggle—will *also* be waged inside the state system at all levels; and it would, incidentally, have to be waged, even if the state had previously been 'smashed'. But how that battle goes depends to a large extent on what happens *outside* the state system as well as *inside* it. Those involved on the conservative side will be deeply influenced in their thinking and behaviour by the manner in which the forces of the left, beginning with the government, are waging the struggle—by their determination, intelligence, and good sense; but also, and crucially, by their capacity and will to rely on popular support and initiative, of which more in a moment.

The class power of the conservative forces in capitalist society at large assumes many different forms—the control of strategic means of industrial, commercial, and financial activity, and of vast resources; the control of most of the press, and many other means of political communication and of ideology in general; large, well-implanted political parties, associations, pressure groups and organizations of every sort, many of which pride themselves on their entirely 'non-political' character, meaning that they are conservative without being affiliated to any particular party; and to a greater or lesser degree, depending on the particular country but nowhere negligible, the churches and their satellite organizations.

Nor is it only a matter of organized, collective power: it is also one of influence and activity on the part of individuals, each making a contribution in his and her own sphere to the strengthening of the conservative forces and the advancement of conservative purposes. It must be reckoned that large numbers of men and women belonging to the middle and upper classes, and occupying positions of relative influence and responsibility in their communities, will be willing to help, in whatever way they can, in the task of saving the country, defending freedom, national independence, their children's future, or whatever.

It may be assumed that a process of acute polarization will have occurred in the weeks and months preceding the accession of the new government to office, and notably during the electoral campaign. But the struggle enters an entirely new phase once the government is in office. There may be a short respite, because of the sense of disappointment and demoralization which besets the defeated side. But this will not last long, and the conservative forces will soon be reorganizing themselves for a task which appears every day more pressing, namely the destabilization of a hated government, and its ultimate undoing. In this task, they will have the precious assistance of powerful capitalist governments and international capitalist interests. As I have noted in a previous chapter, this dimension of the class struggle is of quite vital importance. Indeed, so much is this the case that any socialist 'experiment' of the kind envisaged here would undoubtedly depend very greatly on international solidarity and support, capable of neutralizing or at least of attenuating the impact of the efforts at destabilization that would be undertaken by internal and external conservative forces. Much of the responsibility for countering these latter forces would depend on working-class movements in advanced capitalist countries. In many instances, this would involve a difficult struggle against social-democratic leaders who must, on any realistic view, be reckoned as forming part, and a very important part, of the conservative forces of advanced capitalist countries. The notion that a strongly reforming government in one such European country would mainly face the opposition of the United States is now seriously out of date: there are other countries—Germany and Britain, for instance—with social-democratic governments at their head which could be expected to help in trying to bring the offending government to heel. The responsibility of the left in the countries concerned would clearly be to make their task more difficult, and preferably to make it impossible.

Every reforming step that the government takes will reinforce the determination of its opponents to see it defeated. The opposition will naturally use all the constitutional devices and institutional opportunities which are available to it, for instance in parliament. But this is only one aspect of the struggle and by no means the most significant.

Reference has already been made to the struggle which will be waged in the state system; and what happens here may well be of the greatest importance. There is much that a sullen and hostile bureaucracy can do to impede and discredit a radical and reforming government.

But the struggle will also be waged in every part of civil society—in factories and power stations, dockyards and warehouses, shops and offices, barracks, schools and universities; as well as the press, radio, and television; and also the streets. It will assume an infinite variety of forms, because all forms of social life become 'politicized' in circumstances of great social stress and crisis; or to put it more accurately, their 'political' character, instead of being as hitherto blurred by the general acceptance of prevailing ideas and values, becomes visible and obtrusive by virtue of general contestation, and that 'political' character is further sharpened and extended thereby.

It must be taken, by definition, that a 'reformist' government will try to keep this intensified class struggle within more or less constitutional bounds, and will hope to prevent it from spilling over into class war. It must expect some Fascist-type groups to engage in sporadic acts of violence; but it will hope that this can be confined and contained, and that the conservative forces in general will not encourage, support, let alone initiate and foment, unconstitutional action designed to overthrow the government or in one way or another get rid of it.

But what the conservative forces in general decide to do or not to do must depend in a substantial degree on the government's own attitudes and actions. The fact that it has reached office by way of an electoral victory and that it has constitutional legitimacy on its side gives it a psychological and political advantage which it would be absurd to under-estimate. But it would be equally absurd for such a government to expect that this will necessarily keep its opponents on the path of constitutional rectitude. Some elements among them, and possibly many, who had up to then been constitutionally-minded—since occasion had not arisen for them to be otherwise—will come to find it increasingly difficult if not impossible to keep on that constitutional path, and will persuade themselves that their patriotic duty requires them to stray from it and to encourage others to stray from it.

But the question is not simply one of constitutionalism and legality on the one hand and unconstitutionality, violence, military coups, and civil war on the other. What is involved, at least in the earlier stages and possibly over a prolonged period, is not outright violence and its encouragement, but economic, administrative, and professional forms of disruption and dislocation, which may not be illegal at all and which are certainly not violent. What the government here faces is the pursuit by the conservative forces, with all the means at their command, of many different forms of class struggle, this being sufficiently militant in its intention, character, and consequence to warrant its designation as class war rather than class struggle, yet falling well short of outright resort to arms and civil war.

In this situation, how the government responds is crucial. But it is also the sort of situation which a 'reformist' strategy finds it most difficult to handle. 'Reformist' leaderships know perfectly well that Marx was right when he said that universal suffrage may give one the right to govern but does not give one the power to govern. However, there is a great difference between knowing this and knowing *how* to act upon the knowledge and being *willing* to act upon it.

The government will be strongly pressed to 'be reasonable', to seek compromise and conciliation, to put its more 'extreme' proposals into cold storage until a 'more favourable' time, to consolidate and pause; and there will be those in its midst who will be very tempted to yield to such advice, and who will readily find an apt quotation from Lenin's 'Left-Wing' Communism—An Infantile Disorder to back up their advocacy of compromise, or an apt precedent from Bolshevik history to the same effect.

Nor is it necessarily the case that such advocacy is always mistaken—though the chances are that if it is accepted as a general strategy, it will only be interpreted by the conservative forces as a sign of weakness and indecision, and encourage them to press on with even greater determination their endeavours to destabilize the government; while the government's supporters will be discouraged and demoralized, confused and divided; and the large mass of waverers will be rendered more receptive to the appeals of the opposition.

If however the government does decide to push forward with its programme, it must also as a sine qua non strengthen itself in order to make advance—and survival—possible. Advance and defence are in this instance one and the same thing.

In effect, the government has only one major resource, namely its popular support. But this support, expressed at the polls, has to be sustained through extremely difficult times, and it has to be mobilized. The parties supporting the government will no doubt do this, or try to do it, in regard to their own members; and other working-class organizations, such as trade unions, will play a part. What is required, however, is something very much larger than can be provided by such organizations, namely a flexible and complex network of organs of popular participation operating throughout civil society and intended not to replace the state but to complement it. This is an adaptation of the concept of 'dual power', in that the organs of popular participation do not challenge the government but act as a defensive-offensive and generally supportive element in what is a semi-revolutionary and exceedingly fraught state of affairs.

In this perspective, a 'reformist' strategy, if it is taken seriously and pursued to its necessary conclusion, must lead to a vast extension of democratic participation in all areas of civic life—amounting to a very considerable transformation of the character of the state and of existing bourgeois democratic forms. If this be so, it turns out that the 'reformist' strategy ultimately involves the acknowledgement of the truth of the proposition of Marx and Engels that 'the working class cannot simply lay hold of the ready-made state machinery, and wield it for its own purpose.'

The truth of that proposition does not, however, confer validity on the proposition which Marx and Engels and Lenin linked with it, namely that the existing state must be 'smashed' *in order* to replace it by the 'dictatorship of the proletariat'. As I have suggested earlier, the link that they established between the 'smashing' of the existing state and what they conceived to be the 'dictatorship of the proletariat' *is an illusory one*. What follows the 'smashing' of the existing state is the coming into being of another 'state proper', simply because a 'state proper' is an absolutely imperative necessity in organizing the process of transition from a capitalist society to a socialist one.

That process of transition both *includes* and *requires* radical changes in the structures, modes of operation, and personnel of the existing state, *as well* as the creation of a network of organs of popular participation amounting to 'dual power'. The 'reformist' strategy, at least in this 'strong' version of it, may produce a combination of direction and democracy sufficiently effective to keep the conservative forces in check *and* to provide the conditions under which the process of transition may proceed.

There are many regimes in which no such possibility exists at all; and where radical social change must ultimately depend on the force of arms. Bourgeois democratic regimes, on the other hand, may conceivably offer this possibility, by way of a strategy which eschews resort to the suppression of all opposition and the stifling of all civic freedoms. Such a strategy is full of uncertainties and pitfalls, of dangers and dilemmas; and it may in the end turn out to be unworkable. But it is just as well to have a sober appreciation of the nature of the alternative and not to allow slogans to take over. Regimes which do, either by necessity or by choice, depend on the suppression of all opposition and the stifling of all civic freedoms must be taken to represent a disastrous regression, in political terms, from bourgeois democracy, whatever the economic and social achievements of which they may be capable. Bourgeois democracy is crippled by its class limitations, and under constant threat of further and drastic impairment by conservative forces, never more so than in an epoch of permanent and severe crisis. But the civic freedoms which, however inadequately and precariously, form part of bourgeois democracy are the product of centuries of unremitting popular struggles. The task of Marxist politics is to defend these freedoms; and to make possible their extension and enlargement by the removal of their class boundaries.

NOTES

1 SW 1968, p. 436.
2 Revs., p. 93.
3 Ibid., pp. 92–3.
4 See e.g. H. Collins and C. Abramsky, *Karl Marx and the British Labour Movement* (London, 1965).
5 K. Marx and F. Engels, 'Address of the Central Committee to the Communist League', in SW 1950, I, p. 101.
6 See e.g. K. Marx and F. Engels, *On Britain* (Moscow, 1953), *passim.*
7 See e.g. Collins and Abramsky, op. cit.
8 SE, p. 123.
9 *Address . . .* in SW 1950, I, p. 102.
10 *Two Tactics . . .* in SWL, p. 78.
11 Ibid., p. 82.
12 Ibid., p. 82.
13 SW 1950, I, p. 124; p. 665, in SW 1968.
14 Ibid.
15 H. Gruber, *International Communism in the Era of Lenin*, pp. 241–6 for the full text.
16 *'Left-Wing' Communism—An Infantile Disorder*, in SWL, pp. 549, 551.
17 Ibid., p. 548.
18 See above, pp. 138 ff.
19 H. Gruber, op. cit., p. 106.
20 Ibid., p. 111.
21 See below, pp. 188–9.
22 V. I. Lenin, *The State and Revolution*, in SWL, p. 293.
23 Ibid., p. 293.
24 Ibid., p. 293.
25 Ibid., p. 298.
26 V. I. Lenin, *The Proletarian Revolution and the Renegade Kautsky*, in CWL, vol. 28 (1965), p. 236.
27 Ibid., pp. 246–7.
28 Gruber, op. cit., p. 111.
29 *L'Ordine Nuovo*, 21 June 1919, in *New Edinburgh Review. Gramsci. II*, p. 54.
30 See R. Miliband, 'The Coup in Chile', *The Socialist Register 1973* (London, 1973). I use some of the ideas and concepts put forward in that article in what follows here.

Bibliography

ALTHUSSER, L., *For Marx*, London, 1970.
—— *Lenin and Philosophy and Other Essays*, London, 1971.
ANDERSON, P., *Passages from Antiquity to Feudalism*, London, 1975.
—— *Lineages of the Absolutist State*, London, 1975.
ANWEILER, O., *Les Soviets en Russie 1905–1921*, Paris, 1972.
ARRIGHI, G. and SAUL, J. S., *Essays on the Political Economy of Africa*, New York, 1973.
AVINERI, S., *The Social and Political Thought of Karl Marx*, London, 1968.
—— Ed., *K. Marx on Colonialism and Modernisation*, New York, 1968.
BLACKBURN, R., Ed., *Ideology in Social Science*, London, 1972.
BLOOM, S. F., *The World of Nations*, 2nd ed., New York, 1961.
BOTTOMORE, T., Ed., *Karl Marx*, New York, 1971.
BRUS, W., *Socialist Ownership and Political Systems*, London, 1975.
BUKHARIN, N., *Historical Materialism*, Ann Arbor, 1969.
Bulletin of the Conference of Socialist Economists, London, 1971–.
CARR, E. H., *The Bolshevik Revolution 1917–1923*, London, 1966.
—— *The Interregnum 1923–24*, London, 1969.
—— *Socialism in One Country 1924–26*, London, 1970–73.
CARRÈRE D'ENCAUSSE, H., and SCHRAM, S. R., Eds., *Marxism and Asia*, London, 1969.
CHANG, S. H. M., *The Marxian Theory of the State*, New York, 1965.
CHATELET, F., PISIER-KOUCHNER, E. and VINCENT, J.-M., Eds., *Les Marxistes et la politique*, Paris, 1975.
CENTRE D'ÉTUDES ET DE RECHERCHES MARXISTES, *Sur le 'Mode de Production Asiatique'*, Paris, 1969.
CLAUDIN, F., *The Communist Movement from the Comintern to the Cominform*, London, 1975.
COHEN, S. F., *Bukharin and the Bolshevik Revolution*, London, 1974.
COLLETTI, L., *From Rousseau to Lenin*, London, 1973.
COLLINS, H. and ABRAMSKY, C., *Karl Marx and the British Labour Movement*, London, 1965.
Critique, London, 1973–.
DEUTSCHER, I., *The Prophet Armed. Trotsky: 1879–1921*, London, 1954.
—— *The Prophet Unarmed. Trotsky: 1921–1929*, London, 1959.
—— *The Prophet Outcast. Trotsky: 1929–1940*, London, 1963.
—— *Stalin, A Political Biography*, Revised Edition, London, 1966.
—— *Ironies of History*, London, 1966.
DRAPER, H., Ed., *Marx and Engels: Writings on the Paris Commune*, New York, 1971.
Economy and Society, London, 1972.
ENGELS, F., *Introduction to K. Marx's The Class Struggles in France, 1848 to 1850*, in SW 1950, Moscow, 1950.

—— The Origin of the Family, Private Property and the State, in SW 1968, London, 1968.

—— The Peasant War in Germany, Moscow, 1956.

—— Anti-Dühring, Moscow, 1962.

EVANS, M., Karl Marx, London, 1975.

GERAS, N., The Legacy of Rosa Luxemburg, London, 1976.

GERASSI, J., Ed., Towards Revolution, Vol. 1: China, India, Asia, the Middle East, London, 1971.

—— Towards Revolution, Vol. 2: The Americas, London, 1971.

GORZ, A., Socialism and Revolution, London, 1975.

GRAMSCI, A., Selections from the Prison Notebooks (Ed. Quintin Hoare and G. Nowell Smith), London, 1971.

GRUBER, H., Ed., International Communism in the Era of Lenin, New York, 1972.

—— Soviet Russia Masters the Comintern, New York, 1974.

HOBSBAWM, E. J., Labouring Men, London, 1964.

HOWARD, D. and KLARE, K. E., Eds., The Unknown Dimension. European Marxism Since Lenin, New York, 1972.

HUNT, R. N., The Political Ideas of Marx and Engels, Vol. 1: Marxism and Totalitarian Democracy. 1818–1850, London, 1975.

JAY, M., The Dialectical Imagination, London, 1973.

Kapitalistate, San Jose, 1973–.

KAROL, K. S., China, The Other Communism, London, 1968.

—— The Second Chinese Revolution, London, 1975.

KATZNELSON, I., ADAMS, G., BRENNER, P., WOLFE, A., The Politics and Society Reader, New York, 1976.

KAUTSKY, K., The Road to Power, Chicago, 1910.

—— The Dictatorship of the Proletariat, Ann Arbor, 1964.

—— The Class Struggle, New York, 1971.

KEMP, T., Theories of Imperialism, London, 1967.

KOLAKOWSKI, L., Toward a Marxist Humanism, London, 1968.

KORSCH, K., Karl Marx, London, 1938.

—— Marxism and Philosophy, London, 1970.

LENIN, V. I., Two Tactics of Social-Democracy in the Democratic Revolution, in SWL, London, 1969.

—— Imperialism, the Highest Stage of Capitalism, in SWL, London, 1969.

—— The State and Revolution, in SWL, London, 1969.

—— 'Left-Wing' Communism—An Infantile Disorder, in SWL, London, 1969.

—— What is to be Done?, in CWL, vol. 5, Moscow, 1961.

—— The Proletarian Revolution and the Renegade Kautsky, in CWL, vol. 28, Moscow, 1965.

LICHTHEIM, G., Marxism: An Historical and Critical Study, London, 1962.

LIEBMAN, M., Leninism under Lenin, London, 1975.

LOOKER, R., Ed., Rosa Luxemburg. Selected Political Writings, London, 1972.

LUKÁCS, G., *History and Class Consciousness*, London, 1971.

LUXEMBURG, R., *Rosa Luxemburg Speaks*, New York, 1971.

MANDEL, E., *The Leninist Theory of Organisation*, London, 1971.

—— *Late Capitalism*, London, 1975.

MAO TSE-TUNG, *Selected Works*, 4 vols., Peking, 1965–7.

—— *Mao Tse-tung Unrehearsed* (Edited by S. Schram), London, 1974.

MARCUSE, H., *Soviet Marxism*, London, 1958.

MARX, K., *Critique of Hegel's Doctrine of the State*, in *EW*, London, 1975.

—— *On the Jewish Question*, in *EW*, London, 1975.

—— *A Contribution to the Critique of Hegel's 'Philosophy of Right',* *Introduction*, *EW*, London, 1975.

—— *Economic and Philosophical Manuscripts*, in *EW*, London, 1975.

—— *The Class Struggles in France: 1848 to 1850*, in *SE*, London, 1973.

—— *The Eighteenth Brumaire of Louis Bonaparte*, in *SE*, London, 1973.

—— 'Inaugural Address of the International Working Men's Association', in *FI*, London, 1974.

—— *The Civil War in France*, in *FI*, London, 1974.

—— 'Conspectus of Bakunin's *Statism and Anarchism* (Extract)', in *FI*, London, 1974.

—— 'Critique of the Gotha Programme', in *FI*, London, 1974.

—— *Capital*, vol. I, Pelican Ed., London, 1976.

—— *Capital*, vols. I–III, Moscow, 1959–62.

—— *Theories of Surplus-Value*, 3 vols., Moscow, 1969–72.

—— *The Poverty of Philosophy*, London, 1936.

—— *Grundrisse*, Pelican Ed., London, 1973.

MARX, K. and ENGELS, F., *Manifesto of the Communist Party*, in *Revs.*, London, 1973.

—— 'Addresses of the Central Committee to the Communist League (March and June 1850)' in *Revs.*, London, 1973.

—— 'Documents of the First International', in *FI*, London, 1974.

—— 'Circular Letter to Bebel, Liebknecht, Bracke *et al.*', in *FI*, London, 1974.

—— *Selected Works*, London, 1968.

—— *The German Ideology*, London, 1965.

—— *On Britain*, Moscow, 1953.

McLELLAN, D., *The Thought of Karl Marx*, London, 1971.

MEDVEDEV, R., *Let History Judge* (paperback ed.), London, 1976.

MÉSZÁROS, I., *Marx's Theory of Alienation*, London, 1970.

MILIBAND, R., *The State in Capitalist Society* (paperback ed.), London, 1973.

MILLS, C. W., *The Marxists*, London, 1963.

Monthly Review, New York, 1949–.

NETTL, J. P., *Rosa Luxemburg*, 2 vols., London, 1966.

NEUMANN, F., *The Democratic and the Authoritarian State*, New York, 1957.

New Left Review, London, 1960–

O'CONNOR, J., *The Fiscal Crisis of the State*, New York, 1973.

PASHUKANIS, E. H., *La Théorie générale du droit et le marxisme*, Paris, 1970.

POULANTZAS, N., *Political Power and Social Classes*, London, 1973.
—— *Fascism and Dictatorship*, London, 1974.

RADJAVI, K., *La Dictature du prolétariat et le dépérissement de l'état de Marx à Lenine*, Paris, 1975.

Review of African Political Economy, London, 1975.

ROSSANDA, R., Ed., *Il Manifesto*, Paris, 1971.

RUBEL, M., *Karl Marx devant le bonapartisme*, Paris/The Hague, 1960.
—— *Marx critique du marxisme*, Paris, 1974.

SANDERSON, J., *An Interpretation of the Political Ideas of Marx and Engels*, London, 1969.

SARTRE, J.-P., *Situations VI. Problèmes du marxisme. 1.*, Paris, 1964.
—— *Situations VII. Problèmes du marxisme. 2.*, Paris, 1965.

SCHRAM, S. R., *The Political Thought of Mao Tse-tung*, London, 1969.

SINGER, D., *Prelude to Revolution*, London, 1970.

Socialist Register, London, 1964–

STALIN, J., *Leninism*, London, 1940.

SWEEZY, P., *The Present as History*, New York, 1953.

TROTSKY, L., *The History of the Russian Revolution*, London, 1965.
—— *The Revolution Betrayed*, London, 1967.
—— *1905*, London, 1971.
—— *The Struggle against Fascism in Germany*, New York, 1971.
—— *The Challenge of the Left Opposition*, New York, 1975.

WATERS, M.-A., *Rosa Luxemburg Speaks*, New York, 1970.

WESTERGAARD, J. and RESLER, H., *Class in a Capitalist Society. A Study of Contemporary Britain*, London, 1975.

WILLIAMS, G. A., *Proletarian Order*, London, 1975.

WODDIS, J., *New Theories of Revolution*, London, 1972.

Index